Understanding Diversity

A Learning-as-Practice Primer

ABOUT THE AUTHORS

Barbara F. Okun, PhD, is a professor and training director of the combined school and counseling psychology doctoral program at Northeastern University and a clinical instructor in psychology at Harvard Medical School. She maintains a diverse clinical practice and has authored numerous books and chapters on family and adult development and therapy, gender issues, and psychotherapy theory and practice. Her most recent books include *Effective Helping: Interviewing and Counseling* (5th ed.), *Seeking Connections in Psychotherapy*, and *Understanding Diverse Families*.

Jane Fried, PhD, is an associate professor at Central Connecticut State University and coordinator of the master's degree programs in school counseling and student development in higher education. She has had a lifelong interest in cultural differences, including gender differences. Her most recent publications include *Different Voices: Gender Differences in Student Affairs Administration, Shifting Paradigms in Student Affairs,* and *Ethics for Today's Campus.* She has also written several articles on multiculturalism in learning.

Marcia L. Okun, PhD, currently teaches world history and psychology at Newton South High School. Her professional background is in anthropology and archaeology. She has conducted research in, participated in, and supervised numerous international archaeological field digs and studies. She has presented papers at international conferences and is the author of several reports and articles on Roman archaeology, including *The Early Roman Frontier in the Upper Rhine Area* and *The Process of Acculturation in the Northwest Roman Empire.*

Understanding Diversity

A Learning-as-Practice Primer

Barbara F. Okun
Northeastern University

Jane Fried
Central Connecticut State University

Marcia L. Okun
Newton South High School

Brooks/Cole Publishing Company

ITP® An International Thomson Publishing Company

Pacific Grove • Albany • Belmont • Bonn • Boston • Cincinnati • Detroit • Johannesburg • London
Madrid • Melbourne • Mexico City • New York • Paris • Singapore • Tokyo • Toronto • Washington

Sponsoring Editor: *Lisa I. Gebo*
Marketing Team: *Steve Catalano, Aaron Eden*
Editorial Assistant: *Susan Wilson*
Advertising Communications: *Margaret Parks*
Production Coordinator: *Karen Ralling*
Production Service: *Scratchgravel Publishing Services*
Manuscript Editor: *Jane Townsend*
Interior Design: *Anne Draus, Scratchgravel Publishing Services*
Design Coordinator: *Roy R. Neuhaus*
Cover Design and Illustration: *Terri Wright*
Typesetting: *Scratchgravel Publishing Services*
Cover Printing: *Webcom*
Printing and Binding: *Webcom*

For more information, contact:

BROOKS/COLE PUBLISHING COMPANY
511 Forest Lodge Road
Pacific Grove, CA 93950
USA

International Thomson Publishing Europe
Berkshire House 168-173
High Holborn
London WC1V 7AA
England

Thomas Nelson Australia
102 Dodds Street
South Melbourne, 3205
Victoria, Australia

Nelson Canada
1120 Birchmount Road
Scarborough, Ontario
Canada M1K 5G4

International Thomson Editores
Seneca 53
Col. Polanco
115060 México, D. F., México

International Thomson Publishing GmbH
Königswinterer Strasse 418
53227 Bonn
Germany

International Thomson Publishing Asia
60 Albert Street
#15-01 Albert Complex
Singapore 189969

International Thomson Publishing Japan
Hirakawacho Kyowa Building, 3F
2-2-1 Hirakawacho
Chiyoda-ku, Tokyo 102
Japan

Printed in Canada

10 9 8 7 6 5 4 3

Library of Congress Cataloging-in-Publication Data
Okun, Barbara F.
Understanding diversity : a learning-as-practice primer / Barbara F. Okun, Jane Fried, Marcia L. Okun.
p. cm.
Includes bibliographical references and index.
ISBN 0-534-34810-6 (pbk. : alk. paper)
1. Interpersonal relations and culture. 2. Interpersonal communication. 3. Intercultural communication. I. Fried, Jane. II. Okun, Marcia L. III. Title.
HM132.046 1999
302.3'4—dc21 98-22621
CIP

To Sherman Okun, beloved partner and world traveler.

—B.F.O.

To Donna Fairfield, my constant teacher about the world's many cultures and the historical and economic conditions that shape them.

—J.F.

To Josh Lieberman, a source of comfort and solace as well as a trusted sounding board.

—M.L.O.

Contents

Preface

The Beginning

The concept of this book began in the spring of 1996, after Lisa Gebo, editor, asked Barbara Okun, author, what her next book might be. Having just written two books (published in 1996), this author was not prepared to undertake a new project.

However, the editor and the author began to discuss a way to integrate theory and practice for furthering cross-cultural understanding and communications, subjects of great interest to the author. Within a week, the author recruited two cherished colleagues to collaborate on the project—one who has written and trained graduate students and professional groups in understanding diversity and another who brings a professional anthropological perspective from doctoral study as well as intensive fieldwork in many different countries. Both colleagues shared the enthusiasm and excitement of the editor and the author about this topic. *Understanding Diversity: A Learning-as-Practice Primer* is the product of this mutually stimulating, gratifying, and truly egalitarian collaboration.

The Purpose

The purpose of *Understanding Diversity* is to teach readers how to establish trust and respect by listening, by making profound efforts to understand without judging, and by trying to enter into the worldview of the others. The authors make no assumptions about the cultural, racial, or ethnic backgrounds or characteristics of the readers. The perspective of this book is that all people are strongly shaped by the cultures in which they were raised, including those who consider themselves members of the dominant culture in the United States.

By bridging emotional and intellectual learning to achieve behavioral outcomes, this learning-in-practice model enables people (1) to recognize and modify their own physical and verbal communication styles, (2) to understand how they interact with others, and (3) to appreciate the effects of culture on their own and others' behavior and communication. As readers develop self-awareness, awareness of others, and culturally sensitive interpersonal skills, they will also learn (1) to separate facts from cultural assumptions and beliefs about those facts, (2) to shift between their own cultural perspectives and their understanding of others' cultural perspectives, and (3) to differentiate between personal discomfort and intellectual disagreement. Thus, the major goals of this book are to help readers to become aware of personal comfort and discomfort zones, to recognize how they communicate this comfort and discomfort, and from that to recognize how others communicate comfort and discomfort. The ability to recognize another's discomfort leads to the ability to modify how one is perceived by others and hence the ability to develop positive relations across cultures.

Understanding Diversity: A Learning-as-Practice Primer addresses the issues of diversity from the perspective of individual differences rather than through overgeneralized stereotypes. As a learning-in-practice model that integrates emotional, intellectual, and skill learning, this book is both a conceptual text and an applied workbook. Discussions and exercises help readers assess and understand others' beliefs and behaviors in the context of culture. The first step is to develop a self-awareness, from the inside out, in order to recognize that we are all products of our culture and to understand the power that emotions, values, and personal experiences have in shaping our individual interpretations of information and behaviors.

Through the exercises we encourage readers to compare their cultural assumptions with those of people from other groups in order to enhance their awareness of multiple points of view. We integrate conceptual material with the exercises and develop strategies to overcome structural barriers and individual factors that may hinder positive personal and professional cross-cultural communications. Our guiding premise is that one cannot understand the feelings and reactions of others in a given situation unless one is aware of one's own feelings and reactions in the same situation; an awareness of the similarities and differences will deepen one's insight. Increased self-awareness and self-understanding can enhance one's ability to understand others—from the outside in.

The Organization

Chapter 1 is an introduction to the topic of diversity, discussing how we are all members of many groups. One consequence of this is that "who we are" shifts from situation to situation.

Following this introduction, *Understanding Diversity* is divided into two parts. Part One deals with the self, helping readers learn about how they feel in different situations and how they are most likely to react. New ways of thinking about oneself are introduced in the exercises, encouraging readers to learn their own feelings about the issues and situations addressed in the book and the ways in which culture shapes individual reactions. We have found that North

Americans in this country, whose roots are in the dominant culture, tend to be unaware of the effects of their culture on their own perceptions and behaviors. In addition, people in this country tend to focus on just some, rather than all, of the cultures that shape who they are. The same is true of cultures in other parts of the world. The two chapters of Part One explore the many different ways that we communicate. Chapter 2 deals with the self as a verbal communicator in intimate relationships, in small groups, and in large groups. Chapter 3 focuses on nonverbal, physical communications—both our facial and bodily actions and how we act in and react to different settings.

Part Two helps the reader learn to recognize emotions, intent, and meaning in others. This part of the book deals with learning to recognize and respond appropriately to both verbal and nonverbal cues of comfort or unease from others. Throughout each chapter we incorporate discussion of gender, socioeconomic status, religion, race, and ethnicity, as they affect various aspects of communication. Chapter 4 looks at how and why people express different emotions, focusing on how culture determines the permissibility and expression of various emotions. Chapter 5 discusses different concepts of self among different people and how self-concept changes, depending on circumstances and over the lifespan. Chapter 6 highlights the self-in-relation: the individual as a participant in intimate and nonintimate personal, social, and public relationships. Chapter 7 focuses on how people manage and perceive space and time, the least conscious aspects of culture.

Acknowledgments

Barbara Okun acknowledges her clients, students, colleagues, and family who over the years have contributed to her development of self-awareness and understanding of cultural diversity. She thanks her graduate assistants, in particular Lisa Powell, Sarah Bullock, Wendy Birkman, and Shannon Reed, for their research assistance.

Jane Fried acknowledges Muriel King Taylor, Farah Ibrahim, Chieh Li, Amy Reynolds, and Raechele Pope for their teaching, support, and encouragement.

Marcia Okun thanks all the people who helped her to survive living in different cultures and to learn firsthand what it is like to be a foreigner, in the minority, and different. Several colleagues and friends have provided support and input throughout the writing process. She especially would like to thank Roberta Dollase, Marshal Cohen, Anthony Parker, Carolyn Artin, and her in-laws, Alan and Annette Lieberman, for their support and willingness to listen to her ideas. Her family has also been supportive and helpful in writing this book. First and foremost is her mother (Barbara Okun), without whom this book would not exist. Through thick and thin, she has shown a respect for Marcia's intelligence and ability that most daughters only dream about. She also wants to thank her daughters, Amalia and Michal, for living with her throughout this intense period and for providing her with those moments that make life worth living. Finally, she wants to thank her son, Aryeh, who did not exist when she first started this book but whose presence was always felt.

In addition to our appreciation for each other, we want to acknowledge the continuous support and encouragement from Lisa Gebo and the entire Brooks/Cole staff. Lisa provided chocolate and coffee mugs, to reinforce our diligence, as well as humor and warmth.

Our reviewers' input has been invaluable. Thanks to Bruce D. Friedman; Tricia McClam, University of Tennessee; Twinet Parmer, Central Michigan University; and Edil Torres-Rivera, University of Nevada at Reno.

Barbara F. Okun
Jane Fried
Marcia L. Okun

Understanding Diversity

A Learning-as-Practice Primer

1

Introduction and Background

> I reached out to shake her hand (a female Muslim patient) after the examination and her husband became very agitated. I was just trying to be warm and cordial. I don't understand what happened. (Male Caucasian nurse-practitioner)

> We were disappointed he (a Latino male job applicant) did so poorly in the interview. On paper, he was just what we were looking for. But he never made eye contact; he always seemed to be looking at the floor. (Female Caucasian human resources employer)

The above examples are typical of the kinds of misunderstandings that can occur as a result of our assumptions about our own and others' interactional behaviors. These misunderstandings do not have to occur. With cultural awareness and heightened sensitivity to other people's ethnicity, we can understand that a Muslim man would naturally become upset if his wife were touched by a male who was not a member of the family, and that Latinos characteristically avert their eyes in the presence of "authority" figures.

Thus, the male Caucasian nurse-practitioner could say to the female Muslim patient, "In my culture, one shakes hands and makes eye contact in order to express warmth and cordiality. I know that may not be the custom in other cultures. How do you express warmth and cordiality?" The female Caucasian human resources employer might say to the Latino male job applicant, "I notice that you're not making eye contact. I wonder why. Did I do or say something that offends you?" Sensitivity to cultural differences can enable us to develop more cultural empathy and can result in more gratifying and effective interactions.

In the United States, the rapidly changing demographics of the population have increased cultural diversity at all levels and in all segments of society. In fact, it is estimated that Caucasians, the dominant ethnic group in this country, will become a statistical minority within the next decade (Carter, 1995; Gottfried & Gottfried, 1994; Comas-Diaz & Greene, 1994; Cose, 1992).

Increasingly, members of nondominant cultural groups are asserting their culture-specific needs and values in educational, legal, medical, judicial, governmental, and business environments. Thus, as professional and business staffs, as well as client and customer groups, become more diverse, there is an increasing need for all of us to become more aware of the impact of our own cultural values, beliefs, and assumptions on our interactional behaviors.

In this chapter, we will define and discuss concepts relating to race, ethnicity, culture, and worldviews. These concepts provide a framework for the development of self-awareness, which includes understanding the effects of sociocultural factors on our self-identity, our views, and our interactions with others. We begin with a discussion of stereotyping.

Stereotyping

Stereotyping is a convenient but dangerous type of "shorthand" for interpersonal understanding and communication. A stereotype is a concept "or representation of a category of persons" (Lee, Jussim, & McCauley, 1995, p. 304) that can be inaccurate in terms of how it exaggerates real differences and the perception of those differences.

EXERCISE 1.1 • Ethnic Stereotyping and Empathy

The purpose of this exercise is to help you begin to understand your ingrained assumptions about a different ethnic group.

1. Watch a TV program in a language you do not know; for example, watch a Spanish, Portuguese, or Asian channel.
2. After the program is over, write down what you think was going on in the show.
3. Now assess the factors that influenced your assumptions of what occurred.
   - What cues did you pick up on, and how do these cues relate to your own assumptions about the culture?
   - What notions do you have about the ethnic group you were observing, and how did these notions affect your experience?
   - Write down your feelings about the different characters and their behaviors.

After completing the exercise, imagine for a moment that you are an immigrant in a foreign culture. Every day, when you walk out of your front door, you depend on the same kinds of cues and experience the same lack of knowledge as you did when watching the TV show.

Many cross-cultural texts in the fields of human services and counseling contain chapters about different ethnic groups, particularly those groups that are sizable minorities in the United States, such as African Americans, Asian Americans, Native Americans and Latinos. All these conceptualizations focus on broad categories that are of limited use and that have the potential to cause misunderstandings that can lead to oppression. For example, persons of African descent who were born in the United States often refer to themselves as African Americans. If a white person calls another person African American, what information does that convey about that individual? Does it raise stereotypic ideas about people with relatively dark skin? If the person was referred to as black or Negro, would the white person have some other ideas about him or her based on "racial" category? After all, skin color or race is merely one of a large group of variables that have shaped his or her personality. Consider Native Americans, who subscribe to a value system that honors the earth and holds certain locations sacred, but who vary dramatically in their acculturation to the dominant society, and whose population is divided among several hundred tribes. Each tribe is somewhat different from all the others.

What do you think of when you imagine an "Asian"? Do you have an idea about Asians that helps you understand Korean, Cambodian, Hmong, Lao, Japanese, Chinese, and Vietnamese people? Ask yourself what you mean when you say "Latino." Debate about the appropriate designation for people whose primary language is Spanish is ongoing: Are they Latinos or Hispanics? Does a language designation give a nonspeaker important information about how to interact with that person? Does Latino mean the same thing as Hispanic? Do different assumptions come to mind when an ethnic identifier is used as compared to a "racial" or language identifier? Consider persons of Mexican ancestry whose families have lived in the same place for more than 300 years. Their ancestral home was Mejico, which became part of the United States by treaty in the nineteenth century. What should they be called? How do you think of a Puerto Rican who has lived in New York since birth, speaks very little Spanish, and calls San Juan home?

We have purposely avoided dividing this book into chapters that discuss specific ethnic or cultural groups as if members of those groups can be characterized in general terms. We discuss aspects of all cultures in order to help the reader understand both his or her own culture, which we assume to be one of the dominant or subdominant cultures in the United States, and other cultures.

Race and Ethnicity

Race and ethnicity are both social constructs. *Social constructs* are categories created by a society or culture. What this means is that who belongs or who does not belong to a category is determined by a society. For example, in the United States, anyone with African ancestry is labeled African American, and in Brazil, anyone with white ancestry is labeled white. *Race* traditionally refers to a scientific/biological classification system that differentiates people according to their physical characteristics, such as skin color, facial features, and hair texture. Although the concept of race may help us to understand physical similarities among people, as well as social attitudes, prejudice, stereotypes, and discrimination, it does little to help us understand an individual person's personality, behavior, educational level, social background, or environmental context (Fairchild, Yee, Wyatt, & Weizmann, 1995). Helms (1994) refers to race as a quasibiological concept that can more accurately be considered a "socially defined categorization system that has become the basis of one form of social identity" (pp. 294–295). The concept of ethnicity, based on the Greek term *ethnos,* is based on the characteristics of a nation or tribe. *Ethnicity* refers to the "sense of commonality transmitted over generations by the family and reinforced by the surrounding community" (McGoldrick, Giordano, & Pearce, 1996, p. 4). This concept may be more helpful in terms of understanding one's heritage and value system. It involves socially constructed elements such as language, beliefs, norms, values, behaviors, and institutions, all of which are shared by members of an ethnic group, who have a common ethnic *identity*—the subjective sense of being a member of a certain ethnic group.

A broader concept, which includes ethnicity, race, and other factors, is *culture,* which helps us to understand all the learned behaviors, beliefs, attitudes, norms, and values held by a particular group of people. Cultures continually evolve and change, as we will see in the following discussion.

Ways of Looking at Culture

The peoples of the world are not homogeneous. There is no one group of people that is homogeneous. Our only universal homogeneity is rooted in the fact that all human beings belong to a single species and have basic needs: food, shelter, love, knowledge, and so on. These needs are often manifested in similar ways. However, environmental or individual circumstances cause people to meet these needs in different ways. The tools available to people to fulfill their needs, as well as the methodologies they use, are modified in response to environment and circumstances. This is how cultures and subcultures evolve.

Many ways of looking at culture can be gleaned from various disciplines, including anthropology, linguistics, cultural psychology, history, and the humanities. Western authors have tended to describe cultures in terms of the belief systems they attribute to specific groups of people, including the artifacts associated with those beliefs. This tendency to associate culture with artifacts and to reify a belief system often tells us more about the culture of the authors than it does about the cultures the authors describe.

Culture as a Set of Internalized Influences

D. Ho, a psychologist who has done extensive research on cross-cultural understanding between couples, defines culture this way:

> Internalized culture may be defined as the cultural influences operating within the individual that shape (not determine) the personality formation and various aspects of psychological functioning. (Ho, 1995, p. 5)

Ho's definition of *internalized culture* deserves special emphasis. The dominant belief system in the United States values the creation of categories into which perceptions and experiences can be organized. This is one of the cultural influences that most of us have *internalized.* We like to use broad, descriptive categories as a shorthand method for understanding different kinds of events or experiences. For example, you might categorize vacation as being a choice between "the mountains" and "the seashore." After you decide whether you prefer the mountains or the seashore, you would start to determine which mountain or seashore location you prefer. Then you would consider the details of time, cost, and so forth. In choosing a career, you might begin by asking yourself, "Do I like to work with people or things?" This would be followed by asking what kinds of people or things, in what kinds of settings. This kind of categorical thinking is quite useful under some circumstances, but it can easily lead to stereotyping in other situations. People tend to think by categorizing. The danger is they often pigeonhole people into categories instead of looking at them as unique individuals. Many other cultures take a different approach, moving from the concrete to the abstract, or remaining at the level of particulars, using few abstractions.

Ho (1995) notes that individuals may be members of many cultures, in which case they are enculturated to varying degrees within each one. Enculturation occurs when a person becomes a part of a culture through observation, experience, and instruction. Characteristics related to membership in a particular culture may become significant in specific situations, but may also be irrelevant in other situations. For example, being a white American woman may be irrelevant at a Girl Scout leaders' meeting in the suburbs, but it may become extremely relevant at an international meeting of Girl Scout executives. Therefore, we value Ho's notion of internalized culture as a phenomenon that influences, but does not determine, individual perception and behavior.

Culture and the Universal Human Experience

M. L. Tarpley, a mental health worker who is chairperson of the Metro Boston Department of Mental Health Multi-Cultural Advisory Committee, addresses the impact of culture on everyday human experience.

> Culture, a variation on a standard theme, is the aggregate of ways in which groups of people use and transmit the use of the tools available to them. [Tools consist of physical environment, economic status, sociological factors, education and information, and psychological milieu.] (Tarpley, 1993, p. 12)

Although all cultures share some broad general characteristics (Tarpley, 1993), these general characteristics should be considered indications of typical behavior and guidelines for understanding, rather than absolute descriptions of all members of any group. Tarpley speaks to the universality of human experience. All human beings have basic needs for food, shelter, self-actualization, love, knowledge, and so forth, and share human qualities that form the basis for understanding all people. There is variability, however, among human beings, given their environments, the circumstances of their existence, and the sum of the tools available to fulfill the basic needs. Cultures and subcultures evolve from the variations in the ways people meet their basic needs. Thus, variability among human beings occurs at the cultural level as a product of environmental factors, because of the history of the subgroup—the contexts in which we all live.

The Notion of Cultural Identity

J. Ogbu, a school psychologist who researches learning among inner-city African American children, states that culture is:

> an understanding that a people have of their universe—social, physical, or both—as well as their understanding of their behavior in that universe. The cultural model of a population serves its members as a guide in their interpretation of events and elements within their universe; it also serves as a guide to their expectations and actions in that universe or environment. (Ogbu, 1990, p. 523)

Ogbu (1990), in contrast to Ho and Tarpley, recognizes that individuals within a cultural group have similar perspectives and emphases that are developed through common experience. This is their *cultural identity*. Each culture defines its own criteria for enculturation, socialization, and development of children that will result in what each culture defines as "adequate functioning" through the lifespan.

As we have seen, ways of viewing culture vary greatly, but all agree that cultural variables—which include environment, language, family structure, and tradition—have great influence in determining group differences.

Culture from a Process Perspective

Geographers divide the study of geography into five themes: location (for example, site); place (for example, characteristics of a clapboard singe-family home); interaction between humans and environment (for example, humans farming the land); movement (for example, changes in the environment, perhaps due to storm damage, rezoning, or industrialization); and region (for example, an area of the larger environment, such as New England). The third theme, interaction between humans and environment, is cultural, as are the fourth and fifth themes, movement and regions. These things are the cause and product of culture, which develops as a result of a group of people solving fundamental problems: acquiring food, reproducing, protecting resources, and passing on knowledge.

Culture not only determines how we interact with our environment, but also, through language, it helps us interpret and transmit information about our environment. How would a person obtain information about a situation (environment) if he or she was not able to identify and label the elements that comprise the situation? We see that culture is a complex web, a set of *processes* by which identifiable groups of people make sense of their common life experiences, including the past experience of their groups and their anticipated future.

If you are an American of Anglo-European ancestry, you probably think of things and events, rather than relationships and processes, as typifying American culture. If, however, it comes to mind that people of relatively unmixed European ancestry typically have more credibility as political commentators than do people of African ancestry, or that it is more common for heads of major corporations to be male than female, you are thinking of culture as *process.* Culture from this perspective is "a process of negotiating power and creating shared meaning through talk" (Gailey, 1993). One example is the entrepreneurial relationships that have developed between major corporations and city school systems in the United States. Funding and leadership from corporations have allowed school systems to bypass unwieldy bureaucracies and focus on innovative curriculum and teaching in the schools (Gerstner, Semerad, & Doyle, 1995).

EXERCISE 1.2 • Culture as Process

The purpose of this exercise is to view culture from a process perspective.

1. Identify groups of people who have more credibility or power than other groups in the United States. Explain both the source of their credibility or power and their use of power. Think, for example, about the influence of newscasters and journalists. Discuss your ideas with others in your group.
2. Identify some major groups and relationships that exist in American culture (for example, nuclear family, elected officials–constituents, and so on). Discuss your ideas with others in your group.

Culture from a Content Perspective

Hall (1981, p. 13) considers culture "a series of situational models for behavior and thought." However, he states that studying a particular model of behavior and thought tells the reader more about the person who created the model than it does about the culture it purports to describe:

> In the West, people are more concerned with the content or meaning of the model than they are with how it is put together, organized or performed and the purpose it is supposed to fulfill. (Hall, 1981, p. 14)

In other words, Westerners are accustomed to focusing on things or objects, rather than on processes and relationships. Their descriptions of culture tend to be shaped by this frame of reference. This approach to understanding culture is useful for people who are learning about communication between cultures, as long as the limits of this frame of reference are as clear as its assets. The assets are easily and quickly communicated. The limits are the information that is incomplete—for example, giving a list of ingredients in a recipe, without explaining the process, what to do with them. For instance, Goodenough, a linguist (1981, p. 110), describes culture as a "set of standards for perceiving, believing, evaluating and acting." He uses this idea to understand how specific cultures define human biology, psychology, and behavior. Culture is a "reservoir of resources in knowledge and skills carried by the members of a particular society" as well as "the property of a social group." (Goodenough, 1981, pp. 110–111). Goodenough's metaphors for culture are illuminating. Even though he considers culture to be a set of standards by which people set their expectations of behavior, Goodenough's language talks about culture as if it were a *thing*—a reservoir of concepts or a piece of property. As a linguist, Goodenough's goal is to understand how people categorize their environment through language. This is an example of how an understanding of context (Goodenough's professional perspective as a linguist) enables us to understand and appreciate his meaning.

EXERCISE 1.3 • Perceptions of American Culture

The purpose of this exercise is to help you identify your perception of American culture.

1. Decide which way of looking at culture is the one with which you most identify. Then list the items, events, and locations that you think symbolize American culture.
2. Compare your list with others in your group. Are people's lists identical? What items does everyone have listed? Make a new list of these common items.
3. Have each member of the group write down ten items from the common list that they think are essential for defining American culture. Rank order the items in terms of importance.
4. Now have everyone compare lists. Afterward, write a one-paragraph definition or description of American culture.

The number of objects and ideas that symbolize American culture is limitless. The culture is so large and pervasive that people who attempt to describe it variably describe the same things differently. Many white Southerners in the United States see the Confederate flag as a symbol of a proud period in their family's history. Many black Southerners (and probably northern blacks as well) see the same flag as a symbol of genocide. Everybody has a piece of the story. All pieces are accurate, but none is complete. Therefore, everybody can be correct and still disagree with everybody else.

Common Ideas About Culture

Scholars who study culture seem to agree on several key points:

- Culture includes all aspects of human life and is a process by which groups impose order on and meaning of their life experience (Erchak, 1992).
- Culture is verbal, visual, rhythmic, spatial, temporal, and symbolic (Agar, 1994). It involves communications between all the senses in patterns that are recognizable even though members of any given culture may not be able to express an awareness of the patterns to which they are responding.
- An understanding of how the language is used in a specific culture is essential to understanding the language. Language shapes experience, and experience shapes language. It predetermines modes of observation and interpretation, shaping interpretation of experiences, recreating experiences, and empowering members to imagine and create new experiences (Agar, 1994; Goodenough, 1981; Sapir, 1958).
- The most effective method for understanding one's own culture is to compare it to other cultures. This process forces a person to perceive the various systems embedded in different cultures and to use this understanding of systems, which order and impose meaning, to revisit his or her own cultural system.
- Members of a specific culture typically do not experience their culture as a humanly constructed system. They experience their culture as "the way things are and the way things should be." This phenomenon is generally referred to as *ethnocentrism.* Individuals within a culture tend to believe that their ideas about the universe are simply "common sense" (Geertz, 1983) even though what is common sense in one culture may be unheard of or taboo in another.

As suggested by this list, one attribute of the dominant culture in the United States is the belief in the correspondence theory of truth. This theory asserts that words correspond to objects on a one-to-one basis. A word that describes an object can mean only one thing in reference to that object. For example, the moon can be scientifically defined as a sphere that revolves around the earth, emitting no light of its own and reflecting sunlight during the earth night. That is not an exhaustive definition of the moon's observable characteristics, but those words clearly describe the moon in physically accurate, if somewhat limited, terms. The correspondence theory of truth assumes that this definition or description of the moon can be considered universally valid and true. Attribution of meanings to the moon or moonlight are metaphors or fantasies in this belief system because the real description of the moon is a sphere that revolves around the earth. Within the correspondence theory of truth, there is little or no room for interpretation or examination of alternate meanings or the effect of perspective on meaning. A thing is what it is.

EXERCISE 1.4 • Correspondence Theory of Truth

The purpose of this exercise is to illustrate the limits of the correspondence theory of truth.

Consider the hamburger. What do you see when someone says "hamburger"? What do you smell? feel? taste? What actions and emotions do you associate with a hamburger? Write them down. Now consider that all these perceptions and schemes involve one concrete object, a patty of cooked beef sandwiched between two parts of a soft, round bun, whose purpose is to be eaten. There will probably be no doubt in your mind, as a North American, that the word *hamburger* corresponds directly to the object eaten and that there is no other legitimate interpretation of *hamburger* either as a concept or as an experience.

What perceptions and schemas would someone from a different culture with different values have concerning a hamburger? Let us consider a devout Hindu, who believes that all life is sacred, especially cows. This person not only has never eaten beef, but also considers doing so to be sacrilegious and counter to all his beliefs and values. How would he perceive a hamburger, if he knew that it was beef? He would probably perceive it as a profane, sacrilegious object created by heathens who possess a complete disrespect for life. Eating such an object could no more nourish the body or soul than could eating one's parents!

Implicit and Explicit Behavior

One of the major cultural components is communication. Speech, language, and all forms of communication are embedded in culture, which means that they are not easily separated out. In addition, both explicit and implicit cultural behaviors exist that influence communication. *Explicit* cultural behaviors include dress, language, eating habits, customs, lifestyle, and so forth. These behaviors are easily perceived and recognized by all. *Implicit* behaviors, which lie beneath the surface and are not always recognized, include age, gender, family, family roles, child-rearing practices, socioeconomic class, education, religious/spiritual beliefs, fears, attitudes, values, and perceptions, all of which shape the fiber of a person. One purpose of this book is to make the implicit more explicit. Our understanding of ourselves or anyone else is incomplete without understanding individuals in context.

EXERCISE 1.5 • Cultural Influences

The purpose of this exercise is to help you become aware of the diverse cultural groups to which you belong and that influence who you are.

1. Think back to the time you began to attend school, or earlier if you can, and try to remember all the different cultural influences in your life. Think about your own ethnic heritage from one or both sets of grandparents. Think about your gender, your religion, your race, your class, and other groups that were represented in your neighborhood. List the cultures that you believe had some influence on your own development and your own view of the world.
2. Think about the first time you realized that something about your own upbringing was different from someone else's. What was the difference? How did you feel when you realized the difference? Did you do anything about it? If so, what?
3. Identify the two cultures from question 1 that you think had the strongest influence on you as you were growing up. Now look at the table below. For each topic listed in the left hand column, write down the messages each culture gave you as you were growing up.

	Culture 1	**Culture 2**
Life messages, that is, what to expect from life		
Family relations		
Gender roles		
Education		
Work values and behavior		

Are the values conveyed to you by Culture 1 consistent with the values conveyed by Culture 2? Are there elements in your life now that are uncomfortable or confusing because you received conflicting messages from the different cultures? For example, if you come from a family with Puerto Rican cultural values, you may have been taught that life works in its own way and that you have very little control over the major conditions affecting you. If you come from a family with a British heritage, you may have been told to be the "captain of your fate," to take control of your life circumstances. If you have one Puerto Rican parent and one British parent, you probably have conflicting notions about what to expect from life. As a child, you developed these notions both from the advice your parents and family gave you and from watching how they and all your kin behaved on a daily basis.

Worldviews and Cultural Variability

The term *worldview* refers to one's basic perceptions and understandings of the world (Ibrahim, 1985; Sue & Sue, 1990). This includes views about basic human nature, families, intimate and social relationships, locus of control, time, space, and activity. One's worldview develops out of one's personal experience, through interactions with members of one's culture (Wolcott, 1991). Nonshared, as well as shared, cultural experiences influence an individual's worldview. It is likely that the nonshared experiences account for much of the variability within cultural groups, just as nonshared experiences of siblings account for the variability among siblings within a family system (Plomin, 1993).

Individualism Versus Collectivism

Individualism versus collectivism is one major cultural variable that is used to explain cultural differences in behavior (Triandis, 1994; Matsumoto, 1996a). *Individualism* refers to the importance that is placed on the welfare of the individual person, as opposed to the good or desire of the group. *Collectivism* reverses this, placing more importance on the good or desires of the group.

Individualist cultures, such as those of Europe and North America, value autonomy and independence and rely on objective, empirically validated data as knowledge. The individual is conceived of as independent, autonomous, and self-contained. Power is viewed hierarchically, and values emphasize achievement, productivity, and individual responsibility.

Collectivist cultures, such as those of Africa, Asia, Arab countries, and Latin America, have a collective conceptualization in which human beings function as interdependent members of a group to achieve collective survival. Although collectivism does not reject individual uniqueness, it does reject the idea that the individual can be understood separately from others in his or her social group; there *is* no perceptual separation between the individual and others in the group (Schiele, 1996). Individual identity is conceived of as a way of uniquely expressing a group ethos. Values emphasize sharing, cooperation, and social responsibility.

High-Context Versus Low-Context Cultures

Another major cultural variable is high context versus low context. This variable refers to the amount of implicit information embedded in context. In high-context cultures, such as those that exist in many areas of Africa, Asia, and Latin America, little needs to be stated. One gets most information from the context. In contrast, *low-context cultures,* such as those of North America and Britain, require more explicit, verbal communication, since little or no information is embedded in the context (Triandis, 1994; Matsumoto, 1996a).

High-context cultures tend to be homogeneous, and the worldview varies little among members of the group. People take a great deal of information "for granted" in that they assume that their ideas about almost everything are shared by all members of their culture. There is a strong consensus about what constitutes "common sense." Consequently, members of these high-context cultures make strong distinctions between insiders and outsiders (Hall, 1966a). They assume, in conversation, that their listeners will understand most of what they want to communicate without being told directly. High-context cultures tend to use modeling as a major method of teaching. The student imitates the teacher, learns by experience, and develops a high degree of intuition. Low-context cultures tend to teach by explicit instruction. Little is left to the imagination or the student's intuition. To imagine the felt difference between these two approaches, compare cooking from a cookbook—which gives the chef every detail of preparation, indicating temperatures, times, and measure quantities—with learning from an experienced cook who invites the student into the kitchen and suggests that the student watch while the teacher uses a "little bit of this and little bit of that." Asking a low-context chef for clarification will gain a numerical answer—for example, 350 degrees, two ounces, or eight minutes. Asking a high-context cook the same question gains an intuitive answer—for example, "How much salt? Enough. Stop when it tastes right."

Members of low-context cultures make fewer assumptions about what everybody believes and are far more explicit in their conversational style. The United States is a low-context culture. Credibility is achieved by argumentation with the greatest credibility going to the person who can make the strongest case regarding the meaning of an event. Little is taken for granted, and important communications are as explicit as they possibly can be, in order to avoid misunderstandings or differing interpretations.

Teaching technical information in a high-context culture is very difficult, because technology demands precision, and high-context cultures assume a common understanding and knowledge base, even when communication is not precise. Low-context cultures, on the other hand, seem to be more efficient in teaching technical information, because they employ precise verbal and visual communication. Collectivist cultures—which value the group over the individual—tend toward high-context functioning, because so much of life's experience is shaped by participation in groups (Triandis, 1994; Matsumoto, 1996a; Hall, 1976).

When considering the worldviews of individuals from different ethnic groups, it is important to consider the degree and nature of acculturation of the particular individual, how strong his or her ethnic identity has remained over time, and, if applicable, how his or her experiences as a member of a minority group with lower power and status have affected his or her worldview. Remember, *acculturation* occurs when two separate cultures interact to form a third culture (M. Okun, 1990). For example, the culture of Irish Americans is not identical with that of their relatives in Ireland nor with that of the general population in the United States. Phinney (1996, p. 921) addresses the tremendous heterogeneity among members of American ethnic groups: Ethnic cultures differ in terms of particular country of origin within a broad cultural group (for example, Asian Americans of Japanese versus Chinese versus Korean versus Laotian versus Cambodian ancestry, or Russian Jews versus German Jews versus Yemenite Jews; or Orthodox Jews versus Conservative Jews versus Reform Jews). They also differ in terms of generation of immigration, region of settlement in the United States, socioeconomic status, and community structure. Furthermore, because of their dispersion and because they mix with both mainstream American culture and other ethnic groups in the United States, ethnic cultures are not discrete entities but, rather, part of a diverse cultural mix.

Nonetheless, there do seem to be some generally accepted descriptions of different ethnic groups in the United States. These can be found in Appendix A.

The Dynamics of Human Interaction

We have discussed culture as process and culture as content. In order to understand culture holistically (that is, as one integrated system), it is helpful to use some analogies from physics, particularly the process and content of light. Light in physics is considered to be simultaneously energy and matter, waves and particles, processes and "things" of sorts. Light manifests itself in different forms under different circumstances.

A culture is this same kind of dynamic system. Individuals interacting with each other, particularly when they see the world through the worldviews of one or more cultures, are also dynamic systems. These human/cultural systems are affected by personal experience, socioeconomic status, location, race, ethnicity, gender, sexual orientation, disability, age, language, religion, and many other factors. All these factors interact with each other in the individual's consciousness, with different factors becoming salient depending on the circumstances, or *context,* in which the individual is functioning. For example, an attorney trying a case in an American court is probably conscious of her environment, the social expectations for behavior in that environment, her clothing, the facts she intends to present on behalf of her client, and possibly the age, race, and gender of the presiding judge. She probably is not conscious of her grandparents' ethnicity, her able-bodied status, or her religion. If she has a social engagement later that day, she probably will remain aware of social expectations, age, clothing, and gender, but she also will be conscious of sexual orientation, possibly her race, her family's ethnically focused expectations for her future marriage and childbearing, and even her tastes in food. Context determines, to a large degree, those elements of her cultural worldview that she is aware of at any particular time.

If that attorney were interacting with a client from a different socioeconomic background, race, or ethnic group, she might become conscious of any of the numerous *differences* between herself and her client, as well as of additional attributes of her client's background, attitude, and worldview that might bear on his or her case. She can be considered one dynamic system; the client is another dynamic system; and together they create a third system that develops from their interactions.

What Is a "Holon"?

Ken Wilber has coined the term *holon* to describe "an entity that is itself a whole and simultaneously a part of some other whole" (Wilber, 1996, p. 20.) As the attorney and the client work together, each individual is considered a holon, and the two working together form another holon, which incorporates both of them so that they remain as separate people, or whole, and also form an additional whole in terms of their working relationship. This process of creating holons exists in the natural world from the atomic level to the highest levels of complexity. For example, an oxygen atom could be considered a holon when it becomes part of a water molecule. Every cell in the body is a holon, and each cell is part of an increasingly complex set of organs and systems, which are also holons, and these holons come together to form another holon, a human being.

If you shift your focus from the person as a physical being to the person as an emotional, social, cultural, and spiritual being, you can begin to see each person as a holon that functions within larger interpersonal, family, tribal, ethnic, and faith/belief systems. Each holon shares energy with the larger system in a dynamic relationship. Each holon contributes to the system, is enhanced by it, and participates in an evolving process that transcends its "parts." People who are members of families contribute their time, energy, love, support, and other resources to their families, and they, in turn, are supported by their families. In many collectivist cultures the family is more important than the individual, and "family honor" or family name transcends any other aspect of the family or any individual member of the family, at any time or place.

Agency, Communion, Self-Dissolution, and Self-Transcendence

We see, then, that all holons share two tendencies (Wilber, 1996), and they attempt to maintain these tendencies simultaneously. They maintain their wholeness, their individuality, and they also maintain their "partness," their membership in larger groups. Holons have four characteristics that contribute to these two tendencies: agency, communion, self-dissolution, and self-transcendence. *Agency* refers to the holon's capacity or ability to carry out its purpose or function. *Communion* refers to the holon's capacity or ability to connect with another at the same level of complexity. Agency and communion tend to occur simultaneously and interact cyclically. They create a dynamic process comparable to that of a mother nursing a baby. The mother produces milk, which is part of her agency (that is, her purpose or function) in response to her infant's sucking. Nursing, which is an act of connecting, represents communion for both of them.

Part of the work of each individual holon is to interact, or connect, with other holons that complement its function. When holons fail to engage in communion with other holons, they tend to disintegrate into subholons, units of less complexity. We refer to this process as *self-dissolution.* Self-dissolution is comparable to a multinational corporation spinning off a subdivision, or two people getting a divorce.

Occasionally, holons transcend themselves and make creative leaps to a higher level of complexity. This process does not follow any predictable patterns, but those who undergo it always seem to manifest some higher order of self-organization. Self-organization, also called self-renewal, refers to the capacity of a system, in this case a person, to respond to new information from the environment. The system can simultaneously retain its identity and change its form of information-processing mechanisms in order to thrive in an altered environment. To do this, the system must have strong and active information-sensing mechanisms, a high level of self-awareness and a "strong capacity for reflection" (Wheatley, 1994, p. 91). To transcend a "self" state and reorganize at a higher level of complexity, a holon must dissolve and reorganize. This process is called *self-transcendence.* It is what happens when a caterpillar goes into a cocoon and transforms itself into a butterfly. It disintegrates (the process of self-dissolution), reorganizes, and emerges as a new phenomenon.

When a person moves to a new culture and marries into or otherwise joins a family in that culture, the person will experience elements of dissolution and transcendence. The person will give up key elements of her or his previous ways of doing things and interpreting the world in order to function smoothly in the new environment. This process is also called *acculturation.*

Self-transcendent leaps create new, coherent holons spontaneously, not incrementally. Self-transcendent changes seem to be the result of energy exchanges between holons. When the energy flow between holons reaches a certain level, it generates a structural instability, which "creates the potential for reordering of the system" (Caple, 1985, p. 175). These reorderings create new, more complex holons. These changes are the outcome of competition between systemic stability and systemic turbulence. "The more complex a system, the more numerous are the types of fluctuation that threaten its stability" (Caple, 1985, p. 175).

Feedback Loops

Evolution in these complex, unpredictable systems is continuous. Self-transcendence occurs through the process of continuous *feedback loops* through which the system exchanges energy and information with contiguous systems, and then receives energy and information in return. If an American woman joins an Indian family and cooks with the women, her methods of preparing food will be changed by the continuous feedback given to her by her new relatives as they all cook together. If she returns to the United States and cooks alone, her cooking will reflect her traditional methods as they have been affected by the new methods.

In Western cultures, we have been socialized to think of people in intrapersonal terms. That is, we think about who a person is, and how he or she behaves from the perspective of his or her early upbringing, his or her personality traits, and so forth. When we think about people as holons, our focus on behavior shifts from *intrapersonal* to *interactional* (Sexton, 1994). When we think about people in interaction with each other, we can think of them as holons exchanging energy and information.

Transactions between two persons may ultimately transform both persons/holons into a system of higher complexity. We might also call this process "forming a relationship." Two friends are a system composed of two individuals who are bound by common beliefs, experiences, and feelings. They are engaged in a process that transcends both of them. As long as they continue their relationship, they will be concerned about each one's opinion of the other. Rather than viewing the relationship as one person acting on the other (which is the way a Westerner might view it, the relationship can be viewed as one of *reciprocal causality* (Sexton, 1994, p. 249), in which each action generates a reaction in a continuous feedback loop. In other words, a relationship is in a constant process of modification, with each person reacting to the other and responding to each subsequent action or reaction.

In systems theory, which provides the framework for the notion of a holon, the process is called *iteration*—"repeating a certain function using the previous output as input for the next function" (Wilbur et al., 1995, p. 133). Over time, repeated iterations form patterns of behavior, and friends learn to read each other's moods, facial expressions, and tone of voice so that they know how to respond to each other when particular patterns of behavior appear.

EXERCISE 1.6 • You and Your Environment

The purpose of this exercise is to recognize how you and your personal environment (for example, your home) influence each other.

Next time you arrive home, stop before you enter. Ask yourself how you are feeling, what you are expecting in terms of a greeting, and what feelings you are likely to experience upon entering the house, room, or apartment. Take a mental and emotional inventory before you enter, so that you know your frame of mind and your expectations about what will happen next. Enter the house and speak as little as possible. Walk around and pay attention to your feelings and reactions. If you are spoken to, pay attention to your response and the changes in feelings it creates. If you see some objects out of place and feel as though you want to put them away, pay attention to your feelings and your actions before and after you put the items away. If you have work to do, pay attention to the process you go through as you get ready to do the work and then begin it. Notice your physical activities, your mental commentaries, and your feelings. This is a very slow process, similar to some types of mediation. Its goal is to help you focus the interactive processes between you and your environment, so that you view them as one continuous system of feedback, rather than as one person acting on the world. If you arrive home and everything seems calm and orderly, you will have a different reaction than if you arrive home to a scene of messiness, noise, conflict, and general disarray.

EXERCISE 1.7 • Fantasy Feedback Loops

The purpose of this exercise is to utilize visualization to help you become aware of the influences of different environments and situations on your perceptions and reactions to experiences.

Sit down in a quiet place and take an inventory of your current mental, physical, and emotional states. Pay attention to your state of consciousness at this moment. Now imagine your favorite holiday. Think of events, activities, people, sights, smells, food, music, ceremonies. Allow yourself to really get into the fantasy of that holiday as it exists in your imagination. Now take another inventory of your state of consciousness. The process of becoming aware of your initial state of consciousness, creating the fantasy, and then becoming aware of your subsequent state of consciousness, demonstrates a feedback loop, which was created in your mind and was based on your mental, emotional, and sensory memories. After engaging in this fantasy, you will probably feel happier than you were before you did it. Your system of awareness has been transformed.

We are constantly engaged in feedback loops, which we often think of as "events." The difference between a feedback loop and an event is the way we conceptualize it. When we think of ourselves as engaged in feedback loops, we have an element of influence on the process, as do all the other participants.

We continuously interact. When we think of ourselves as participants in events, we are either the initiators or the recipients, the agents or the respondents. Feedback loops involve continuous interaction and are composed of malleable and nonreplicating processes. You cannot repeat or go back and fix something that occurs in a feedback loop. You can, however, go forward and improve or change the situation. In contrast, agents acting on objects are more likely to consider themselves causative, nonreciprocal participants who do good things and feel good about their actions, or who make mistakes that they then must fix, without assistance from others. This attitude leads to feelings of individual responsibility, which may involve pride, blame, guilt, and "ownership" of outcomes, as opposed to involvement in a feedback loop, which leads to constant and simultaneous feelings of empathy and mutuality.

EXERCISE 1.8 • Relationships as Feedback Loops

The purpose of this exercise is to examine the concepts of being part of a feedback loop or an event.

Find a friend with whom you can do this exercise. Recall a recent time when you participated in an activity together and things did not go exactly as planned. It might be a situation where you went to a party and one of you had a good time, while the other did not. It might be a time when you agreed to go shopping or to a ballgame together and one of you forgot or got the date wrong and did not show up. Talk about the ways your feelings evolved as the situation evolved, how your feelings changed as you realized that your expectations were not going to be met. Remember what you thought, what you felt, and what you did. Talk about this and compare your different responses to this unpredictable situation. How did you react to each other the next time you saw each other? Did you try to figure out whose "fault" it was? That would be an agent/action/object conceptualization. Or did you discuss what happened, which would be a feedback loop conceptualization? Did you try to figure out who to blame, or did you try to figure out how to make sure something similar did not occur the next time? How did the situation affect your friendship? Have your feelings for each other changed? Have you taken any steps to minimize future misunderstandings?

EXERCISE 1.9 • Friendships as Holons

We have talked about the concept of holons. Friends constitute a holon. Through an examination of how you and a friend interpret the world, we will explore further the concept of holons.

Try to find a friend whom you have known for a long time and with whom you have shared a lot of different experiences. This person should be somebody you can count on for support in difficult situations. Each of you should answer question 1 alone; then answer question 2 together.

1. Make a list of similarities and differences between you and your friend. Include hobbies, values, life priorities, preferences in clothing, food, recreational activities, relationships with families, living conditions, career choices, and anything else you can think of. Now review the similarities and try to remember if you ever had different preferences or attitudes regarding any of the items on the list. Try to remember when and why you changed your attitudes or opinions.
2. Compare your lists of similarities and differences with each other. Pay particular attention to your similarities and to the changes that have occurred to make you more similar since you have been friends. Discuss why you changed your preferences or viewpoints.

The process by which you have influenced each other over time was one in which you created a holon in the form of a friendship. The two of you are simultaneously separate and connected. Your two separate selves interact to form connections. Sometimes, on a particularly important issue or choice, you may disconnect a part of the relationship, but as long as you are friends, you are maintaining your connectedness, even though its form or content may change. If one of you chooses a life partner, becomes a parent, or moves far away, the nature of your connection may change and evolve. In extreme cases, you may disconnect because you have chosen some new connections, which create new holons/relationships for you and permit this one to dissolve.

Intentionality and Cross-Cultural Communication

People are products of their cultures. Most people in the United States are multicultural, either because of their ethnic ancestry, their membership in one of the nondominant groups in the United States, or because of other life-shaping circumstances, such as disability, divergent sexual orientation, gender, or age. Americans have multiple frameworks or worldviews, which shape their behaviors in social situations, family roles, work environments, and, possibly, faith communities.

Intentionality is the human framework through which objects and circumstances acquire meaning. Mentally, emotionally, and behaviorally, we all live in overlapping "intentional" worlds (Shweder, 1991, p. 74). *In intentional worlds, people create or construct meaning from the objects, people, and processes with whom and with which they interact.* For example, "stealing" in one situation is "liberating" in another and "borrowing" in a third, although the action of appropriating an object without permission of the owner is objectively the same. "Intentional things have no natural reality or identity separate from human understandings and activities. Intentional worlds do not exist [independent] of the intentional states (beliefs, desires, emotions) directed at them and by them, by the persons who live in them" (Shweder, 1991, p. 75).

Intentional worlds have cultural dimensions to them, so persons from similar cultural backgrounds are more likely to share intentional worlds than are those from dissimilar backgrounds. In an intentional world of African American people who have been abused by numerous white members of a police force, all white cops are considered dangerous. The world they have constructed does not contain benign white cops.

The concept of intentionality is illustrated by this anecdote about baseball umpires and how they call balls and strikes:

> The first umpire says, "I calls 'em as I sees 'em." The second says, "I call 'em as they are." The third says, "They ain't nothin' til I calls 'em." (Shweder, 1991, p. 356).

The intention of the first umpire is to use his perception to construct reality. The intention of the second umpire is to match his words to his perceptions as closely as possible. His world is shaped by a correspondence theory of truth, which he does not question. He assumes that his words reflect, but do not create, reality. The third umpire lives in an intentional world, and he is conscious of his own intentionality. Truth does not exist until he names it and decides what it is.

The enormous difficulties generated by humans' efforts at cross-cultural communication are in large part a result of our unawareness of the complexity and intentionality of the human being. When one person faces another person and says "Good morning" or "Inshallah" or "Your paper is late" or "Namaste" or "I have no food for my children" or "I can't find a job," that person is speaking from and through the intentionality of his or her previous attitudes, beliefs, expectations, norms, socialization and life experience.

For example, if a person from India, recently arrived in the United States, says "I can't find a job," it may mean that his relatives have not found a job for him and he does not expect or know how to find one for himself, but that he believes things will work out in time. In the meanwhile, he is living with his extended family and all resources are shared. If a white or black American says "I can't find a job," it may or may not mean that she or he has looked in the want ads, has or does not have employable skills, expects an unreasonable level of compensation, does not know how to interview, or is not willing to accept the types of employment currently available.

Western cultures believe in an objective model of reality that represents an intentional world. The implication is that words refer to things or experiences on whose meaning we all agree. We pay little attention to context, intentionality, previous experience, or expectations. Thus, in order to communicate across cultures, Americans (with whatever additional cultural elements accompany this primary designation of "American") would enhance their ability to understand and communicate with cultural others if they moved from objective perspective to constructed perspective. In other words, all communications should be understood from at least two perspectives: yours (the objective perspective) and what you imagine (or construct) the other person's to be (the constructed perspective). For example, a dandelion is a weed to a gardener and a flower to a naive observer. Pork may look like dinner to a Christian, but it looks like sin to a Muslim or a Jew. A dog may look like dinner to a Korean, but it looks like a pet to an American.

Thus, cross-cultural communication is a continuous feedback loop in which the participants are creating new holons. Each person wants to retain agency—the ability to achieve his or her goals—and communion or effective communication, all at the same time. This is possible only if each participant is willing to engage in the feedback loop and improve the quality of understanding as the relationship evolves. In addition, the participants must try to grasp and understand which elements of each person's intentional world are active in the particular interaction. In this process of attempting to understand each other, each person is reconstructing his or her meaning system, as well as learning how to understand future behavior and conversation from the other, simultaneously. If participants in the conversation are responsive to each other, they are operating from stable intentional worlds, or meaning systems that have the capacity to "reconstruct themselves when destabilized by new information" (Barton, 1994, p. 9). This capacity exists on all levels of human experience, from the physiological, to the psychological, to the spiritual.

EXERCISE 1.10 • Activities and Value Statements

The purpose of this exercise is to look at some of the activities you engage in during a typical day and to try to evaluate them from a different cultural perspective.

1. Make a chart that will allow you to describe a typical day in your life. Set it up like this:

Activity:

Reasons:

Activity:

Reasons:

(and so on)

On the chart, list the types of things you usually do ("Activity") and then indicate why you believe it is important to do those things ("Reason"). When you finish, you should have a list of some of the ways in which you spend your time and some of the main values that shape your decisions about the ways you spend your time.

2. Now review your list from the point of view of a person from another culture, preferably someone you know. Imagine that person's reaction to each activity. Imagine his or her response to each value statement. Show your list to the person and evaluate the accuracy of what you perceived as his or her point of view. How accurate was your understanding? Where did you miss out? Is there a pattern to your distortions or misunderstandings? If there is a pattern, how is it related to your own viewpoint?

A major dilemma that North Americans face when coming to terms with interactional feedback loops is the common belief that "personality" is stable across time and space. Thus, there is no way to accommodate circumstances under which changing behavior might change one's ability to function effectively (that is, one's personality) in a particular situation. For example, one of the authors of this text recently delivered some "diversity training" to community police in a city with a large, economically disadvantaged Puerto Rican population. The police were all North Americans of European ancestry who had achieved middle-class status and held middle-class values. They had enormous respect for law and order, and they expected everyone who met them as police officers to respond to them deferentially. One young officer was horrified that a 9-year-old boy, who was doing something unacceptable on the street, did not stop when the officer told him to. In fact, the youngster told the officer "where to get off" and to "leave him alone." The 9-year-old boy stated that he saw no reason to pay any attention to the officer's request. The officer knew he could not hit the child or arrest him for mouthing off, and he was so tied to his self-perception as a good person who was maintaining order and who deserved to be respected that he was unable to change his approach to the child. He had little idea of how he appeared to the boy or to the other children who were gathering around him. Therefore, the officer left the scene feeling frustrated, and the child continued to engage in dangerous activities. If the officer could have kept in mind his goal of stopping dangerous behavior, and if he had understood how a large man in a blue suit with a gun might appear to a 9-year-old sitting on the ground, who only partially understood the officer's words, he might have been able to find another approach to achieve his goal. These two holons—the boy and the officer—retained agency (that is, they retained the ability to achieve their goals), but did not figure out how to connect.

Cultural Development and Adaptation

As people mature within their own culture and particular set of experiences, their thinking and functioning become more complex. Infants mature by enculturation, adapting their individual proclivities to the details of their surrounding culture, and (usually) enhancing those elements of their personality that the culture values and suppressing those elements that the culture does not value or recognize (Matsumoto, 1996a).

EXERCISE 1.11 • Cultural Shaping of Children

We are all socialized as children. The purpose of this exercise is to begin to understand how our individual families socialized us.

Try to remember something you loved to do as a child, which your family discouraged you from doing. What was the behavior? What cultural norm did it violate? When did you decide to stop doing it, or have you? Do you remember how your family discouraged you? Did they embarrass you in public? Shame you in private? Tell you that they were disappointed in you? What forms of discouragement are used in your culture to shape the behavior of children?

Development can be considered as a series of fluctuations between agency (the ability to carry out one's purpose or function) and communion (the ability to connect with another). Periodically, people transcend themselves, becoming motivated by a higher goal, a challenging experience, or a new vision of who they want to be. Also periodically, people dissolve toward a previous state of less complexity. This usually occurs when one is faced with extreme stress or an insurmountable challenge. For example, in times of difficulty, many of us resort to eating "comfort food," the food our families gave us when we were children to make us feel good. If intense stress endures, people are likely to revert to earlier coping mechanisms, such as rocking or thumb-sucking.

People who are seriously ill both need and want to be taken care of. People who are chronically ill or are confined to any type of institution for extended periods of time often lose confidence in their ability to take care of themselves. In contrast, some people are willing to risk their lives to save others, or to share valued resources when others are at risk. This is a form of self-transcendence.

The Chaotic Nature of Human Interaction

Holons are dynamic, chaotic systems. Chaos in this sense means complexity and unpredictability, not complete disorder. Interactions, according to chaos theory, tend to occur in patterns that recur or reiterate for a certain number of cycles, and then become unstable. This phenomenon can be observed in the flow of smoke upward from a stick of incense. The smoke forms a column up to a certain point, then becomes wavy, and finally dissipates. Ripples flowing out from a pebble tossed into a calm pond remain regular for a period of time, and then become irregular and finally disappear. Changes in chaotic systems are a result of sensitivity to initial conditions, or strange attractors. *Strange attractors* are conditions that prevail at the beginning of a process and amplify as the process evolves. Strange attractors map the order that is inherent in chaotic and evolving systems. Often that order is "only visible over time and history" (Wheatley, 1994, p. 79). In terms of interpersonal relationships, values, beliefs, and norms can be considered strange attractors. They shape initial interactions and demonstrate increasing but unpredictable power as the relationship evolves. Only in retrospect can the people involved unearth the pattern that has been shaping their interactions. The more variety in the initial conditions, the more variation in pattern. The farther the pattern moves from the initial conditions, the more extreme and unpredictable the variation. Finally, the system destabilizes, integrates the new dynamic, and reorganizes itself at a higher level of complexity (Barton, 1994).

When people interact as chaotic systems, they follow this pattern, although the workings are far less visible than they are in a column of smoke. "Psychosocial systems are best understood as repeated patterns of interpersonal interactions" (Sexton, 1994, p. 250), which are organized according to roles, rules, cultural values, expectations, behavior patterns, and interpersonal history. This complex set of interacting variables forms each person's intentional world (Shweder, 1991) as well as the co-created intentional worlds that exist in relationships and communities (Sexton, 1994). As people form intentional worlds, they live and interact according to their intentionality. As people's intentions, beliefs, perceptions, and values change, their behavior and ascribed meanings change as well.

For example, as long as Michael Jordan is a public sports hero, the athletic shoes he endorses will have great value in the United States. If Jordan were to change sponsors or drop his association with the shoe company, the meaning and value ascribed to those shoes would change among his fans. Fashion among teens in the United States seems to be an intensely intentional world. People have been killed for their leather jackets because the desire to own one was so high. An outfit covered in brand names is far more valuable than a similar outfit bought at a discount store, even if the appearance at a distance is the same.

Any personal preference, cultural value or practice, or family custom can become a strange attractor. As such, it affects both the initial assumptions of people interacting with each other, as well as subsequent patterns of their interaction. For example, if George meets Ashok at a social event, and George greets Ashok with a handshake and says "Pleased to meet you," their subsequent interactions will be shaped by Ashok's perception of what, to Americans, constitutes an appropriate response in social situations. If George greets

Ashok with "Namaste," placing his palms together at his forehead and bowing slightly, Ashok will make a different set of assumptions, based on George's use of Indian greeting patterns. The location of this meeting also will affect its progress. Are the participants in New York? or Calcutta? Is either the guest? Or the host? Any one of these circumstances could become a strange attractor, affecting subsequent iterations of the pattern, topics of conversation, types of activities, future meeting places, and so forth.

EXERCISE 1.12 • Emotional Expression within Conversational Styles

The purpose of this exercise is to recognize the different degrees of emotional expressiveness allowed within different conversational styles, with the understanding that these styles are culturally shaped.

1. Find a friend or willing acquaintance who was raised in an environment that had different cultural elements from those in your own environment. Go to a place where you are out of earshot of other people. Start talking about any subject you like in a serious manner. With each successive interaction, raise your voice. As soon as one of you becomes uncomfortable, signal the other. Discuss the ways in which people expressed anger in your home or cultural community, and what level of expression and intensity was acceptable. Discuss differing kinds of expression that were permitted to people by virtue of gender (for example, men could express anger, but women could not), status (parents could express anger, but children could not) or any other relevant factor.
2. With this same friend or with another, express positive feelings about each other. Talk about why you like each other, what aspects of each other's behavior and personality you find attractive, how you respond emotionally to being with each other. Anytime either of you feels uncomfortable with the conversation, stop and discuss your discomfort. If you are able to identify the rules about expressing positive emotion that governed your cultural community, discuss and compare them.
3. Try bragging about yourself to your friend. Cultures vary drastically in their willingness to permit people to express their happiness at their own individual achievements or skills. If you can do this, try it out, and discuss your friend's reaction to your bragging. If this kind of bragging is too uncomfortable for you, discuss your discomfort. Thinking of your friendship as an evolving holon or chaotic system, discuss what changes would need to occur for either of you to become comfortable expressing these feelings in the presence of the other. Discussing and analyzing your reactions demonstrates how two holon systems can reorganize their organizational patterns in order to incorporate new information.

EXERCISE 1.13 • Chaotic Interactions in Social Settings

All social rituals and interactions have unstated rules and regulations. The purpose of this exercise is to begin to recognize their existence.

Think of a party you have attended in the past few months. Try to remember as many details as you can. How were you invited? How far in advance did you receive the invitation? Were you expected to bring food or drink to the party? Were you expected or permitted to bring a guest? If you were permitted to bring a guest, did you have to ask permission in advance? Were any assumptions made about the gender of your guest or your relationship with that person? How did you greet the host or hostess? Did you arrive at a particular and specific time or within a general time period, or was only the time of day designated (for example, "Tuesday evening")? How did you know what to wear? What did you think people would be doing at the party?

Think of the party as a particular form of North American ritual gathering. After you have reviewed all of the expectations, create a monologue in which you explain to a friend from some other part of the world what a North American party (among your group of friends) is like and what the friend could expect if he or she attended the party as your guest. Remember, you need to inform your friend about appropriate use of time and space, proper clothing and forms of greeting, acceptable relationships between the sexes, assumed connections or relations among all the people who attend, and so forth. After you have finished your description, try to imagine your friend's reactions to these social requirements.

If you do have a friend from another culture, discuss his or her reactions to your list. If you do not, compare North American expectations for socializing with what you know about similar expectations among people of the same class in India, Japan, Nigeria, Saudi Arabia, or some place whose culture is dramatically different from that of the United States. If you are a university or college student, go to the office of an ethnic club for students from another country and find somebody with whom you can discuss this exercise. If possible, ask to be invited to one of their social gatherings so that you can sense and observe the differences in socializing patterns. Expect this analysis of a complex social event to take quite a long time.

Establishing Equilibrium

The complex social event in the previous exercise is a type of chaotic system. Each person at a party arrives with his or her intentional world in an operative state. All of the guests' intentional worlds begin interacting. Initial circumstances, as we have seen, profoundly affect outcomes. For example, if the room is too crowded or if somebody does not understand somebody else or interprets somebody's behavior according to another meaning system, a fight can occur or feelings can be hurt. Strange attractors can change the dynamics. You will recall that a strange attractor is an initial condition that might seem insignificant at the beginning of an interaction but has increasing influence as the interaction progresses. If a fraternity is throwing a stag party for a brother who is about to get married and his fiancée arrives uninvited, or if a bisexual male goes to a gay bar for the first time, gets drunk, and yells in a loud voice "Where are the women?" the tone, feelings, and activities in the room can change immediately.

Consider the bisexual male who yelled about wanting women in a gay bar—an event that actually happened. The dynamics of socializing in the room changed immediately. He had pushed the system from a state of equilibrium, in which everybody knew how to act, to a state far from equilibrium, in which nobody knew what was going to happen. Some people tried to hit him. Some people pulled him back into his chair and surrounded him in order to protect him. Fear and anger, which had not been apparent before the man yelled, became palpable in the room. People did not know if he was simply drunk and unaware of his surroundings, or if he was dangerous and likely to pull out a weapon. Should the people in the bar humor him? Attack him? Or just remove him? In such situations, the immediate response is always unpredictable, but subsequent action always restores equilibrium to the system. In this case, the man's friends surrounded him and, after the noise quieted down, escorted him from the bar and took him home.

If an Israeli student went to a gathering of Arab students and suddenly began singing the Israeli national anthem, a similar disturbance would probably ensue, although the outcome might be different. In both cases, the level of cohesion, friendship, and concern in the group would also affect the outcome.

When two people communicate, they can be considered as two complex holons, exchanging energy and information between systems. The greater the difference between the two people, the more likely it is that information from one system will disrupt the dynamics of the other system. For example, imagine a Scandinavian female, who is normally rather reserved, meeting a gregarious male from Southern Europe. He kisses her hand. She is at a loss for an appropriate response. She has to create a response that will minimize her discomfort and not increase his, all within seconds. If a Japanese woman who is accustomed to quiet and order goes shopping in a marketplace where bargaining is conducted in very loud voices, she may become upset, because the tone of the voice conveys danger to her, even though she does not understand the words and content.

Communication between people, across cultures, varies in complexity, depending on the depth of the relationship and the type of work or business that must be performed. In business relationships, people must learn the social forms appropriate to the cultures that have shaped their business partners. This includes information about gift giving, time usage, deference to authority, proper modes of address, work schedules, and so on. A person who has repeated transactions with members of a particular group must understand the norms of that group. For example, a grocery store owner in a neighborhood that has many people from the Middle East must learn the appropriate forms of public communication between unrelated men and women, as well as how to exchange money, how to address customers, and so on. In more intimate or personal relationships, such as sharing a room in college, dating, or even being invited to join someone's family for a social occasion, an individual needs an even greater awareness of norms, expectations, values, forms of address, time, and ways of showing respect.

Chaos theory is very helpful in giving us a framework for understanding the dynamism, the unpredictability, and the vitality of efforts made between people to communicate across cultures. Nothing can be taken for granted, yet over time, patterns emerge. Once a pattern is noticed, it continues to evolve, sometimes in very surprising ways. These patterns are nonlinear and irreversible. Rather than being able to go back to a previous situation and try to improve it, we are forced to go forward and continue to manage it until we learn to sense the pattern and contribute to mutual understanding. Cross-cultural communication is comparable to improvisational music, in which harmony may be disrupted by discord, which adds interest and moves the melody along to the next harmonic resolution. Harmony and discord form an evolving pattern; one without the other is far less interesting than both in relationship to each other. As harmony and discord weave their melodies, the repeating themes that stabilize the process over time are respect and understanding.

Conclusion

In the 1950s, Lederer and Burdick (1958) coined the term "Ugly American" to describe North Americans who travel throughout the world, ignoring the social customs of all other cultures and assuming, ethnocentrically, that their North American system is the most civilized and the best. We have come a long way from the Ugly American, but most of us still have a long way to go to become Beautiful Americans. Since the 1950s, the level of interaction among people from all over the world and the demands, by members of nondominant groups in the United States, that their cultures be recognized, have escalated exponentially.

We have created extremely complex systems of interaction among different cultures for purposes of travel, study, business, and socializing. Some of these systems, such as multinational corporations, exist in many places over extended periods of time, and their processes, although dynamic, are well articulated. When a person joins a multinational corporation, she or he is trained in company expectations and in ways of doing business wherever the company is actively involved. Universities have established relationships with "sister" institutions around the world, and students and faculty travel back and forth, teaching and learning in different locations and cultures. On a smaller scale, people meet each other while traveling or studying and learn how to relate to each other in a limited time frame. Every cross-cultural connection requires the creation of a new holon in time and space. The creative process requires dual awareness of self and other, as well as attention to the interactive processes of communication and to the strange attractors of strongly held values, beliefs, and norms. Although a person can learn a lot about a different culture before actually meeting people from that culture, no cross-cultural interaction is completely predictable.

The Ugly American did not feel the need to understand other cultures, because he thought the North American system was the best, the most culturally advanced, and the most civilized. He lived in a hierarchical world in which North American and Eurocentric values dominated all others.

We live in a would in which everything is connected to everything else, and the pattern, in its own, unpredictable way, becomes evermore complex and fascinating as it evolves. The brief overview and sample exercises in this chapter are intended to challenge your assumptions, to heighten your attention to verbal and nonverbal cues, and to show you the importance of viewing people and events in their sociocultural context. In this way, you can watch the pattern evolve and find the harmony.

PART ONE

Developing Self-Awareness

From the Inside Out

2

Self and Verbal Interactions

Communication involves two people: the sender, or transmitter, and the receiver. It involves a message that has both verbal and nonverbal components. Communication requires the receiver of the message to listen, pay attention, perceive and respond verbally and nonverbally to the other person, the sender, so that that person knows that he or she has been accurately understood (Okun, 1997, p. 23). Communication also requires the sender to express his or her thoughts and feelings in verbal and nonverbal language so that the receiver can understand the message.

Effective communication between people usually means speaking the same language. It also means understanding expectations regarding tone of voice, distance between speaker and listener, amount of physical touching that is considered appropriate, rules for eye contact, body movements, and facial expressions.

The focus of this chapter is on language and tone of voice, the verbal aspects of communication. The objective is to develop self-awareness of your verbal communications in small, intimate groups, in small, nonintimate groups, and in large groups. The ecological perspective—which considers an individual as embedded in his or her family system, which is, in turn, embedded in larger sociocultural systems—assumes that our self-awareness, comfort, and discomfort differ in each of these different contexts.

People who communicate effectively also understand cultural norms regarding which topics of discussion are considered comfortable and appropriate for people who are colleagues, friends, or relatives, or who differ in terms of gender, age, sexual orientation, or social class. Implicit expectations exist about the "rules" of communication; these vary by culture. For example, counselors and therapists are trained to avoid self-disclosure about their personal views and experiences to clients. A gay man may know that a discussion about his sexual orientation at Christmas dinner will make his family uncomfortable, even if he has "come out" to individual family members. An Asian high school teacher may be dismayed and feel personally affronted by the angry tone of voice used by her supervisor when they are talking about a particular issue.

Take a moment to sit back, close your eyes, and think about how people communicate. Start with the members of your immediate family. What particular communication traits come to mind? What about the people with whom you associate at school? At work? At parties and other social gatherings? Try to identify tones of voice, gestures, closeness or distance, facial expressions, and body language.

Effective communication is complicated and difficult, particularly between people who have different assumptions about what is appropriate. One of the biggest challenges facing people in the United States today is learning how to communicate with people from different cultural, ethnic, or racial backgrounds, as well as with those of different religions and different economic classes.

Self as a Verbal Communicator

The terms *self* and *identity* take on different meanings in different cultures. *Identity* has been described as knowing who you are as a person and as a contributor to society—maintaining "personal coherence or self-sameness through evolving time, social change and altered role requirements" (Hoare, 1991, p. 47). *Self* has overlapping meanings with identity, and this idea will be discussed comprehensively in Chapter 5. In many cultures, "self" implies a larger connection that involves relationship with the cosmos and with the current and historical community in which a person is embedded. This definition of self is particularly salient in certain areas of Asia, where community roles, family roles, and continuity of self over a lifetime are important. In this text, we have chosen to use the terms *self* and *identity* interchangeably, because in the United States they tend to be synonymous.

Psychological and anthropological literature (as summarized by Agar, 1994) define language as a reflection of a person's identity. Experience, reflection, and language are reciprocally influential. Language influences the way we think about ourselves, and the way we observe, and interpret the world around us. It determines what behavior is expected of us in any particular situation (Sapir, 1958; Whorf, 1956). We learn both our language and our ideas about who we are from those around us in our earliest years. These primary experiences, which Cooley (1956) and G. H. Mead (1964) called "the looking glass self," lay the groundwork for our self-identity. When considering language, we must take note of possible differences in proficiency and comprehension that may exist between one's primary language, the first language one learns, and one's preferred language, which might be, but is not necessarily, the language of the dominant culture, as well as semantic differences. Some languages are better than others at expressing specific types of information. People choose the language with which they will be most comfortable in social context. For example, people often speak one language at home and another in the workplace.

We begin this section with an exercise on self-identity. Exercises like this one are designed to help us become more aware of the influences of ecological variables (those involving the relations between individuals and their environment) and cultural variables on our socialization, which, in turn, influences personality development and consequential behaviors (Triandis, 1994).

EXERCISE 2.1 • Self-Identity

The purpose of this exercise is to help you become aware of the different groups and cultures to which you belong and the different roles you play in each of these groups and cultures.

Examine the sample ecomap in Appendix B. An *ecomap* is a map that shows all of the sociocultural systems in which you are embedded. An ecomap is an extension of a family *genogram*—a map that lists family members, their age, their relationship to you, their special characteristics, age at death, time of divorce, and so on. A genogram covers at least three generations of one's family. In an ecomap, we display our roles within our former and current families in the inner circle. In the outer circles, we display those institutions and sociocultural systems that have affected our development.

Construct an ecomap for yourself by examining the groups in your microsystem and beginning to label the roles you play in each group in that system. For example, in your family-of-origin (the family into which you were born) you may be a brother or sister, a son or daughter, the oldest child, the youngest child, the only son, and so forth. In your current family, you may be a spouse, a parent, or a significant other. At school, you may be identified according to your areas of interest or skill, such as journalism, biology, athletics, music, and so forth, or by your nonacademic role such as leader, peacemaker, or clown. At work, you may practice similar functions. Those involving teamwork and group achievement may become more prominent, leading you to assume the role of consensus builder, decision-maker, or organizer.

Now that you have drawn your ecomap and have identified some of the roles you play in the associations and groups that are most significant in your life, complete the following steps. (You may make your ecomap as extensive as you wish, but be sure to *analyze* your microsystem in great detail.)

1. Make a chart that includes a list of *statements* that describe you.
2. Now identify your membership, relations, activities, and accomplishments in each group (the *external function* of your association with the group).
3. Finally, consider what that aspect or role contributes to your sense of self (the *self* function of your association with the group). In your family of origin, for example, were you the mediator? The placator (avoiding conflict)? The opposer (resister)? The initiator? The

bystander? The "smart" one? The "athlete"? What about your friendship system? Your work system? Your school system? Your religious system? Your recreational systems? Your chart should look something like this:

Role (Internal)	**External Function**	**Self Function**
I am a mother.	relation	nurturer
I am a teacher.	activity/relations	nurturer/judge
I am an American.	membership	pride/values
I am a Catholic.	membership	values/beliefs
I am a daughter.	relation	commitment
I am a musician.	activity	expression
I am a college graduate.	achievement	pride

This assignment should help you become aware of your involvement and participation in a multitude of social systems (groups) and how that participation contributes to your sense of who you are. These roles may occur by choice, by accident, by assignment, or by selection. In each of these systems and roles, your conversational style may differ. This chart can be transcribed into a new ecomap or map that shows the relationship of your self in relation to these other social systems (see Appendix B for an example). Each role and function may be associated with subtle or overt changes in conversational style, tone of voice, type of vocabulary, and so forth. Return to this ecomap as you continue reading this book, and add dimensions to it that reflect your increasing awareness of the complexity of your self-identity in a social/historical context.

Self in the Context of Early Groups

One's self-definition develops within the context of one's family of origin, the family into which one is born. That family, embedded in larger sociocultural systems, is formed in the context of the larger communities in which it resides. Gender, socioeconomic class, religion, race, ethnicity, geography, and generational values, attitudes, and beliefs all impact the family system that shapes your own self-construction. Recent developmental theories, as summarized by Rutter and Rutter (1993), posit that our self-identity is fluid over the lifespan and is subject to other influences. These influences may include changing sociocultural variables, such as our changing role as we grow in our family of origin; the establishment in adulthood of our own family and career; participation in various community activities; place of residence; and so on. Some characteristics of our self-identity remain relatively constant, but some disappear, and others emerge or reemerge over time.

As you look over your chart from the previous exercise, consider the effect that eliminating any particular role or function might have on your self-identity. Do you have a core set of roles, beliefs, and values that seem to have defined your sense of self over an extended period of time, or is your self fluid and highly responsive to context? Which roles and functions are most important with regard to how you see yourself?

People who are born in the United States and who are part of the dominant culture tend to see the self as constant over time and context. They tend to think of modifying their behavior to fit a situation or context as "role playing," as falsifying one's "true self" in order to fit in, impress others, or achieve fairly selfish goals. In other cultures, fitting in is a very high priority, and one's behavior is determined by the role one is expected to play in a particular situation. For example, in traditional China or India, a woman as a young wife is expected to defer to her mother-in-law. In contrast, she may become very domineering as an older woman, once she has given birth to sons and has become a mother-in-law herself. She is not considered to have changed, but merely to be behaving in a role-appropriate fashion.

EXERCISE 2.2 • Others' Views of Who You Are

The purpose of this exercise is to compare others' views of who you are with your own views.

Ask five or six people who know you in different contexts (relatives, close friends, colleagues) to write down ten adjectives that they believe describe you, and put them in a blank envelope. Ask one person to collect these envelopes (by mail or in person). At the same time, write your own list of ten adjectives that describe you. When you receive the others' lists, make a table in order to compare them with each other and with your own list.

Which adjectives occur most frequently? Categorize the words. For example, *good, nice, pretty, smart, helpful, friendly,* and *warm* are personal attributes. *Hard-working, diligent, ambitious, workaholic, productive,* and *efficient* have to do with work or industry. What categories shape or describe the important aspects of your self? Do your adjectives apply to all of these categories? How much congruence is there among others' views of who you are? Do others' views mesh with your own self-views? With which aspects of your identity are you most comfortable? With which are you uncomfortable? Consider the people whom you asked to help you. What group membership do you share with them? Where do they belong on your ecomap? Most people tend to choose people whom they know well and with whom they feel comfortable. Would people from other systems have chosen the same words to describe you?

It might be interesting for you to redo this exercise, picking people who do not know you well or who come from different systems, such as colleagues with whom you do not work directly, a spouse's friend, or your doctor. Proceed as you did before. After you have tabulated your responses, compare the two sets of responses. How can you explain the similarities or differences?

The final part of this exercise involves self-analysis. How do your beliefs about yourself fit your aspirations of who you would like to be? Are they congruent with the ideas you received growing up about who you were supposed to be? How do your self-views differ according to the system in which you find yourself? For example, some people describe themselves as active with their families and passive at school or work.

Our presentation of self-identity changes not only over time, but also across contexts. It is influenced by the different people with whom we interact within different systems. It is contextual. We may present one person to our families, another to our colleagues, and still another to the general public. Some people tend to be more fluid than others. People who have rigid self-identities and who resist adapting to new people, circumstances, and situations frequently find their growth and development restricted. Most people typically have a core sense of self that emanates from childhood. This sense of self is the frame of reference we use for replication, repudiation, or modification. If, for example, we were labeled as the "stubborn" one in the family, we may fulfill that script by becoming increasingly stubborn as we pass through adolescence and adulthood, or we may try consciously to be anything but stubborn in order "to prove them wrong," even becoming too placating. Or, we may continuously struggle with what has become a propensity for stubbornness. The point is that there is always a dialectic struggle between stability and change. In some contexts, it may be easier for us to be easygoing; in others our "stubborn" tendency will prevail.

Verbal Communication: Speaking

Verbal communication has many facets: our use of language; our tone of voice; our punctuation; our rate of speech; our topic selection; our timing; our redundancy. The term *verbal communication* also refers to our ability to listen effectively and provide adequate feedback. All of these aspects together make up our conversational style. A wide variety of conversational styles is possible.

EXERCISE 2.3 • Definition of Conversation

People not only have different conversational styles, but also have different definitions of conversation. The purpose of this exercise is to compare personal definitions and come up with possible inclusive definitions.

1. Write down your definition of "conversation."
2. In a small group, compare your definition with those of others. Create a group list of definitions.
3. Consider the following questions:
   - How do different group members view the role of silence in conversations?
   - Discuss what messages "silence" can give and how it makes people feel.
   - How do different members view the role of interruptions, of loudness, or of other conversation characteristics?

Every one of us has a dominant or primary conversational style, a style that we feel most comfortable with, and that we use in comfortable situations. Like our "self-construction" (the way we view ourselves), this style develops when we are young, and it is strongly influenced by our family of origin. Unlike personality, in which some traits or characteristics continue throughout life, we can possess or master several distinct conversational styles. We continue acquiring these styles throughout life as we become exposed to new styles, different social settings, and new goals or tasks. Our conversational styles have some consistencies, even if we have had training or have consciously sought to change some aspects. For instance, if one tends to talk quickly, or in clipped phrases, these traits carry over from situation to situation. At the same time, clear differences occur, which are due to context. For example, when you are with peers, your conversational style may be less formal than when you are with teachers or supervisors. You may note that you talk to children differently than you talk to other adults—more slowly or in a higher pitched voice. You may talk more slowly, talk louder, and enunciate more clearly when you are with the elderly or someone from another country. You may be more casually conversational with friends than with co-workers, and even more so with friends who share your cultural heritage. These differences depend on our perceptions of the people, situations, and contextual systems with whom we talk, perceptions that unconsciously shape and determine our conversational styles.

Making judgments about which conversational style to use is important and can become difficult in ambiguous situations. For example, a white North American meeting a person of Asian ancestry has to decide quickly how to speak with that person. This decision is based on an immediate assessment of the other person's place of birth and level of competence in speaking English. The white North American is responding to the visual cue of facial features, and is making assumptions about what those cues might mean. Similar judgments are made when responding to the visible cues of dress or hair. For example, persons who are considered black in the United States, but who were born in the Caribbean Islands, do not share the same cultural history, self-image, or conversational style as African Americans. Inaccurate assessments can lead to painful social embarrassment. Becoming aware of our own conversational styles is much more difficult than thinking about other people's styles. As you look over your ecomap, reflect on whether you have received feedback from anyone about your conversational style. Did anyone tell you that you talk too fast? Too slow? Too loud? Too soft? If so, make a note of such feedback in the appropriate place on your ecomap. Has anyone told you that you do not listen? That you do not understand? That your vocal tone does not match the affective (feeling) quality of the content of what you are saying?

It is difficult to come up with a typology of conversational styles, primarily because the number of factors involved would lead to too great a number of styles to be able to process and work with. Therefore, we will focus instead on a representative array of traits, with the understanding that individual styles can fall anywhere along the spectrum of each trait.

Conversational Traits

Conversational traits include *formality, intimacy, directness, acknowledgment and tolerance of conflict,* and *involvement.* With regard to *formality,* people may find themselves at the formal end of the spectrum in which they address others by their formal title (such as Doctor, Mr., or Ms. in the United States), to the most informal end of the spectrum, where people may address each other by pet names or descriptions (such as "sweetie," "love," "peanut").

Intimacy is related more to informality than to formality. The characteristics of the intimacy trait refer to the amount of personal information that is revealed in the course of the conversation (self-disclosure). In other words, intimacy refers to the degree to which one is comfortable with exchanging information of a personal nature or talking about sensitive issues. The definition of "personal information" is, at the same time, determined by the participants and by the context and the prevailing cultural norms (Triandis, 1994). Cultural definitions exist as to what are considered sensitive issues. For example, in some cultures, discussing money is viewed as inappropriate, whereas in other cultures it is acceptable.

A trait with which many people have problems is *directness.* Some people can be extremely direct, saying exactly what they think and feel at the moment, or they can be very indirect, not saying what they mean or feel and assuming that the listener will understand the hidden message. For people who are accustomed to directness, indirect speech can be difficult to decipher. We will see in a later discussion that this trait is a major cultural difference between high-context and low-context cultures.

Acknowledgment and tolerance of conflict is strongly influenced by culture. Arab cultures, for example, tolerate conflict in the bargaining arena, where raised voices and insults often are used. In contrast, Japanese people rarely say no to anything and have numerous ways to convey their negative feelings without expressing them verbally. Awareness of the powerful influence of culture helps us to understand different people's behaviors in context.

Some aspects or traits of conversational style are compilations of characteristics or behavior patterns. For example, tolerance of conflict is a process that involves the degree to which conflict or disagreement are acceptable, as well as the degree to which arguments and insults are acceptable. At one end of the spectrum, the high-tolerance end, conflict is not only acceptable, it is expected. This means that saying no and arguing are acceptable, as are expressing negative feelings, whether through insults, silences, or jokes. People are expected to become emotional, and it is not necessary for everyone to agree. At the low-tolerance end of the spectrum, conflict is not allowed. "No" is to be avoided at all costs and no negative feelings can be expressed. Everyone is supposed to agree.

One trait that evokes strong responses is the amount of *involvement* or enthusiasm. Characteristics of high involvement include overlapping and tagging. Overlapping occurs when people talk simultaneously, elaborating on the same topic. Tagging involves adding onto another's incomplete sentence. An easy identifier of high involvement among North Americans is the lack of silence. At the other end of the spectrum (low involvement), people wait for "breaks" and two people never talk at once (Tannen, 1990).

Involvement and enthusiasm can be related to the degree of frivolity or seriousness. At one end, this trait reflects an excessive, strictly serious manner or presentation. As a result, it can be seen as linked to a formal or impersonal style. At the other end, this trait reflects excess frivolity, resulting in an abundance of jokes, humor, and related behaviors.

EXERCISE 2.4 • Preferred Conversational Styles

The purpose of this exercise is to identify your own preferred conversational style.

In order to personalize the above discussion about conversational styles, rate your behavior or preferred style on the following chart. A 3 means you behave equally in both ways, whereas a 1 or a 5 means you behave according to one extreme or the other. Keep this chart in mind as you continue reading about communicating.

Formal	1	2	3	4	5	Informal
Impersonal	1	2	3	4	5	Intimate
Considerate	1	2	3	4	5	Inconsiderate
Direct	1	2	3	4	5	Indirect
Controversial	1	2	3	4	5	Noncontroversial
Intolerant	1	2	3	4	5	Tolerant
Frivolous	1	2	3	4	5	Serious

EXERCISE 2.5 • Personal Conversational Styles

The purpose of this exercise is to understand how you change your conversational styles to fit the social context.

From the following list, identify the verbal characteristics or behaviors that you would be most likely to use with the individuals included on your ecomap:

deferential forms of address and titles (such as Dr., Mr., Mrs.)
disclosure of personal information
joking
insulting
humor
gossiping
boasting
talking about feelings
disagreeing
arguing
clamming up
changing the subject

See if you can determine what it is about each relationship and/or situation on your ecomap that enables you to use these conversational characteristics/behaviors.

Now review Exercises 2.4 and 2.5. What have you learned about your conversational style(s)? What behaviors make you feel comfortable? uncomfortable? Cast your mind back to your family of origin. Using a different color of pen or pencil, indicate the conversational style of the members of your family of origin on the chart that you made in Exercise 2.4. Is your style like your family's or different? How would you explain this similarity or difference?

As you review this data, try to figure out when you experience particular comfort and ease and when you experience discomfort. When is it safe to be direct with people and when must you be indirect? What do you think are the patterns and preferred modes of verbal communicating that you have learned over the years? With whom and when are you able to share your feelings? Your secrets? With whom and in what circumstances do you avoid conflict? With whom and in what circumstances can you disagree? With whom can you argue? With whom can you openly express your views?

EXERCISE 2.6 • Language Values

The purpose of this exercise is to understand the hidden values and connotations of everyday language.

People have different experiences with language and therefore assign different values to words. Consider the following list of words: *direct, secret, loud, whispering, muttering, fast, distant, whining, yelling, swearing, touching.* Each of these words describes a way of communicating. On the chart below, label each word as good, bad, honest, dishonest, right, wrong, powerful, inept, intrusive, or considerate. (You can assign more than one label to each word.) Now, consider how you judge people with whom you associate by using these words. For example, if someone is direct, and you have labeled this word as good, honest, right, or powerful, then you will consider that person in a positive manner. If directness is seen as bad, dishonest, wrong or inept, then a person who is direct will be viewed negatively. These views will shape your expectations about your interactions with this person.

	good	bad	honest	dishonest	right	wrong	powerful	inept	intrusive	considerate
Direct										
Secret										
Loud										
Whispering										
Muttering										
Fast										
Distant										
Whining										
Yelling										
Swearing										
Touching										

EXERCISE 2.7 • Your Verbal Behavior

The purpose of this exercise is to enhance further your awareness of your personal conversational style.

Make a tape recording of a conversation with a friend, classmate, or colleague. You may pick a particular topic or allow one to evolve naturally. Plan on taping for at least 45 minutes. Be sure that both of you are audible on the tape before proceeding. At the end of the taping session, listen to your tape. Note the following:

- Your use of language. Do you use simple words? Descriptive? Complex? Long sentences? Short comments?
- Are there many pauses in your sentences?
- Do you sound hesitant? Sure of yourself?
- Are you speaking too slowly? Too fast?
- Do you seem to stumble over your words?
- Do you think about what you are going to say before you say it? Or do you think out loud?
- How would you describe your tone? Friendly? Intimidating? Sure? Unsure? Aggressive? Argumentative?
- How well do you listen? Are you reflecting on what your partner said? Does it sound as if you are thinking more about what you will say next than what he or she is saying? Does it sound as if you are trying to solve the problem rather than listen?
- Are there any periods of silence?
- Do you talk more about your views or your partner's? Do you find that you reveal much about what you are really thinking or feeling?
- Do you joke? Use humor? Insults?
- Do you sound as if you are boasting?

Finally, how do you feel about the way you sound? Do you recognize yourself? Sometimes people cannot identify with their recorded voice; it sounds like someone else. What would you like to change about your verbal behavior? Do you think you expressed yourself the way you wanted? How direct/indirect were your verbal messages? Putting yourself in the position of your partner, how easy would it be for someone to receive your messages accurately?

It may be helpful to listen to the tape again after a few days to see if your later reactions to it match your earlier ones. What later reactions do you have? How do you think other people hear you? If possible, ask your partner to answer the above questions about your verbal conversational style and think about the similarities and differences in your appraisals.

Literal and Analogic Messages

Although becoming aware of the characteristics of your conversational style is important, the congruence or lack of congruence between your *literal* messages and your *analogic* (hidden, or underlying) messages is equally significant. Each communicative message has two levels: (1) the literal content of your words and (2) the underlying "message about the message," the analogic message conveyed by both your verbal and nonverbal messages. For example, you might say, "It's really raining heavily." That message is an observation about the weather. But what if you are saying that not just to inform the recipient of your message about the weather, but because you want that person to offer you a ride home so you do not have to stand in the rain waiting for the bus? If the recipient of your message does not get the underlying message and therefore does not offer you a ride home, you may be annoyed and think to yourself, "He/she is so insensitive and selfish." It is the "message about the message," the *metacommunication,* that shapes and controls relationships. Recognizing that we often send several messages and that they are not all received is an important step in understanding how people communicate. It is important for you to recognize the literal and underlying analogic messages within your own conversational style.

As discussed in Chapter 1, there are high- and low-context cultures. In a low-context culture such as the United States, one tends to believe that if a person wants something, he or she should ask for it openly and directly. Conversation is literal. In high-context cultures such as Asia, messages are more analogic; that is, if a person wants something, they imply it indirectly and expect the other person to "know" the underlying meaning of the message. For example, a North American might ask a close friend whether she and her spouse were planning to have children. A person from a high-context culture might remark to a close friend that couples these days seem to be postponing having children—and let the subject drop.

EXERCISE 2.8 • Verbal Feelings

The purpose of this exercise is to help you become aware of the kinds of verbal behaviors you use to convey your feelings.

Choose a partner. Generate a list of words that you use to communicate feelings of "glad," "sad," "mad," and "scared." Write the words on a chart such as the following one. How descriptive and expansive are your word lists? Compare your list with that of your partner and then combine with others in your group. Are there differences? Now list other verbal behaviors associated with these four major categories of emotion. When you are "mad," for example, do you swear? use short, clipped sentences? retreat into monosyllables? yell?

	Mad	Sad	Glad	Scared
Descriptive Words				
Verbal Behaviors				

EXERCISE 2.9 • Analogic Messages

This exercise should be done in pairs. The purpose is to recognize the analogic messages we are sending.

The table below contains a list of sentences (on the left) and a partially filled in column of possible analogic meanings on the right. Each person should complete the right column individually. Then, take turns saying the sentences on the left with the intention of conveying the messages on the right. Did you or your partner pick up on the analogic meanings? Exchange lists and compare your results. How similar were your lists? Were you surprised by any of the analogic meanings? Do these sentences remind you of any past misunderstandings?

Sentence	Analogic Meaning
It's raining outside.	Can I have a ride?
It's stuffy in here.	Open the window.
That smells good.	Can I have one?
Oh yeah, oh yeah.	
This is a very difficult lab.	
Well, what do you want to do?	
What time is it?	
Well, I have a lot of work to do.	
I don't like computers.	
I'm confused.	
I want to please you.	
I'm bored.	
We're late.	
I'm tired of waiting.	

Verbal Communication: Listening

Listening is also an important part of communication. Listeners must attend to the apparent and underlying meanings of the verbal communication—to the literal *and* the analogic messages. They must assess the tone, punctuation, rate of speech, and clarity of message, as well as their understanding of the actual words.

EXERCISE 2.10 • Listening Skills

The purpose of this exercise is to assess how accurately you hear what other people mean.

Listen again to your tape. This time, assess your listening skills. How well do you think you heard your partner? Were you able to decode his or her messages accurately, grasping the analogic as well as the literal messages? Did you ask clarifying questions when you were unsure of his or her meaning, or did you act as if you understood even when you did not? Was it hard to attend to your partner? In other words, did you find that other thoughts crossed your mind? Did you communicate interest in what your partner had to say? If so, what verbal behaviors did you use to communicate this interest? Did you answer his or her questions directly? What questions did you evade, and how? Was your vocabulary easy to understand? As a listener, when do you think you felt most comfortable during the taping session? When were you least comfortable?

Given the same language, two people can easily agree on the literal meaning of a statement but have different analogic meanings. How we interpret hidden messages is related to our role in the group and to the role of the person making the statement. The same statement made by two different people in two different contexts may be interpreted differently. Both context and the roles of the participants determine both meaning and interpretation. Unfortunately, the sender's meaning and the receiver's interpretation are not always the same.

EXERCISE 2.11 • Multiple Meanings

The purpose of this exercise is to increase your understanding and appreciation of multiple possible meanings and interpretations of verbal messages.

Look at the following chart. On the left side of the page is a list of statements. On the right is space for you to identify each statement as an order, request, question, statement, and so on.

Consider how your interpretation would change if the person making the statement was (1) your boss, (2) your colleague at work, (3) your subordinate at work, (4) your spouse, (5) your parent, (6) your child, (7) a close friend, (8) female, (9) male, (10) Latino, (11) African American, (12) white, (13) a stranger, (14) someone you dislike.

Discuss how your role relating to the sender affects your statement identification.

Statements	**Type of Statement**
Please take a seat.	
Stay here, please.	
Would you mind waiting a moment?	
Could you help me, please?	
Would you please get me a cup of coffee?	
What you need to do is . . .	
Where are you going?	
No, I can't go for a drink with you.	

Now, use the awareness generated by this exercise to go back over the tape you made earlier and decode your partner's statements. Make a table like the one above with your partner's statements in one column and the type of statements in the other.

What do you think he or she was feeling or really thinking or wanting from you? Check your answers to these questions with your partner to determine if you are correct in your interpretations. See if you can get in touch with the internal process—what you say to yourself to understand meaning and to decode others' messages.

Along with learning how to evaluate one's own listening skills, it is useful to consider how we interpret other people's listening skills. Did you feel that your partner listened to you throughout the conversation? At what points did you feel listened to? What actions, behaviors or characteristics caused you to feel this way? How do you know when someone is hearing and understanding you? Make a list. When did you feel as if you were not listened to? Now make a list of those actions, behaviors or characteristics that caused you to feel as if you were not being listened to. Consider both of your lists. How does one know when one is being listened to and understood?

Understanding Your Verbal Conversational Style

Our primary verbal style is strongly influenced by our family of origin. We first begin to learn the rules of conversation around age 3. We make certain assumptions about verbal communication while we are growing up. Remember, you were influenced not just by the family system in which you were raised, but also by your gender, class, religion, race, ethnicity, educational opportunities, and the community in which you resided. Let us see if you can identify the "communication rules" that govern your verbal behaviors. Rules, as previously noted, tend to cover the following areas: forms of address, expression of feelings, distinction between public and private information, self-disclosure, and so forth.

EXERCISE 2.12 • Family Rules (Part 1)

The purpose of this exercise is to identify your family-of-origin rules about conversation.

Consider the following questions as you reflect back on your experience growing up in your family of origin:

- Were you encouraged to talk about your feelings? If so, what was permissible and what was not?
- Was anyone in your family allowed to swear? Yell? Argue? Disagree? Call people names? Were these behaviors restricted to certain members or allowable for everyone? Were there special names for certain people in the family? What roles did they indicate?
- Did family members ask each other questions about their interests, feelings, views, and activities?
- Did you call adults by their first names? Did you use titles?
- Were children allowed to talk freely, or were they expected to be silent except when asked direct questions?
- Who talked to whom about what?
- What topics were not to be talked about within the family? Could they be discussed with those outside of the family?
- Were people expected to apologize? How? Were these expectations based on one's role in the family?
- Were there certain familiar words or sentences that you recall characterizing your family communications?
- Were certain ethnic words or phrases (from other languages such as Yiddish, Ebonics, Greek, Chinese) frequently used within your family?
- How did your parents talk to each other?
- Do you recall differences in the ways your parents talked to their sons versus the way they talked to their daughters?

- Who was the most silent in your family?
- How did people verbally express defiance?
- What verbal behaviors enabled you to get what you wanted?
- What were the pathways of communication; in other words, did you have to ask for something through another person?
- What verbal behaviors communicated power? Who had the most power in your family when you were growing up? How did you know?
- What differences did you notice among the verbal behaviors in your family, your school, and your friends' families?

When you recall some of the operating rules of the family in which you grew up, you can begin to identify the communication rules that you internalized. For example, some families operate by the rules: "Children should be seen and not heard"; "Never express your feelings or you'll get blamed or criticized"; "Don't give too much information"; "Try to joke your way out of trouble." Again, compare your rules with those of others in your group. What kinds of gender, race, ethnic, or class differences can you identify? If you are married, compare the rules of your family-of-origin with those of your spouse's.

EXERCISE 2.13 • Family Rules (Part 2)

The purpose of this exercise is to further explore your family's rules about conversation.

In order to identify our rules of communication, we need to look more closely at our family of origin. The following is a modification of "Discovering Ancestors' Shadows," an exercise developed by Joel Crohn (1995).

On a large piece of paper, create a family tree, using a circle to represent females and a square to represent males. Include all members who lived with you in the same house. Leave room underneath each symbol to write down what each member would say in response to the following two statements:

> The primary rule for conversations in this family is: ____________.
> The most common criticism about your conversational style is: ____________.

After completing your chart, choose members of your group to speak each part. Have them practice their lines until you feel that they say them with the correct intonation, phrasing, and emphasis. When you are satisfied with their mastery, have them all stand in a line facing you and speak their parts. Then have them say their lines as a chorus. Repeat several times. Which voices stand out? Which resonate or make you feel comfortable? uncomfortable?

Politeness is a category of speech or action that is culturally determined. It can be the source of major insults and misunderstandings. What is considered polite in one culture may not be considered polite in another culture. For example, shaking hands is expected during a polite greeting in some cultures but is frowned upon in cultures where personal contact is considered intrusive.

EXERCISE 2.14 • The Meaning of Politeness

The purpose of this exercise is to help you become aware of your own concept of politeness.

Can you recognize your own feelings about using and receiving politeness?

List some verbal examples of politeness. In what situations do you feel comfortable using these examples or receiving them? Consider politeness in different situations or spatial settings. Consider your own discomfort and recognize how you display it. Apply these same questions to boasting, joking, insulting, arguing.

Next, consider what verbal behavior rules you learned in your neighborhood, with your peers, and in elementary school. Ask yourself the same questions as above, apropos to each of these other settings. Were there differences? How has your verbal conversation style been shaped by your experience in these systems?

Consider how your conversational style may have changed over the years. Which relationships and group settings have been most influential? How have your own choices and decisions affected these changes? Are there some elements that remain constant?

EXERCISE 2.15 • Development of Conversation Style

The purpose of this exercise is to learn about the developmental path of your conversational style.

Draw a time line from birth to where you are now in your lifespan. Along this line, mark the influences that served as milestones in the development of the verbal rules by which you now operate. At the end of the line, where you are now in your life, write down five current verbal rules for speaking and listening that guide your behaviors.

Verbal Interactions in Small, Intimate Groups

We all belong to groups, large and small. A group is a specific type of social collection of individuals distinct from a party, crowd, or mass. A group is further defined by the presence of an external boundary, which creates a sense of "us" and "them," and by at least one internal boundary. Internal boundaries exist between different categories of membership. An external boundary delimits the group from the rest of society. For example, a school class has a distinctive, external boundary separating members from nonmembers. There are also internal boundaries between the teacher and students within the class and, perhaps, between various subgroups of students. Whether small or large, a group has a definable membership. Members interact and need each other in order to achieve any shared goals and objectives. As a result of these traits, a group consciousness forms (Knowles and Knowles, 1965, pp. 39–40.)

Intimate relationships can be the source of extreme joy and pleasure as well as deep, excruciating pain. The main difference between intimate relationships and nonintimate relationships is our level of emotional involvement. In our intimate relationships, we reveal our best and our worst behaviors, because we feel safe enough to relax and be more authentic. In Western cultures, intimate relationships have the primary aim of fulfilling our capacity to love and be loved. We choose to be in intimate relationships with those people who reinforce the image we have of ourselves (our self-identity). Thus, we gravitate toward those people who bring out our ability to love and be loved and who encourage us to be whom we want to be. We tend to feel closer to people with whom we can share some aspect of our being, whether it be values, activities, interests, beliefs, or whatever. We may have intimate relationships with siblings, parents, lovers, friends, or children. They may be one-to-one relationships or small group relationships.

Roles and Rules of Communication

Different cultures have different notions about intimate relationships, as we will discuss further in Chapter 6. Each culture has different roles for participants in intimate relationships, and these roles translate into communication rules. For example, many Asian cultures script complementary spouse roles, where the wife is expected to subordinate her needs and interests to those of her husband and derive pleasure from caring for him. One unspoken communication rule that derives from this role is "Good wives do not contradict their husbands in public." Most Latino cultures tend to prescribe matriarchal roles for women with regard to child rearing, but patriarchal roles for men with regard to the overall direction and management of public spheres. In both Asian and Latino cultures, the patriarchal power differential is assumed, and there are likely to be clear boundaries between men and women, and between parents and children. (McGoldrick, Giordano, & Pearce, 1996). One Asian colleague expressed concern that her Asian friends felt that her daughter was becoming "too Americanized" because she was so outspoken. The verbal behaviors that communicate disrespect to members of the Asian culture are viewed in many parts of North American culture as representing appropriate individuation.

In the dominant, mainstream, middle-class white North American culture, communication difficulties in intimate relationships can be seen as power struggles for symmetry (Haley, 1963). These power struggles are less about dominance and submissiveness than they are about who decides what and how the roles and rules of the relationships will be. For example, the roles and communication rules determine distance regulation (to whom you can be close, and how you can be close), how feelings are or are not expressed, how disagreement is or is not tolerated, how conflict is approached or avoided, what types of negotiation and problem-solving strategies are acceptable, how positive reinforcement is communicated and received by all parties, how one copes with one's anger and with others' anger, who can criticize whom, and how, and so forth (Okun and Rappaport, 1980). How are these roles and rules determined? Whose expectations prevail? Different ethnic and racial groups have traditional ways of determining these roles and rules. In our diverse culture, with so many intermarriages and cross-cultural friendships, people no longer feel obliged to follow traditional scripts and often create new scripts to fit specific relationships (Okun, 1996).

Thus, what differentiates intimate relationships from all other relationships is the intensity of our expectations, needs, and wants. We reveal more of our "true" selves to intimate others, and there is, therefore, a greater potential for feeling exposed and vulnerable. In other words, our emotional investment is greater; thus, the risk of disappointment, pain, and loss is higher. If someone in whom we have invested emotionally withdraws from us or is acutely critical, we feel a sense of shame or loss, as if some part of our core self is not good enough and acceptable. If a colleague responds to us in the same way, we may feel very hurt, but because our needs for love, acceptance, and affirmation of our sense of self are not invested in that person, we are less devastated than we would be with an intimate other. In short, our response is in part determined by the intimacy of the relationships.

In Western societies, interactions of intimate relationships are often more relaxed and spontaneous than interactions of nonintimate relationships. Intimate interactions represent the open, authentic "I–thou" relationships (which belong to our more "private" self), rather than the less personal, more role-prescribed relationships (which belong to our more "public" self). Recall Exercise 2.1, in which you charted the roles that you play in different groups and in different systems. Clearly, some roles are more public than private. Our public self is evident with people with whom we go to school, work, sport events, and so on. Our private self is reserved for more intimate relationships. How much we reveal of our public or private self exists on a continuum, so that we are more emotionally intimate with some of our co-workers than with others, and more formal with some of our distant relatives than we are with a spouse.

EXERCISE 2.16 • Comfort Levels

The purpose of this exercise is to make explicit how comfortable, in terms of different topics and issues, you are with various people in your life.

Think of the person(s) to whom you feel the closest at this time in your life. In the following chart, rate your comfort level with regard to sharing your true feelings and thoughts about the following topics. Rate your comfort level from 1 to 5, 1 being the lowest and 5 the highest.

Name of Person:

Topic			
boredom			
sex			
money			
family			
religion			
politics			
children			
cheating			
abortion			
feminism			
race			

Look at the topics you rated as low comfort areas and see if you can identify the source of your discomfort. For example, are you afraid of an argument? Of being disliked or rejected? What would have to happen in this relationship in order for you to feel more comfortable talking about this topic? When you talk about these topics with other people (talking about is different from sharing your own personal views and experiences), how restricted or expansive do you feel?

We often engage in more intense verbal communications with those with whom we feel the most comfortable and relaxed, those whom we trust. We are more likely to talk less personally about controversial subjects with nonintimate others.

EXERCISE 2.17 • Intimate and Nonintimate Verbal Behaviors

The purpose of this exercise is to recognize differences in our verbal behavior when interacting with people to whom we feel close and with those to whom we are not close.

Look at the following chart. For each verbal behavior, list the people with whom you would be most likely to engage in that behavior. Then list the people with whom you would never engage in that behavior. Then classify the people with whom you would and would not engage in these verbal behaviors as "Intimate" or "Nonintimate." What are the differences in your lists? What do you think and feel about these differences?

Verbal Behavior	People Most Likely to Engage in the Behavior	People Least Likely to Engage in the Behavior	I = Intimate; N = Nonintimate
Arguing			
Confronting			
Blaming			
Nagging			
Teasing			
Threatening			
Shouting			
Swearing			
Apologizing			

EXERCISE 2.18 • Intimate Discussion

As with the above exercise, the purpose of this exercise is to make apparent how intimacy and familiarity affect how we interact verbally.

Make a tape recording of a talk you have with a small group of intimate friends or at your family dinner. Again, be sure that everyone is audible on the tape. Keep the tape recorder on throughout the meal. After a few minutes, you and the other participants will be unaware of the tape, and the discussion will feel less stilted. You may pick a topic or just let the conversation develop naturally.

When you listen to the tape, note the same verbal characteristics or behaviors that you focused on in Exercise 2.5: disclosure of personal information, joking, insults, humor, gossiping, boasting, talking about feelings, disagreeing, arguing, clamming up, changing the subject. Then compare the two tapes on the following dimensions:

interruptions
pauses
confident tone
hesitant tone
friendly tone
intimidating tone
argumentative tone
aggressive tone
offering solutions
expressing feelings
silences
"mm-mm," "uh-huh"
subvocal actions
questioning
informing
confronting
reassuring and supporting
joking/teasing
expressing empathy and understanding
pet names

What kinds of differences can you discern about the way you interact verbally with intimate others and with nonintimate others? In which group do you talk more about yourself? Which of the tapes seems to be "the real you"? How do you feel about the tapes? Which do you like better? Some people like themselves better in more formal relationships, because they are more self-controlled. Others feel more secure "letting their hair down" with intimate others.

Think about how you influence people. How do you get others to do what you want them to do? Do you harangue? Debate? Argue? Offer concrete information? Threaten? Cajole? Negotiate?

How is your sense of power and influence in your personal relationships similar to or different from that in your other relationships? How do you respond when you are disappointed? When you are angry? When the other person is angry? When you are delighted? How well do you think your intimate others know you? How well do they read you? What verbal behaviors do you think you can use to improve your intimate relationships? Look back at your ecomap and see if you can tell how you interact differently according to which system you are in.

Gender Differences

Much literature exists (Tannen, 1990; Gray, 1993) about gender differences in intimate communications. Couples therapists typically hear "He doesn't listen to me" or "She just wants to talk everything to death." For example, she comes home and vents about how difficult her day at work was, and he responds by telling her what she might do about the problem. She's furious—she does not want to be told what to do, she just wants to be heard. He's confounded at her anger; he was just trying to be helpful and constructive by offering a solution to her problem. This is rather a classic example of how two well-meaning people of different gender have different expectations and assumptions about how their relationship should be. How do your verbal interactions differ with same-gender and opposite-gender intimate relationships? What differences do you see that can be attributed to gender as opposed to individual personality? What kinds of assumptions do you have about women? About men? About same-gender and opposite-gender relationships? Do you think there must always be a sexual dimension in opposite-gender intimate relationships?

EXERCISE 2.19 • Gendered Verbal Characteristics

Having recognized the effects of familiarity and intimacy on verbal communications, we will now explore the effects of gender on verbal communication.

Divide up into small mixed groups. Have each person write a list of what he or she thinks are "female verbal characteristics" and "male verbal characteristics." Compare your list with those of others in the group and develop a group list. Then merge with another group and compare the two group lists. Continue until you have one large group list. Discuss what the gender differences mean to different members of the group. How much can be attributed to socialization in one's family of origin? To socialization in the larger culture? How much can be attributed to ethnicity? How do you explain the variation within male and female groups?

Listening in Intimate Relationships

One of the main difficulties in intimate relationships is that because we think we know the other person so well, we often do not really listen to them. And listening is probably the most important communication skill for creating and preserving intimacy. When you are listening well, you are expressing that you care about the other person and truly want to know what he or she thinks and feels. You are able to put aside your own thoughts, feelings, and views in order to be open to the other person's.

EXERCISE 2.20 • Attending and Listening (Part 1)

An important component of communication is listening. The purpose of this exercise is for you to become very aware of how you listen.

Listen again to the tape you made in Exercise 2.16. Note whether or not you ever:

- read the mind of another participant, deciding for him or her what was meant
- listened to some of what was said but not all of it, filtering out what you did not want to hear
- became preoccupied with thinking about what you wanted to say
- jumped in with your advice before the other person finished their sentence
- caught your attention wandering off to something totally irrelevant to the discussion
- felt annoyed and judgmental about what others were saying because you had made up your mind in advance
- searched for opportunities to argue, debate, or disagree
- tried to control the conversation by talking incessantly or by changing the subject or trying to distract the others from a subject that was uncomfortable for you
- found yourself agreeing too readily in order to be viewed as the "nice, supportive one" in the relationship

At times, we all have difficulty attending and listening to intimate others. This is because of our vulnerability: We are afraid of rejection or abandonment, of feeling unworthy or unlovable, lonely, controlled, or engulfed. We are also fearful of feelings associated with guilt, shame, failure, jealousy, humiliation, emptiness, and loss. When these feelings are triggered, we tend to *avoid* (by turning off and withdrawing), to *deny,* (by not acknowledging or responding to what the intimate other has said), or to *act out* (by attacking, demanding, or finding fault).

EXERCISE 2.21 • Attending and Listening (Part 2)

In this exercise you will practice your listening skills and, with that fresh in your mind, attend to how you are being listened to.

With an intimate friend or partner, block out a 20-minute period of time when you both are undistracted and can sit facing each other. Have your partner talk for five minutes about whatever he or she wants to discuss. Your task as the listener is to attend to both the literal and the analogic messages. You may not interrupt except to ask clarifying questions. At the end of the five minutes, tell your partner what you heard him or her saying, what you decoded your partner's thoughts and feelings to be. When your partner reports that he or she feels accurately heard, reverse roles. Discuss with your partner how you know and feel when you are being accurately heard and what the difficulties are in listening to each other. Come up with an agreed-upon list of verbal cues that indicate that you are listening to each other.

Just as we often speak in a more carefree manner in intimate relationships, we also may not attend to listening as carefully as we would in other contexts. Familiarity often leads to the assumption that we do not have to try as hard as we would in more public relationships.

Verbal Interactions in Small, Nonintimate Groups

Most people in their school and work life spend a lot of time working in groups. The tasks of the groups include communicating information, negotiating formal and informal contracts and expectations, making decisions, and organizing, executing, completing, and evaluating group projects. A nonintimate group may be a working group. It may be small (as when a doctor and patient meet to confer about treatment), or it may be larger, when eight to ten people convene to negotiate policy for a corporation or arrange an international conference. We are more likely to interact with people of different cultures in a working group than we are in intimate groups, where we have the option of selecting those whom we view as more "like us." (There are many exceptions. Many interracial, intercultural, and interfaith couples exist. For discussions specifically about mixed couples, please see Okun, 1996.)

People from different countries who have been forced to interact across the boundaries of different languages, expectations, and norms are familiar with the idea that little can be assumed, that there are no cross-cultural "givens." People who are used to working in culturally encapsulated environments, as is true in large areas of the United States, must continually remind themselves that people from other backgrounds may not interpret or understand language or forms of communication in the same way that North Americans do. In short, there are many different cultures within the United States, and we need to recognize their existence.

The exercises in this section are designed to help you become aware of how your own verbal interaction style and content are influenced by North American cultural expectations. A primary assumption of North American culture is that each person should be an individual, self-determining and guided by a personal belief system founded on the value of autonomy. This core assumption of North American culture makes developing awareness of the effects of culture on our behavior and values rather difficult, because it masks the potential effects of environment on self.

Some elements of verbal communication that vary across cultures have already been identified. These include forms of address, use of humor, level of personal emotion to be revealed or discussed, teasing, disagreeing, and the use of silence. Additional elements that influence communication include culturally based notions of power and status in relationships, gender relationships, the role of individualism versus collectivism in the culture, ideas about time, definitions of family and its function as a public or private element in a person's life, and the role of the sacred in the life of the culture. All of these elements are combined in the notion of "face." "Face is the negotiated public image, mutually granted each other by participants in a communicative event" (Scollon & Scollon, 1995, p. 35). Within cultures, people understand what constitutes face, what courtesies must be extended, how to use humor, how to acknowledge deference or status differences, and how to convey respect or disrespect. Procedures for maintaining face across cultures vary widely.

EXERCISE 2.22 • Power and Status Differential

At this point we will investigate the effects of power and status on verbal communication, alternately as powerful and as powerless.

Imagine yourself in two different types of situations, one in which you have higher status than those who are with you, and one in which you have lower status. Make a list of situations in which there is a clear imbalance of power and status (for example, student–teacher, doctor–patient, mother–daughter, boss–secretary, and so on). Now describe what you would do in a situation where you had superior status or power. How would you address the participants? How would you control the topics to be discussed? How would you indicate that the meeting or interaction was complete? Would you speak slowly or quickly? Would you ask the other participants about their families, their physical condition, or whether they attended religious services in the past week? What subjects would you consider acceptable, and what subjects might be taboo? Are there topics that you as the dominant member of the group might bring up but that nondominant members might not bring up?

Now reverse the situation. Describe what you would do in a situation where you had inferior status and power, and answer the same questions. Compare your responses to the two situations. How does your form of verbal interaction vary according to your status in the group?

EXERCISE 2.23 • Degree of Congruence Between Imagined and Actual Verbal Behaviors

The purpose of this exercise is to compare your lists from Exercise 2.22 with your actual behaviors.

Begin to observe your verbal interactions in nonintimate or working groups. Do you behave in the manner that you thought you would when you made out the lists in the previous exercise? Compare your actual behavior to your imagined behavior and try to identify the source of any differences.

Now try to find a person with whom you can collaborate. Plan to attend a group meeting together. Before the meeting, make up an observation sheet like the one that follows. (Each of you should have a copy of the sheet.) Include topics such as speed of conversation, topics of conversation, who is allowed to change the subject or get the group "back on track," who speaks first or brings up new topics, who summarizes or concludes topics or meeting, and which topics each of you seems willing to bring up or close off.

Sample Observation Sheet

Who opened the meeting by indicating that the time to do business had arrived?

Status/role of that person in the group:

Who typically finishes a subject by summarizing or changing the topic?

Status/role:

What is the relative volume of participants? Who speaks loudly, who more quietly?

Does anybody keep talking or talk louder when somebody else tries to get into the conversation?

Status/role of loud speakers, conversational overriders:

What is the general speed or intensity of the conversation? Who talks fast? Slowly? Who appears more intense than the others?

Status/roles of fast and slow talkers:

Do any topics affect the pace of the conversation (that is, do they cause the conversation to speed up or slow down)?

Do any nonverbal cues accompany the change in pace?

Who brings the meeting to a close and how?

Status/role:

You and your partner should attend the same meeting and fill out your observation sheets. After the meeting, compare your observation sheets. Notice the effects of status and role on group members' behaviors. Make a list of the rules that seem to govern verbal interactions in this group. Label those rules that are status dependent and those rules that are role dependent.

EXERCISE 2.24 • Humor and Gender

Humor plays a large role in verbal interactions. As an aspect of verbal communication, humor is perceived differently by different social groups. In this exercise we will look at gender differences with regard to humor.

Get together with a group of three to eight people who are the same gender as you. Write down several jokes or stories about humorous situations. You might also want to make a list of the TV shows and films that you find funny. Be sure that you have a high level of agreement that these stories, jokes, and films are indeed funny. Now try to identify the reasons why your group thinks these stories are humorous. (You may not be able to identify reasons. You may simply have intuitive agreement.) Then, individually, tell these stories and jokes to members of the opposite gender. Ask your respondents what they think about the humor in each case. Finally, reconvene your original group and examine your results. Try to draw some general conclusions about gender differences and humor.

You might invite your respondents to make this a cross-gender conversation. If you do have a cross-gender conversation, observe the differences and similarities in the ways that males and females manage conflicts or differences of opinion and how they handle the use of power.

EXERCISE 2.25 • Cross-Cultural Interactions

The aim of this exercise is to help you become aware of how you interact in different cultural groups.

If you are a student on a college campus, attend meetings of several different student groups that are organized around ethnic or other cultural concerns, such as religious affiliation, race, or gender. Ask permission to attend. If you are not a student, go to a local NAACP meeting, visit an ethnic community center such as the Armenian Association or the Jamaican Cultural Center, go to a religious center other than your own in terms of ethnicity, race, and religion, or attend a cultural event sponsored by some group of which you are not a member. Enjoy the event as an observer. Observe the informal interactions among members of the dominant group. Compare their behavior to your typical behavior in public. In formal meetings, observe the ways in which the members of the group reveal themselves to each other by noticing topics of conversation, assumptions about family and religion, status arrangements in the group (that is, who the formal and informal leaders are), ideas about the amount of time devoted to different subjects, and promptness of starting and ending. Do the participants talk only about the group's business, or do they talk about themselves, their values and beliefs, and the current issues in their personal lives? Do people speak directly to each other or only to the designated leader? Do group members tease each other or relate to each other more formally? Does one gender dominate discussion or hold all the formal offices? How do people with less power in the group relate to people with more power?

Write down ten statements indicating how your behavior and conversation in a typical group to which you belong differs from the behavior and conversation of people in these groups. Repeat the experience in other contexts.

EXERCISE 2.26 • Different Generation Groups

At this point we will look at how your verbal communications differ with members of different generations.

Observe yourself in different generational groups. Place yourself in situations where there is a significant difference between your age and that of one or more others, such as in class or in a meeting with a doctor, a professor, or the parent or child of a friend. Think about what type of impression you want to make on the older person or the younger person and what aspects of yourself you choose to present in conversation. Do you speak only about the subject that brought you together, or do you introduce additional aspects of your life into the conversation? If you introduce more information, what do you talk about? Is this information designed to enhance the other person's image of you or to present some of your flaws, or do you try to strike a balance? Are some topics simply out of the question? Do the two of you use the same vocabulary in describing similar situations? How would you characterize the differences? Do you consciously change the words you use, as well as the topics you choose to discuss? If you feel comfortable, ask the other person what he or she expects from people in your age group as "proper" behavior. If you are with people older than you, ask how ideas about how young people should treat older people have changed since they were young. Have the topics of conversation changed? Have the forms of address changed?

EXERCISE 2.27 • Self-Awareness of Verbal Behaviors

The purpose of this exercise is to help you focus on the ways that you present yourself in different contexts, particularly in terms of your verbal forms of expression.

Write some statements describing your verbal behavior in small groups (working or public). What do you speak about? What do you want people to know about you? How much do you reveal about your personal life and your emotional reactions to events? How much do you ask others about personal issues? How do you speak to people who have different power or status than you do? Do you vary the ways in which you present yourself to members of your own sex and members of the opposite sex? Are there some aspects of yourself that you "instinctively" would not reveal to anyone else in a public setting? What are your assumptions about appropriate disclosure of self in small public groups? How comfortable do you feel with other people's self-disclosure?

Verbal Interactions in Large Groups

Look at your ecomap. How many groups do you belong to? What types of groups do you belong to? In other words, are they voluntary or involuntary? We all belong to both types of groups. For example, we are born into involuntary groups such as family, race, and gender. These group affiliations cannot be changed. Voluntary groups, on the other hand, can be changed. We can change our nationality, religion, professional affiliation, our group of friends. Think of groups to which you no longer belong, and add them to your ecomap. Past affiliations can still affect current behavior.

How do the groups on your ecomap interact, and what is the result of these multiple memberships? Understanding these questions and your verbal interactions in these groups is the focus of the rest of this chapter.

Having determined which groups you belong to, the next step is to look at how you function in these groups. Before doing this, it is important to understand how groups function. There are two aspects of group functioning. They are *group maintenance* and *group tasks* (Johnson & Johnson, 1997; Olmstead & Hare, 1978; Knowles & Knowles, 1965; Berne, 1963). *Group maintenance* involves all actions, beliefs, and so on that exist in order to maintain and preserve both group identity and cohesion. For example, groups often have their own lingo and terms, forms of address, and conversation styles. These help identify who belongs, and they give members a sense of shared identity. *Group tasks* are goal-oriented activities and behaviors—that is, behaviors and activities necessary for achieving a specific goal or purpose, as opposed to simply maintaining group identity.

The focus in this chapter is on group maintenance, with the understanding that group tasks may also be involved. The reason for this is that group culture develops out of group maintenance. How we communicate as members of a group is, in part, determined by how we feel about our membership. People who are content tend to uphold and rigorously practice group ideals, values, and norms, while those who are not content often reject the ideas, values, and norms of their group. In addition, a person's function in a group will to some extent determine his or her behavior. Each specific position in a social system results in a special, position specific type of norm called a role (Triandis, 1994; Johnson & Johnson, 1997). In order to understand our behavior, we need to know both our group memberships and our roles in those groups.

EXERCISE 2.28 • Group Membership: Involuntary and Voluntary

The purpose of this exercise is to help you recognize the variety of groups to which you belong and to begin to look at how those groups are formed.

Work in groups of four. Have each group divide into pairs. One pair should create a list of all types and categories of groups into which we may be born. The second pair should create a list of all types and categories of groups to which we belong by choice.

The pairs should then come together and present their lists to each other. The listening pair should be sure that each group meets the criteria for that list. Some groups may belong on both lists, because people are born into a specific group but can, at a later date, make a choice as to whether to retain that alliance. The listeners also should add to the list, if they can, in order to make the list as complete as possible.

Starting with the list of involuntary groups—for example, those into which we are born—determine the characteristics the members of a group must possess. How is group membership determined and recognized? Now repeat this process for the list of voluntary groups—those to which we choose to belong.

Now take a moment to consider your characteristics. Do they fall into obvious categories and groups? Try to sort them along different traits and variables.

Discuss your findings with other groups. Did each group come up with similar lists? Did you agree on what was voluntary or involuntary? Would members of different societies have come up with similar lists? What determines if group membership is voluntary or involuntary? Do people have similar definitions of these terms? How do these terms make you feel?

Now look at the final lists. Using the lists, fill out the following table. Decide which groups you belong to or have belonged to in the past. Keep this list of membership for further exercises later in the book.

Past Membership	Present Membership	Lifelong Membership	Voluntary Membership	Involuntary Membership
Involuntary Groups example: family of origin				
Voluntary Groups example: Knights of Columbus				

EXERCISE 2.29 • Group Roles

We have already looked at the groups we belong to, voluntary and involuntary. The purpose of this exercise is to consider the roles we play in these groups.

Review your chart of voluntary and involuntary groups. Decide what roles exist in each group. Consider that many groups have general types of roles like taskmaster, mediator, jokester, or tension reliever. Other groups have group-specific roles like mother, teacher, or president. How does one's role affect one's verbal behavior? Would a taskmaster talk about the same things that a joker talks about? What topics are taboo for those in certain roles to broach? Are all roles equally empowered to initiate conversation? To change topics? Discuss the verbal behaviors and tasks associated with each role.

Of the roles that you identified, decide which ones you have played throughout your life, and note the periods of your life in which you played them. In which roles do you feel comfortable? Uncomfortable? Adequate? Inadequate? What makes you feel this way? Is it the norms associated with the role? Is it that you have a hidden agenda? Is it the specific events associated with the role? Which roles have you never had that you would like to try? Which would you prefer never to have again?

Having determined which groups we belong to and the roles we play in those groups, how do we verbally identify ourselves as members of a specific group or as playing a specific role? As mentioned, groups develop cultures, which consist of acceptable values, beliefs, and norms. These cultures also determine how we act or react in various situations. If we understand our group's culture, can we then understand how we act and communicate? No, because we belong to various other groups at the same time. Therefore, it is necessary to identify both how the setting of the moment may affect our behavior and how we, as conscious, decision-making creatures, choose which group identity is primary, which is secondary, and so on. In other words, we do not always act as members of *all* the groups to which we belong. This means that we need to learn to recognize which group is salient in a given time, place, or situation. For example, terms like *girl* and *boy* have different meanings in different contexts. When talking about children, the terms are considered descriptive. If used to refer to a grown person, the terms can become pejorative. If our parents or someone clearly superior to us uses one of these terms, we may grit our teeth and accept it. If someone whom we consider our equal or inferior were to use it, we probably would interpret the terms as insults and react accordingly. For example, there are racial implications for the term *boy* and gender implications for the term *girl*.

EXERCISE 2.30 • Terms in Context (Part 1)

The purpose of this exercise is to recognize how context influences meaning. Context determines how we interpret language and actions.

Following is a table with a list of terms down the lefthand side. In the column labeled "General Rating (positive or negative)," identity whether or not the term is positive or negative on a scale of 1 to 5, with 1 being completely negative, 2 being mostly negative, 3 being neutral, 4 being mostly positive, and 5 being completely positive. Next, look at each term as it relates to the context mentioned at the top of each subsequent column, and give it a qualitative value in terms of positive or negative connotation, using the scale given above.

Look at the table you have created and identify the changes in your feelings about the terms as their context changes.

	General Rating (positive or negative)	In church, temple, mosque	At work	At home	At a party	In a restaurant	On the street
boy							
girl							
sir							
madame							
devil							
angel							
workaholic							
laid back							
follower							
leader							

EXERCISE 2.31 • Terms in Context (Part 2)

The purpose of this exercise is to help you recognize how certain terms and phrases make you feel in different situations. In this way, you will recognize how your reactions shift from context to context.

1. Divide into groups of 6. Come up with a list of descriptive terms like *boy, girl, rich, white, tall.*
2. Have each group divide into pairs. Have each pair conduct a conversation in which the terms that the group came up with are used. Members of the pair should note how they felt when they either said or heard each term. Did the words have any affect at all? Did they make you feel uncomfortable, embarrassed, pleased, or something else? Now switch partners with members of the other pairs until you have gone through the exercise at least three times.
3. Reconvene as a group, and discuss your feelings. Did they change depending on who the other person in the conversation was? Did they change over time?
4. Now make a list of the situations or contexts in which these terms would make you feel comfortable, uncomfortable, or neutral. Discuss your findings.

These exercises demonstrate that how we interact is determined in part by context. Now Let us look at the specific forms of verbal communication in large groups. As you read the following, please keep in mind the various groups to which you belong and the roles you play. Remember that each situation plays out differently depending on context.

EXERCISE 2.32 • Group Conversation Styles

Each group has its own verbal style, which influences the personal style of its members. (Recall the different conversation traits discussed earlier in the chapter.) The purpose of this exercise is to determine the normative conversation styles of groups to which you belong.

Review the chart that lists the groups that you belong to and the roles you play (Exercise 2.26). From each category of membership, pick two groups (preferably one voluntary and one involuntary) in which you have different roles. Copy the following chart so that you have two charts. Then, for each group that you chose, rank each conversation trait by circling a number from 1 to 5.

Formal	1	2	3	4	5	Informal
Impersonal	1	2	3	4	5	Intimate
Considerate	1	2	3	4	5	Inconsiderate
Direct	1	2	3	4	5	Indirect
High-Level Controversy	1	2	3	4	5	Low-Level Controversy
Frivolous	1	2	3	4	5	Serious

You should now have a much better understanding of the groups to which you belong and of the conversational styles of those groups. Let us now look at specific aspects of conversation in terms of group membership.

The size and tasks of a group often determine its conversational style. Voluntary small groups tend to be more horizontal in structure, with the conversational style being an informal conglomeration of members' individual styles. Task-oriented large groups tend to be more vertical in structure, with specific roles assigned to various members. They have leaders—sometimes one, other times a small number of people—who set the agenda and monitor who talks, when, and how long. In these situations, the authority figure determines who speaks and if that person has spoken appropriately (Olmstead and Hare, 1978). A typical example of such a group with which everyone has had experience is in the classroom.

In order to understand how we behave and communicate in large groups, it is necessary first to collect data about general conversational practices found in our groups. This means that when participating in a large group, one must step back and be an observer, at least for a short while. The following exercises are to be conducted in as many group situations as possible. If possible, more than one exercise should be conducted for each group.

EXERCISE 2.33 • Who Talks?

The purpose of this exercise is to identify which members of a group talk and what types of things they talk about.

Before starting, make a table like the one below, with group members' names in the lefthand column and attributes along the top row. It is not necessary to put down all the member's names. Only those who talk need to be included in the table. Observe the group in action. Each time a person talks (including yourself), put a checkmark in the appropriate column according to what type of communication occurs.

Name	Talks	Starts New Topic	Answers Question	Offers Ideas or Information	Tells Joke/Humor	Defends	Confirms

How much did you talk in comparison with other members of the group? Did you talk more than most or less? What types of talking did you do?

Most of the interaction that occurs between members of large groups actually happens in smaller groups, maybe even in dyads, but it is the norms of the group that determine one's behavior.

EXERCISE 2.34 • How We Talk in Group Settings

The purpose of this exercise is to become aware of how our verbal interactions differ according to the group context.

As we have said before, how we communicate is a result of the groups we belong to. It is also a result of the roles we play. Consider the following actions and practices in terms of the different groups you belong to:

- In which groups are you free to initiate talking?

- How frequently do you talk in each group?
- Do you ever joke or lighten the mood?
- Do you always state your opinion?
- Do you seek clarification or offer it?

Review the role(s) you said that you play in each group. What patterns do you see? Do your conversation patterns support your roles? Discuss your findings.

Conclusion

You now have a clearer awareness and understanding of your own verbal behaviors in different contexts. Your idea of your self may or may not coincide with what you have learned from these exercises. As we progress through this text, your self-awareness as well as your awareness of others' communicative behaviors will continue to evolve. You also have learned from the group exercises in this chapter that there is great variety of conversational styles within and among groups. Before we move on to nonverbal aspects of communication, it might be helpful for you to reflect and summarize what you have learned about your verbal behaviors.

3

Self and Nonverbal Interactions

The dominant culture of the United States can be described as high verbal, low context (Hall, 1981). This means that the United States culture emphasizes verbal communications, particularly the *literal* meaning that words convey. There is little attention on a conscious level to the metaphoric, analogic, or contextual meanings of words conveyed by the accompanying nonverbal communication.

This emphasis on literal verbal communication dates back to the European Age of Enlightenment. During this period, men decided that they could unravel the mysteries of the physical world by counting, measuring, and describing literally all the important phenomena in it. Thus, for at least 300 years, our Euro-American culture has valued precise, empirical description, and verbal (as opposed to nonverbal) communication.

Western culture has also emphasized ideas and objective general principles rather than subjective experiences, processes, and specific contextual information (Fried, 1995). This orientation causes us to pay much more attention to *what* people say than to *how* they say it. The dominant Euro-American cultures are far more skilled at understanding the meaning of words than at decoding the meaning of nonverbal communication. The "how," the methods by which people communicate, includes their emotions, posture, gestures, pace or rhythm of speaking, voice level, and timing.

In this chapter, we will discuss the significance of nonverbal communications, and the development of self-awareness of our own nonverbal behaviors in families and small, intimate groups, in nonintimate, small groups, and in large groups. We will examine the cues we use to decode others' nonverbal messages, such as emotion, physical gestures, facial expressions, touching, silence, and space. Our language, both verbal and nonverbal, develops in family and cultural contexts; we will discuss the influences of gender, race, class, religion, and sexual orientation. The exercises in this chapter, as with those in Chapter 2, are intended to develop self-awareness of your own nonverbal cues and messages in order to understand better those of others.

Learning About Language and Culture

If you ask a language teacher why it is easier for young children than it is for adults to learn two or more languages and to speak them with native fluency, the scientific answer will be that children's brains are more "plastic," or flexible, than those of adults. This is an accurate, but incomplete, answer. It seems to imply that learning a language means learning words, syntax, and grammar. Learning language is a complex, multilayered process that is very similar to learning a culture. This type of complex learning is simultaneously technical, formal, and informal (Hall, 1959). It involves absorbing the stated rules about what can and cannot be discussed in the culture, which implies learning the morality of the culture (*formal learning*). It also involves learning the unstated but implied rules and behaviors, as well as the exceptions to the rules that all "natives" understand (*informal learning*). Finally, it involves learning the technical details of implementing the rules or speaking about specific topics in specific situations (*technical learning*).

Language and culture learning also demand absorption of an enormous amount of nonverbal and paralinguistic material, including: intonation and rhythm of spoken words; subvocalizations, such as "hm hmmm," "uh uh," and "mmmm"; and tone, pitch, and volume of voice in specific situations. Purely physical aspects of communication, such as facial gestures; eye contact; posture; hand motions; the distance one stands from persons one knows intimately, knows formally, or does not know; the areas of another person's body may be touched, for how long, under what circumstances; and so forth—all of these comprise the total context of nonverbal communication. The typical ways in which members of a specific cultural group use space and decoration also are part of that group's code of nonverbal communication. Verbal and nonverbal communication are woven into a wholistic tapestry or orchestration, which conveys a speaker's message to a listener. People who learn this information informally, often as children or as a result of long exposure as adults, can understand a speaker's complete message. This kind of learning can be called high-context learning because the speaker knows much of the implicit context of a message by reading or decoding the nonverbal portion.

Nonverbal communications create the foundation of human relationships (Okun, 1997). Accurate perception and interpretation of patterns of gestures, posture, spatial relations, silence, emotions, personal appearance, and cultural characteristics are crucial elements in the definition and maintenance of personal, social, and work relationships. In this chapter, we will focus on developing your self-awareness of these elements in small, intimate groups: in small, nonintimate groups; and in large groups. You will begin to notice your own patterns of nonverbal communication and also to attend to the patterns of nonverbal behavior demonstrated by people in your environment who speak in different rhythms.

Placing more importance on the implicit context of a message by reading or decoding the nonverbal portion is characteristic of high-context cultures

(Triandis, 1994). Members of any given culture know which aspect of communication is given the greater weight by the speaker; listeners then interpret accordingly. As previously noted, the dominant United States culture is low context, emphasizing the verbal, literal message. However, many of the nondominant cultures in this country (and many cultures of countries with whom we deal regularly in business or other arenas) are high context.

Self as a Nonverbal Communicator

Understanding how we communicate nonverbally not only shapes our self-identity; it also is an important step in learning how to communicate effectively with members of our own and other cultures. Rarely are we aware of how we communicate nonverbally, for we cannot see ourselves as others can. For example, are you aware of what your facial expression is right now as you read this chapter? Are you aware of how you look? Most likely you are not aware of it, because you are not paying attention to your own expression. As members of a primarily low-context dominant culture, most of us focus our attention on what we say, often analyzing every word, its meaning and location, and possibly the tone of voice or pace of the verbal message. Unless one is an actor or politician—someone who is unavoidably concerned about his or her public image—it is rare for individuals in the United States dominant culture to give equal attention to facial expression, posture, or distance from the intended audience. One reason for this lack of awareness is the fact that we learn to communicate nonverbally on an unconscious level. We are all unaware of some of our nonverbal behaviors. For example, you may not be aware that you scowl at certain times.

EXERCISE 3.1 • Nonverbal Self-Awareness

The purpose of this exercise is to reflect on how your family shaped your nonverbal communication and what verbal and nonverbal methods of shaping were most influential.

Take a moment to think back to how you learned your first language. Chances are you do not remember much. Now think about how your parents expressed approval of an action, behavior, activity, or whatever. Did their expressions of approval differ for each family member? For those outside of the family? What aspect of their approval do you remember most clearly? Their words? Their smiles? Their hugs? A special meal just for you? Some other form of nonverbal communication? Now consider how your parents expressed disapproval. Again, what aspects of the communication do you most clearly remember? What were the differences between your parents' nonverbal expressions of approval and disapproval?

How do you express approval and disapproval? What do you consider the most effective method of expressing each? Is it enough to just say "You did well," or must certain expressions and actions accompany the verbal message? Or, is it even possible to convey the message solely through expressions and actions? If you think the latter, than you use a high-context form of communication. If the verbal message is the sole communication, then your communication is low context. If you chose both, then you fall somewhere in-between the two extremes.

Regardless of whether your family system is embedded within a high-context or low-context culture, individual differences may exist among family members. In the following diagram, identify where you think each family member falls in terms of his or her communication style.

Low Context	**High Context**
uses few nonverbal cues	uses lots of nonverbal cues
uses explicit descriptions	uses vague descriptions
ignores common history	assumes accurate recollection of common history
describes meanings explicitly	assumes agreement about meanings

EXERCISE 3.2 • The Meaning of Nonverbal Behaviors

The purpose of this exercise is to recognize how dependent we are on nonverbal communication.

Pick a partner and sit so that you are facing each other directly. Together, select a controversial topic, such as abortion, euthanasia, the legalization of marijuana, or capital punishment. Discuss the topic for five minutes. Take a few minutes to write down what you believe your partner's views are and what the partner's salient communication behaviors—both verbal and nonverbal—were. Then pick a different partner and sit back-to-back. Discuss the same topic without any visual contact for five minutes. Again, write down your perception and interpretation of your partner's thoughts, feelings, and attitudes. Then select a third partner and communicate face-to-face *nonverbally* about the same controversial topic. You may not *say* anything: All of your thoughts and feelings must be expressed through posture, gesture, facial expression, and so on. At the end of the five minutes, write down your perceptions of the third partner's views.

Compare the communication behaviors of your three partners and share your feedback with each partner. What have you learned about the importance of nonverbal communication? In which situation were your perceptions most accurate? Why?

Hall (1981, p. 71) describes the processes by which infants learn language and people from the same culture speak to each other as "sync-ing" or "being in sync." He asserts that all cultures bind verbal communication into rhythmic verbal and nonverbal patterns that convey a complete message that can be decoded only by persons who can perceive the entire pattern. The particular aspects of each synchronization are culture specific. He also maintains that people who are "brought up in the northern European tradition are underdeveloped rhythmically" (p. 77) and are, therefore, less aware of the audible and visual rhythms of communication than are people from other cultures.

EXERCISE 3.3 • In-Sync

The purpose of this exercise is to begin to recognize the fact that sharing a culture facilitates understanding and ease of communication.

Select a partner who shares your gender and culture. Engage in a ten minute dialogue about whatever topic you wish. After the dialogue, discuss with your partner how "in sync" you are—how easy it was to understand the nuances, subtleties, and literal verbal and nonverbal communications that passed between you. Then, select a partner of different gender and, if possible, different cultural group. Repeat the exercise and see if you can identify the difference in your ability to both decode and be decoded.

EXERCISE 3.4 • Family Nonverbal Expressions

The purpose of this exercise is to begin to investigate nonverbal practices within your family of origin.

Look at family photographs dating from your infancy up to now. Pay particular attention to people's expressions. How well can you discern what they and you were really feeling? Can you remember the context of the photographs? What were the themes in your family concerning nonverbal communication? See if you can come up with three adjectives to describe the nonverbal behaviors of each family member, including yourself. Overall, how would you describe the rules for nonverbal communication in your family?

Emotions

We all have emotions. In fact, all humans experience the basic emotions of enjoyment, anger, fear, sadness, disgust, and surprise. Research has shown that people across cultures use the same facial expressions when experiencing these emotions (Ekman, 1993; Poortinga, Shoots, & Van de Koppel, 1993). These emotional reactions are involuntary, which means that they are innate and unlearned. In other words, people express these basic emotions with the same facial responses throughout the world, but how openly they express the emotions varies depending on the culture (Ekman, 1993; Triandis, 1994). For example, in the United States, it is considered acceptable for men to show anger, but not fear. Women, on the other hand, can show fear but not anger (Lerner, 1985; Gilligan, 1982). Gendered differences are embedded in larger cultural contexts. Some cultures fall at the high-intensity end, believing that feelings should be expressed, while others fall at the opposite, high-formality end, believing that emotional self-control is critically important (Crohn, 1995). Potential differences in the permissibility of displaying emotions can hamper communications and cause misunderstanding in all types of relationships.

Although research suggests that the basic emotions listed above elicit the same facial expressions irrespective of culture, many other emotions are culture specific. Vocabulary is a good way to determine the range of emotions in a culture, or to discern how much importance is placed on an emotion or group of emotions. The more words there are to describe a group of emotions, the more importance there is placed on that emotion by the culture.

EXERCISE 3.5 • Emotion Lists

The purpose of this exercise is to investigate the permissibility of expressing various kinds of emotion.

1. List all the negative emotions that you can think of within five minutes.
2. Now list all of the positive emotions that you can think of within five minutes.
3. Classify them on the chart below according to the basic emotions of enjoyment, anger, fear, sadness, disgust, and surprise. If you have listed any emotions that do not belong to any of these groups, come up with a new category. Which list of words is longest?

Enjoyment	Anger	Fear	Sadness	Disgust	Surprise

4. Now compare your list to the lists of others who share your culture. How are your lists similar? Now compare your list to the lists of people from other cultures. How do your lists differ?
5. Consider your list of emotions. Do you feel comfortable expressing each of these emotions? In what circumstances would you feel that expression is not permissible? For example, is it okay to express sadness when you are alone? When you are at home? With friends? At the office? While watching a movie? Walking down a street? In other situations? With which types of people is the expression of emotions okay? With those of the same sex, the opposite sex, or both? With parents, siblings, or children? Superiors, colleagues, or subordinates? Friends or strangers? In-group people (that is, those of the same ethnicity, race, religion, nationality, sexual orientation, and so on) or out-group people?

Facial Gestures

The human face is an extremely important site for the expression of feelings, and the eyes and mouth seem to be the center of expressiveness and response. Involuntary facial gestures associated with the basic human emotions discussed earlier have universal meaning. Other, voluntary facial gestures convey different meanings in different cultures. For example, a smile is generally taken to convey happiness in most Western cultures, but in Japanese culture, people more typically smile when they are feeling nervous or uncomfortable. A smile or a giggle may be a polite way of saying "no" in Japan, where verbalization of disagreement is often considered the height of rudeness (Triandis, 1994). Westerners sometimes smile when they are nervous, but the cultural interpretation of a smile's predominant meaning is different in Japanese and United States cultures. Imagine how a Japanese person visiting the United States might feel if everyone she or he was introduced to smiled. Even if we "know" that smile means welcome in the United States and indicates discomfort in Japan, our knowledge is formal, intellectual, and technical, and our informal, emotional knowledge inserts an element of confusion into the communication process. In short, we smile automatically.

EXERCISE 3.6 • Smiling

The purpose of this exercise is to become more aware of when and how you use smiling to communicate.

Keep a journal and note the times you smile during one full day. What provokes your smiles? Do you smile intentionally? How often do you smile spontaneously and in what situations? For example, do you smile to express agreement? In what situations do you consciously smile? Choose other facial expressions, such as scowling, frowning, biting your lip, rolling your eyes, and whatever else you can think of. Note your use of each expression for at least one day. Again, how consciously do you use them and in what situations? How easy or difficult is it for you to become aware of your own facial expressions? What have others told you about your facial expressions?

EXERCISE 3.7 • Interpreting Facial Expressions

The purpose of this exercise is to become aware of your own facial expressions.

Stand in front of the mirror and make faces at yourself. Think of a specific emotion you intend to convey and then arrange your features to convey that emotion. You might have to think of a situation or event that elicits the desired emotion. Do this with as many feelings as you can think of. Realize that one facial expression on its own can convey several different emotions and that verbal communication of the emotional message may be inadequate or confusing. You may also try this exercise with a friend. Each of you make a face at the other, and then ask the other person to interpret your expression. Discuss the differences between your intention and the other person's interpretation. Try to determine if any patterns exist in your understandings and misunderstandings. Experiment with a "sincere" smile and a "phony" smile and see if you can tell the difference. Note that the former involves involuntary muscles and therefore will look different (Ekman, 1993). Identify the source of the cues you used to differentiate between sincere and phony smiles.

EXERCISE 3.8 • Self-Awareness: Facial Expressions

The purpose of this exercise is to further your awareness of your facial expressions in a more natural situation.

If you can get hold of a video recorder, videotape yourself having a conversation with a friend. Watch the videotape with the sound off, focusing on your face. Were you aware of your facial expressions at the time that you made them? Watch the video again, still focusing on your face, this time with the sound on. Do your facial expressions match what you are saying? Have your friend watch with you. Discuss the "fit" between your verbal and nonverbal communication.

EXERCISE 3.9 • Mirroring

Again, the purpose of this exercise is to increase your awareness of your facial expressions, this time as perceived by others.

Sit facing a partner. Select a topic that you can discuss for five minutes. Your partner is to not to engage verbally with you, but should attempt to *mirror* all of your facial expressions, gestures, and posture. After this five-minute dialogue, share your feelings and reactions with your partner and ask him or her how natural, unnatural, comfortable, or uncomfortable these gestures or expressions were for him or her to mirror. What emotions did your partner perceive you to be expressing? Repeat the exercise reversing roles.

Silence

Silence is an extremely powerful form of verbal and nonverbal communication. *Verbal silence* is the lack of speaking. But one can still continue to communicate, to be connected, on a nonverbal level—for example, through gesture or facial expression. *Nonverbal silence* refers to the absence of any connection—for example, crossing the street, moving to the corner of a room, or immersing yourself in a book. Nonverbal silence often takes the form of a flat expression, wooden stance, lack of movement or response, or some other "non" nonverbal message. Unlike verbal silence, which can be interpreted as (1) an invitation for someone else to speak, (2) a person thinking, (3) respect, or (4) agreement, nonverbal silence always has a negative connotation. It is a way to distance oneself from the speaker, to show disapproval or anger. In the dominant white male United States culture, we are trained to leave our emotions out of discussions. Emotions are viewed as being extraneous, as clouding the issue and obstructing productivity. High-context communicators, who tend to speak emotionally and feel that passion strengthens an argument, will respond to a nonverbal "lack" of response more readily than they will to a verbal communication (Kochman, 1981). High-content communicators do not just listen to the words; they take in the whole picture, including the visual cues, the tone of voice, the speed of delivery.

Therefore, it is necessary to become aware of our "non" nonverbal communication, our silences, in order to be able to use them appropriately when we choose to. The following short exercises were designed to help you understand how you both use and respond to nonverbal silence.

EXERCISE 3.10 • Discomfort with Silence

Now that you understand what silence is, it is important to recognize your comfort level with silence.

Choose a partner and sit facing each other, silently and motionless for five minutes or until one of you feels uncomfortable. Which one of you feels uncomfortable first? How is this discomfort experienced? Is this a familiar feeling? What does it remind you of? Consider your choice of partner. Would you respond differently if your partner had been a different gender, or if he or she had been of a different age, race, or different in some other way?

EXERCISE 3.11 • Verbal Communication without Nonverbal Cues

In order to further your awareness of the importance of nonverbal communication, this exercise will investigate its absence.

With the same partner, have a five-minute verbal conversation. Both of you keep your bodies and faces still and emotionless throughout the conversation. Discuss your feelings about every aspect of this situation. What was comfortable? What was uncomfortable? How did you read each other's messages?

EXERCISE 3.12 • Self Awareness of Physical Expressiveness

Having become aware of how the lack of nonverbal communication affects a conversation, you will now explore your awareness of your own physical expressiveness.

With the same partner, engage in a normal five-minute conversation, being as expressive and physical as you normally are in conversation. Did you feel more self-conscious about facial expression or about moving your hands? Compare this conversation to those in the previous two exercises.

EXERCISE 3.13 • Delayed Responses

The purpose of this exercise is to further explore the role of nonverbal expression in communication.

Pick a specific time in your day, perhaps an hour or two in which you will be interacting with others. During that period, make a conscious effort to delay or slow down your nonverbal responses when people speak to you. When someone addresses you, take a deep breath before responding, silently count to ten, or use some other delaying tactic. Carefully observe the reactions of the other people to your silence.

EXERCISE 3.14 • Physical Silence

Having explored the effects of nonverbal silence, consider it now in different social situations.

Observe the use of physical silence in different situations. What does it mean if a superior is stone-faced? A subordinate? How is physical silence used between colleagues? Within your family? When you were a child, how did your parents use physical silence to influence you? What were the rules you learned about silence?

Space and Decoration

Gestalt psychology's notion of *figure and ground* suggests that our perceptions are organized by our psychological needs (Yontef, 1982; Perls, 1969). In Western cultures, we tend to see objects and people as *figure,* and space as *background.* They are distinct from each other. Thus, when we look at something, we perceive a dominant figure against a less dominant background. In other parts of the world, particularly East Asia, either space is perceived as dominant figure, *or* the whole visual setting—figure and ground—is perceived in an integrated fashion. Figure and space are noticed holistically and equally.

In this particular section, we will consider space as part of the physical context of human activities. Proxemics, the amount of distance that is comfortable between people, will be discussed later in the chapter.

In different cultures the concept of space is perceived differently. Thich Nhat Hanh (1992), a noted Vietnamese Zen Buddhist teacher, states that space can be perceived only in juxtaposition to that which potentially fills or surrounds it. He asks his students how they can know that a bowl is empty unless they know what it is empty of. How can you imagine the top of your hand without imagining the bottom of your hand? Space is defined and perceived by that which surrounds it, but space is inconceivable without its borders. In beginning to notice space and its uses, it will be helpful to observe those objects that can be defined as the borders of space.

EXERCISE 3.15 • Comfort and Discomfort in Space

The purpose of this exercise is to determine your personal definition of clutter.

Find a space, such as a room, lobby, or store, that you consider uncluttered. Then find a space of comparable size that you consider cluttered. Look at the objects in both spaces. Compare the number of objects, size of objects, proximity, and location. Stand or sit in each space long enough to get a sense of your own feelings about comfort or discomfort in "empty" space. ("Empty" space refers to areas without living beings.) How reminiscent are your feelings to those you felt about space in the home of your childhood?

EXERCISE 3.16 • Effects of Space

Continuing from the previous exercise, explore further personal comfort levels in terms of space.

Visit a museum gallery. Museum galleries are arranged meticulously by people who are trained to use space for particular effects. Again, stand in different parts of the gallery long enough to get a sense of your own feelings about comfort or discomfort. How does someone else's arrangement of space for a particular purpose work for you? Would you make any changes?

EXERCISE 3.17 • Enclosed in Space

The purpose of this exercise is to continue your exploration of levels related to personal space.

Find an elevator in which you can ride several times a day, both when it is empty and when it has several other people in it. When you ride the elevator alone, pay attention to your feelings about being alone in an enclosed, "empty" space. If you were to make the elevator more comfortable for one person, how would you decorate it or use its space? What elements of the environment would make this space more comfortable for you?

EXERCISE 3.18 • Spatial Arrangements: Comfort and Discomfort

Homes are by contemporary definition places where one should be at ease or feel comfortable. This exercise will explore whether or not this is achieved.

Walk through your home or the home of a friend. Spend some time in each room. Decide which room is most comfortable for you and which room is least comfortable. Look at the amount, type, and arrangement of furniture, at the color of the walls, at the types and colors of the decorations, at the windows, mirrors, and the level and type of light. Make a comparative list of spatial arrangements you find comfortable and those you find uncomfortable. Compare the spatial arrangements of your current home with the home in which you grew up. Ask several friends or colleagues to do the same and then compare lists.

If you are all natives of the United States, you may have fairly similar criteria for comfort. Differences in the size of your family of origin and the part of the country where you grew up may account for any dissimilarities. If some of you are natives of other cultures or members of nondominant United States cultures, your comfort criteria may be different. If they are, spend some time discussing what elements of space usage you find comfortable and what early experiences in your own life you associate those elements with. For example, if your grandmother had overstuffed chairs in which she sat and read to you, you will probably find overstuffed chairs very comfortable. If you grew up in a home where everybody sat around the kitchen table and shared important events and figured out family problems, you will probably find sitting around a table with lots of people comfortable. If everybody in your family ate TV dinners alone whenever they got home, the round table setting will probably be less comfortable for you.

Space as an Extension of Self

We tend to fill the spaces we use most often with objects that convey something about our interests, our ideas of beauty, our values, and our sense of comfort. We also arrange those objects in a manner that reflects our idea of esthetic attractiveness. The entrance to a home is a place where the residents of that home convey a level of welcome to visitors. One's bedroom conveys a sense of comfort and security in intimate or vulnerable settings. The living room is arranged according to the occupants' ideas of what should go on there—conversation, watching television, listening to music, performing music, reading, and so on. Large homes often have living rooms that are arranged formally and are used for formal, non-family functions.

EXERCISE 3.19 • Inferences About Meaning of Space (Part 1)

The purpose of this exercise is to investigate how the division of space and the location of objects within space are manipulated to make both conscious and unconscious statements.

Look around your home again, going carefully through each room. If you live in a residence hall, look around your room at the way the space is divided between you and your roommate (if you have one). Look around the rooms of other friends. In each room you examine, use a chart like the following to write down the items in the room that convey something about the occupant(s) and/or the use of that room—their personality traits, their values, or their intended activities.

Item	Location	Traits, Values, Activities

EXERCISE 3.20 • Inferences About Meaning of Space (Part 2)

In this exercise, you will look at the use of space in your parents' home.

Now look around your parents' home. Use the chart below to write down what you notice about the items in their house.

Item	Location	Traits, Values, Activities

After you have completed both charts, compare what you have inferred from the use of space in each house to what you know about the personality of the people (including yourself) who use the rooms you cataloged. How closely do the objects in the room correlate with your impressions of that person's personality, likes, and dislikes?

Nonverbal Interactions in Small, Intimate Groups

One's attitudes and beliefs about self, about partner, and about significant others in small, intimate groups influence all aspects of communication. As previously noted, however, because we are less aware of our nonverbal behaviors than we are of our verbal behaviors, we may be unaware of how much we actually reveal of our true feelings and attitudes. For example, one may say the appropriate words to one's intimate other, but one's body language may convey messages that are discrepant. When one asks one's spouse "Are you angry at me?" and the spouse responds verbally with "No," but has a clenched jaw and tight fists, the spouse asking the question does not feel reassured. The anger is felt, even though it is verbally denied. With nonverbal behavior as with verbal behaviors, we are less constrained with intimate others. In fact, we may actually be irresponsible by assuming that we have license to "let it all hang out" with intimate others. Our less inhibited nonverbal expressions are more easily read by those with whom we are familiar and intimate.

Research shows that in intimate relationships, nonverbal expression through self-disclosure seems to be more important than verbal self-disclosure, although the association between relationship quality and intimate expressions may vary considerably over time (Brown, Werner, & Altman, 1994). It is likely that partners do not disclose at equal levels; intimate self-disclosure varies among individuals. Some people have learned that revealing one's feelings is not safe; others find it stress-relieving. In intimate relationships, fear of rejection is the primary inhibitor of self-disclosure. Our perception and interpretation of others' nonverbal behaviors either elicits our fear of disapproval and rejection or reassures us.

Eye Contact

Eye contact has a great deal of power in all cultures (Triandis, 1994). The eyes have been described, in Western culture, as the windows to the soul. Lovers presumably can spend hours gazing into each other's eyes, trying to absorb a mental image of the beloved. Direct eye contact can be an invitation to further conversation, empathy, or a sexual liaison, while a stare—continuous direct eye contact over an extended period of time—often is interpreted as a statement of defiance, as a challenge, or as an invitation to conflict. In many cultures, people are forbidden to look directly at holy images and rulers or into the eyes of those who have more power. In Muslim cultures, for example, it is inappropriate for a woman to look directly at nonfamily males. In Western cultures, women's staring at men is often interpreted as a sexual invitation, which explains why, in many cultures, downcast eyes in women is considered evidence of sexual virtue. The amount of direct eye contact between two people is determined by their cultures, their personal relationship, and the topic of conversation.

EXERCISE 3.21 • Eye Contact

The purpose of this exercise is to recognize when and how you make eye contact.

1. List the types of situations in which you look at people. Now list the types of situations in which you avoid direct eye contact.

2. Over the next few days, observe yourself and modify your list according to your experiences. In what types of situations did eye contact occur? How comfortable were you with the contact? Who initiated it? How long was contact maintained and how frequently? Most likely, the more intimate a situation you were in, the more eye contact occurred and the more comfortable you felt with the contact. In United States society, eye contact with parents, spouses, children, and close friends is expected and returned. In fact, lack of contact is often interpreted as anger, withdrawal, or disapproval. Eye contact with strangers or one's boss is not expected and is often not returned.

EXERCISE 3.22 • Observation of Eye Contact

The purpose of this exercise is to consider the use of eye contact as a conversation initiator or as a signal of interest.

Go to a place where people are socializing for the purpose of finding potential sexual partners or mates. This might be a bar, a fitness center, a social club, or any other activity designated as an opportunity for singles to meet. Observe eye contact, particularly between people who are meeting for the first time or who do not know each other well. You will be able to observe an entire nonverbal conversation. Try to identify the signals people use to indicate either that they are or are not interested in verbal conversation, that they want to be noticed or ignored. If possible, find a situation in which two women are interested in the same man or two men in the same woman. Assuming that standards of civility and friendliness govern the norms of the group, these people will jockey with each other for the attention of the person of the opposite sex. Because nonverbal communication is an integrated pattern, the signals used to indicate attention will include use of space (how close each is willing to stand or sit near the others), posture, facial gestures, tone of voice, use of laughter, and subvocalizations. This phenomenon would be considered a courting ritual. It also occurs between lesbians and gay men, typically in segregated settings. If you have the opportunity to observe lesbians or gay men in a similar social setting, do so and compare your observations of eye contact and other nonverbal courting behavior. Become aware of your own eye contact in this setting. With whom do you initiate eye contact? How do you respond to others' gazing at you?

Touch

Touching in United States culture is typically an act that conveys either intimacy or dominance, and sometimes both. Touch is a powerful form of communication, ranging all the way from expressions of love to efforts to assault and subdue (Argyle, 1988; Barnulund, 1975). A third type of touch, which is used widely in the United States, can be called "clinical" or "diagnostic" touch. In this type of touching, the person being touched has given permission for the person doing the touching—usually a member of a health profession—to touch him or her for purposes of understanding some physical problem and prescribing a method of healing.

The boundaries among the different forms of touching are difficult to describe. In the United States, we do not have a precise set of rules for who can touch whom, on which part of the body, and under what conditions. An attempt to formalize these rules is now taking place in government and workplaces as consciousness about sexual harassment and other forms of intimidation increases. The rules of touching are part of our informal "you'll get the hang of it" (Hall, 1959, p. 87) learning system, and they differ according to context. Men and women learn very different informal rules, which leads to a great deal of confusion about what types of touching are permitted and what they mean.

On several university and college campuses, the problem of differentiating between invited and uninvited sexual touching has led to some rules that outsiders find amusing and difficult to imagine using. In any potentially intimate encounter, the aggressor, usually presumed to be the male, must verbally ask permission of the recipient, usually a female, by asking "May I (do this) with/to you?" In order for the behavior to occur, the recipient must verbally agree. At each stage of increased arousal, permission must once again be asked. These rules assume that participants know when they have moved from one stage to the next, that they both follow the same script in sexual encounters, that men are usually the aggressors in sexual relationships, that sexual encounters are heterosexual, and that verbal and nonverbal messages have the same meaning.

The same problem of ambiguity applies to the issue of acquaintance rape. At one end of the continuum of sexual touching, both partners have given consent. At the other end, one has forced sexual touching on the other, a pattern that is considered to be sexual assault. Because these encounters generally take place in private, there seems to be no unambiguous way to define acquaintance rape in many of the situations where it is alleged to have occurred. Only verbal communication can clear up the confusion and prevent undesired behavior. Simplistically, this verbal clarification has been characterized by the sentence "What part of 'no' did you not understand?"

National efforts to teach children how to differentiate between "good touch" and "bad touch" have also been difficult. Good touch is intended to convey love and protection to children, while bad touch has sexual overtones or involves explicit sexual stimulation. Children are touched constantly, because they need protection and reassurance. Good touch is essential to healthy human development. Teachers are hampered profoundly in their efforts to communicate with children if they cannot touch them, but recent reports of abuses of children in school and day care settings have made touching children a potentially dangerous act for adult caregivers. The most effective ways to teach children the differences between good and bad touch involve role playing, using dolls in an effort to help children label their own feelings of comfort or discomfort with particular kinds of touch.

Touch is also used to establish or reinforce dominance. If one person wants to convey that another person is "with" him or her socially and signal the competition to back off, she or he will put an arm around the partner. Or, if one wants to signal an intimate other that a certain topic of speech is forbidden, a slight pat or touch might communicate this authority. Although touch can be positive or negative, it often is used to control the other's behavior.

EXERCISE 3.23 • Intimate Touching

The purpose of this exercise is to explore your comfort level in terms of touch.

What types of touch do you use with people who are your sexual intimates? With people who are intimate with you in nonsexual ways, such as family members or close friends? Make a list of the people with whom you have nonsexual intimate relationships. Think about when and where you feel comfortable touching them and when and where they seem to feel comfortable touching you. Consider what types of touching take place and what you feel comfortable and uncomfortable with. For example, when and how do you initiate holding hands? Hugging? Putting your arm around someone's waist or shoulder? Sitting on someone's lap? How do you feel when someone else initiates these touches? Discuss this with friends as well as with intimate others, and find out if you have similar informal rules about touching.

One's private behavior with intimate others is more governed by family history, cultural norms, and personal preference than is public behavior, which is governed by the dominant United States culture. In private, any form of touching is permissible as long as all participants agree.

Proxemics

Proxemics is the study of the distance between people. "We each possess zones of territory. We carry these zones with us and we react in different ways to the breaking of these zones" (Fast, 1970, p. 26). There are four zones of proxemics: (1) intimate distance, (2) personal distance, (3) social distance, and (4) public distance. These distances determine how close we stand when we talk to people or feel that we need to recognize someone's presence. In intimate relationships, our personal space is likely to be more permeable than in nonintimate relationships. We develop our comfort zones regarding physical and emotional intimacy, and our styles of distance regulation, as we are growing up in our families. Within the same family, individuals may have different personal boundaries; these boundaries range from extremely close to distant and cut-off. Obviously, we can let people with whom we feel safe and secure come much closer than those with whom we experience anxiety or doubt. It is likely that our comfort levels are influenced by our earliest physical and emotional attachments. People who were raised in families with a lot of emotional and physical expressiveness are more comfortable with this kind of closeness in adulthood than are people who were raised in homes where there was little physical or emotional expressiveness. But we are also influenced by our culture, gender, and age and by our associations with people who have different inclinations.

EXERCISE 3.24 • Personal Boundaries

The purpose of this exercise is to help you gain self-awareness of distance control as well as an awareness of individual differences.

Stand across the room from someone you consider to be an intimate other. Ask that person to walk toward you slowly in a friendly manner. When that person is as close to you as you feel comfortable with, put your hand up to stop him or her. Now ask the person to return to a spot across the room and to approach you in a more menacing manner. Again, stop him or her when you begin to feel that your space is being invaded. Now reverse roles. If possible, repeat this exercise with as many intimate others as possible. Notice whether or not your distance regulation changes with different people. Now think back to your family of origin. Who was comfortable being physically close to whom? Who was the most distant? Who was the most predictable? Who was the most unpredictable? How comfortable are you letting intimate others know whether or not you are comfortable with the degree of physical and emotional closeness in your relationship.

Nonverbal Interactions in Small, Nonintimate Groups

In small, nonintimate groups, we tend to be more accommodating to our perceptions of group norms, those aspects of expressiveness shared by group members. Obviously, the nature of the group will create different structures and social space. A work group might have different norms than a school or neighborhood group. The purpose and context of the group will shape the roles of the members as well as the rules of verbal and nonverbal communication.

Eye Contact

In nonintimate groups, eye contact may be less intense than with intimate others. As with intimate others, however, eye contact can be the means for structuring alliances and boundaries among group members. For example, if your boss comes into the room where you are working with some of your colleagues, you and a colleague may give each other all-knowing looks, indicating that you both understand something and that the boss does not understand. If you work in an organization that is in the process of downsizing, you may find that people avoid eye contact, fearful of revealing what they are truly thinking and feeling. As discussed previously, eye contact, or lack thereof, is one of the most powerful communicators of the power structure of a group. We avoid eye contact with those we do not know or want to interact with, and we gaze at those we know or want to know. We also use eye contact as an acknowledgment or response.

EXERCISE 3.25 • Eye Contact and Space Negotiation

In this exercise we will explore how eye contact is used to control the negotiation of space.

Any type of waiting line or any instance of space negotiation offers the opportunity to observe the use of eye contact for establishing dominance. If you eat in a cafeteria, watch how people get in line during heavy-use hours. Typically, when two people are heading for the end of a line, each will see the other coming and, by the time they arrive at the end of the line, both will have decided who is to go first. This process is typically polite and uneventful at uncrowded, unhurried times, and results in more conflict during peak hours. When two people approach any object that both want and that is in short supply, such as the last CD on the rack or the single copy of a journal in the library, an "eye-contact conflict" often occurs over who gets it.

EXERCISE 3.26 • Leader's Eye Contact

Now we will learn how eye contact is used by various types of leaders to achieve their objectives.

At a work meeting or in your classroom, observe the leader or teacher. With whom does this person seem to make eye contact most consistently? At whom is everyone else in the group looking? Who seems to be off in his or her own world? When the teacher or leader asks a question, who indicates that he or she hopes not to be called on to answer by looking down or away? How do you get the leader to acknowledge you? Do you ever find yourself staring at others? What happens when someone catches you staring at him or her?

If possible, keep a record of people's eye contact and write down your feelings about your own participation in a classroom or work-related group over the course of time. What patterns emerge? What roles and rules become evident?

Touch

In both social and work settings, dominant people are permitted to initiate touch with subordinate people, but not vice versa. If a person who is perceived as subordinate wants to increase her power in a business situation, one method of doing so is to extend her hand in a handshake, which establishes her as an equal. Men of equal power or status greet each other with handshakes, while a subordinate male waits for the dominant male to extend his hand in welcome. Because handshakes are typically nonsexual, the issue of who extends the hand first is probably more related to establishment or demonstration of dominance in a work situation than it is to gender.

Women are more likely to greet each other with a hug in social settings and, perhaps, in less public work settings (Gilligan, 1982). Because of the history of male dominance and female subordination in work and social settings, there is currently great confusion about men touching women now that women have entered the work world and have begun to achieve increased power. In fact, today if a male puts his arm around a female's shoulders, it can be interpreted as sexual harassment. The "you'll get the hang of it" (Hall, 1981) approach does not work well in nonverbal communication when the roles men and women occupy and the relative power relationships have changed. However, automatic, unconscious touching gestures occur before a person can "catch" him or herself. We have seen enormous activity in the legal sphere as efforts have been made to define sexual harassment and sexually inappropriate behavior, and to draw the line between sincere, possibly well-intentioned gestures (which can be handled by clarifying the rules for touching) and the malicious use of touching, which is intended to intimidate.

Individual, gendered, and cultural variables affect our comfort level with touching and being touched. Do not assume that someone of your same gender, for example, has the same rules as you about touching.

EXERCISE 3.27 • Intimidation by Touch

Touch is not always a positive connection. In this exercise we will investigate its negative side.

Think back to a time when you felt intimidated by another's touch. It may have been with a fellow worker, a professional such as a doctor, therapist, lawyer, supervisor or boss, teacher, and so on. Recreate the scene in your mind and recall the thoughts and feelings that the situation aroused in you. What did you say or do then? What did you think? How would you perceive the exact same situation if it were to occur today, and what would you do? Now, recall a time when you touched someone who tensed up or recoiled from your touch. What did you think, feel, and do then, and what would you think, feel, and do now?

EXERCISE 3.28 • Rules for Touch

The purpose of this exercise is to survey how various people use touch in their professional lives.

Ask some of the dominant public people in your life, such as your supervisor, a professor, or the head of an organization to which you belong, when or under what circumstances they touch subordinates or students. Ask them if they have a conscious set of rules that governs their behavior or if they are operating on an informal level. If you have public responsibilities, such as teaching, caring for people, or supervising, write down the rules you use for determining when to touch people. Also familiarize yourself with whatever professional code of ethics governs your current or anticipated profession. Once again, because of the power of touch and its potential for abuse, every helping profession has some type of statement that is intended to guide its members as to the rules for touch in the professional setting.

Gestures, Posture, and Spacing

As with facial expressions, some gestures are universal, and some are culture specific. Often, usage varies from individual to individual. This is a result of the combined factors of personality, culture, and environment. Our gestures, especially our hand movements, have often become an integral part of how we communicate (Hall, 1959, 1966a, 1981; Argyle, 1988). Although our gestures, posture, and spacing may be more relaxed and informal with intimate others, our characteristic styles are quite consistent among different contexts. They become so much a part of our communicative styles that we are often unaware of them unless someone points them out to us.

EXERCISE 3.29 • Self-Awareness: Use of Hands (Part 1)

In this exercise you will become aware of the role your hands play in your communications.

Try talking without using your hands for extended periods during the day. Clasp them or put them in your pockets. How does it feel? Do you find your hands creeping out on their own to "start talking"? Next, try talking just with your hands. You might want to limit this to situations where you are with intimate friends. You will probably be surprised how much you can communicate without uttering a word. Discuss your use of hands with friends. Do they think that you use your hands frequently? Not enough? Do you use them only for certain situations or for certain types of communication?

EXERCISE 3.30 • Self-Awareness: Use of Hands (Part 2)

Building on the previous exercise, in this exercise you will now validate what you have learned.

Review the video of the conversation you made earlier (in Exercise 3.8). This time, pay attention to your hands. First watch with the sound off and then with the sound on. Discuss your observations with a partner. Now look at gestures other than those you made with your hands.

Gestures blend into how we use and position our whole body—in other words, our posture. Differences in posture exist both within and among cultures. Some people tend to have open-bodied postures: arms and legs are uncrossed, often open. Other people are more closed-bodied, with arms and legs crossed, head and shoulders forward. The open-bodied posture in our society is considered more masculine and persuasive. Our posture communicates how open, how trusting, and how giving we are to others.

EXERCISE 3.31 • Self-Awareness: Body Posture

The purpose of this exercise is to become aware of how you hold your body.

At different times of the day, check how you are holding your body. What type of position feels most comfortable, standing or sitting? Which do you find preferable in a conversation, standing or sitting? Spend some time learning how you use your body in conversations. Are you in complete control of how you use your body in conversations. Do other people, such as a boss or a friend, influence how you hold your body? Experiment and try different body positions and postures. If you usually converse with certain people while sitting down, try standing instead. If you usually stand, try sitting instead. How do these changes feel? On another day, if you are normally open-bodied, try using a closed-bodied position. How does it feel? Does it affect how people react to you?

Distance is another communication factor that often relates to gender. In general, women tend to stand closer together in most cultures than do mixed partners or men. When talking, women face each other directly. Men, on the other hand, sit at angles to each other, or even parallel (Triandis, 1994; Tannen, 1990). Distance is also an indicator of differences in status and power. One interesting piece of research (Triandis, 1994, p. 201) has shown that the distance between speakers is also language-dependent. Venezuelan and Japanese foreign students were asked to speak with members of their culture in their native language and in English. When they spoke English, the difference between speakers changed to approximate the distance Americans use.

EXERCISE 3.32 • Self-Awareness: Preferred Distance

Everybody has a preferred conversational distance. The purpose of this exercise is to recognize your personal conversational distance.

Consider your preferred distance when you talk. Keep a journal for one full day, and record how close you stand when you talk to people. Are you a forearm's distance apart, a full arm's distance apart, or further apart? Does the distance change depending on gender, intimacy, age, status, or topic of conversation? Record how you sit when you talk to people of the same gender or of different genders. Do you face the other person or sit at an angle? How closely do you sit? Does how well you know the person, or your respective status and power make a difference?

EXERCISE 3.33 • Personal Space

In this exercise you will consider how you negotiate the division and use of space in order to maintain your personal space.

Look back at Exercise 3.18, in which you observed the spatial arrangements in your home and in others' homes. Consider what happens when two people from different systems decide to live together. If you are living with someone else (not necessarily a spouse or significant other), how did you negotiate the arrangement of space in your shared dwelling? Which rooms did you arrange? Which rooms did the other person(s) arrange? Which spaces in the house do you consider your own? Are there certain activities that you feel can be undertaken only in certain rooms? Why? Is it that the division of space is functional or territorial, or do certain activities only "feel right" in some places?

EXERCISE 3.34 • Functions of Space

In this exercise we will consider how space is divided up by function.

Look at the list you made for Exercise 3.18. If you have not done so, list the functions of each room that you observed. For example, a kitchen may be used to prepare food, serve food, talk on the phone, do art activities with the children, work, and socialize with friends. Some functions are site specific (that is, can be done *only* in that site),while others are not. Consider what aspects of certain spaces lend those spaces to certain functions. Some reasons that the kitchen serves so many functions may include the presence of a table, its size, and the amount of light. Having recognized the organization and usage of space in your home, consider how this arrangement came to be. Did people work together and explicitly state their preferences? Was one person in charge of "decorating"? Are members of the household given equal opportunity to make changes? How do you communicate your spatial preferences?

People usually gravitate to the same location, whether it is at the dining room table, at home, in the classroom, in the cafeteria, or in the work place. Without realizing, we become fixed to one perspective. Changing this perspective can be most instructive. You may find opportunities to talk to different people, or to experience the whole situation differently.

EXERCISE 3.35 • Self-Awareness: Changing Positions

In this exercise we will see how changing one's territory or position can change one's perspective.

The next time you meet in a work group or a classroom, change where you typically sit. How do you experience the session? What do you observe that you could not observe before? How do the roles and rules change?

Most people who work in offices use that space to convey something about themselves to visitors—from hanging the family picture on the wall of a small cubicle to arranging expensive furniture, art, and plants in an executive's office. The direction a desk faces, whether the person sits behind the desk, separated from visitors, or in a chair, facing visitors, the type of upholstery or the lack of upholstered furniture—all of these communicate to the visitor the attitudes, beliefs, and values, of the occupant of that space.

EXERCISE 3.36 • Personal Versus Public Space

The purpose of this exercise is to see how you arrange personal space in a public setting.

Make a chart like the one you used in Exercise 3.18. Now observe the special arrangements at the place where you work and study. Look at your personal space, but also look at meeting rooms, places to eat, utility rooms, other people's office areas, and so on. Consider how differently personal space and public space are structured. What types of differences are there between your own personal space and others? How does the arrangement of space at work relate to that at home? What about your comfort level? In what space are you most productive?

Recently, there has been a trend among large businesses toward eliminating office space for employees. In some cases, people work on computers in an open area. They may spend most of their days in face-to-face interaction working on projects. In other cases, sales personnel, who are highly mobile, no longer have any designated space. A building is converted to a series of work stations, and is equipped with fax, modem, computer, and other telecommunications equipment. Employees who need indoor work space and access to electronic hook-ups simply reserve space in the building, but have no place that is specifically designated as their personal work environment. Whether or not these new work arrangements support creative productivity remains to be seen.

Nonverbal Interactions in Large Groups

Our behavior in large groups may differ dramatically from our behavior in dyads or small groups. Much depends on the purpose and nature of the group, on whether our attendance/participation is voluntary or mandatory, and on the history of our experiences. Some people automatically feel uncomfortable and shy in large groups, even though they are perceived as the "life of the party" in small groups. Other people are uncomfortable with the scrutiny of small groups and much prefer the excitement or anonymity of large groups. Touch is not usually a different issue in large groups than in small groups; eye contact is easier to avoid in large groups. The elements of nonverbal interaction that may differ in large groups include gestures, postures, space, and facial expressions.

Gestures, Postures, and Space

In groups, often only a minority of members actually talk. Even if everyone talks, long periods of silence occur on the part of each member, at least in terms of verbal communication. Nonverbal communication, however, constantly occurs. If members are in agreement, they nod their heads, look more attentively at the speaker, smile, or find some other silent way to convey their concurrence. Disagreement is also expressed by shaking the head, looking away, frowning, or doing something else.

EXERCISE 3.37 • Gestures in Public

Given that the majority of people in large groups do not talk, gestures and other nonverbal signals are important. In this exercise, we will look at how gestures are used in large group settings.

Make a list of all the gestures you use to express agreement or disagreement in group settings. Next time you are in a group, notice how often you and other members of the group use these gestures.

Gestures are also used to indicate that one wants a turn to speak, is not finished, or feels interrupted. They are important parts of conversation in that they help determine the order and process of changing speakers.

EXERCISE 3.38 • Gestures in Context

In this exercise we will consider the role of gestures in small groups.

1. Have a ten-minute conversation with at least two friends. Notice all the gestures used to change or maintain the speaker, the topic, or any other element of the conversation. Check your list against your conversation partners' to see if they noticed anything that you missed. Discuss these gestures. Did you all interpret them the same way?
2. Next, have a ten-minute conversation with at least two people who are not good friends. Did you use the same gestures? Discuss the gestures that were used and see if the others interpret them the same way you do.
3. Finally, observe a meeting that has a formal agenda and a definite hierarchy, such as a school council meeting or a department meeting. What gestures are used to control the conversation? Are they the same as were used by the informal groups? Is everybody equally entitled to used them? Or is the conversation controlled by verbal cues?

EXERCISE 3.39 • Crowding

The purpose of this exercise is to define what crowding means to you.

With a group of friends, set up a space of about 4 ft. by 4 ft. and mark the boundaries either with tape or with furniture. Allow one person at a time into the space, stopping to notice how you feel with the addition of each person. When does the space feel comfortable? How many people does it take to feel crowded?

EXERCISE 3.40 • Space Negotiation

The purpose of this exercise is to observe how others negotiate space.

Negotiation for space between strangers continually takes place in our urban societies. Go to a supermarket at a time when you know a lot of people will be shopping. If there is a general supervisor in the checkout area, introduce yourself and tell the person what you intend to do. Then stand off to the side of the checkout lines and observe people as they approach and stand in line. People will make judgments about which line to stand in based on nonverbal cues related to posture, use of eye contact, speed of the checker, and other elements of the total picture. Try to identify the cues that cause people to choose a certain checkout line. Then watch what they do while in line. Do they read magazines and block out the environment? Maintain vigilance to be sure nobody cuts in? Try to cut in themselves? You will probably observe are least one instance of two people rushing for the same "space." Usually, they do not speak unless conflict develops. They also do not hit each other, although they may push. Try to identify the cues that are used in determining dominance. Finally, observe the closeness of people in the line and the cues they emit to one another as they observe the checkout person. What does one person do if another person invades his or her comfortable "space bubble"? How does the person who feels crowded push the invader back? This might also be an interesting exercise to conduct in a bus or subway, in a food line, at a sports event, or at a concert.

EXERCISE 3.41 • A Stranger in a Group

The purpose of this exercise is to experience what it is like to be a stranger.

Go alone to a large party or informal group meeting where you know few, if any, people. Become aware of how you feel entering the room. Do you try to make eye contact with someone? What is your posture? How do you enter the group? How do others enter the group? Do you find yourself standing aside and observing, like a wallflower? Do you latch on to someone, engaging him or her in conversation so that you do not stand out alone? How do you signal people that you want to be included in their conversation? Do you smile? While you observe yours and others' behaviors, keep track of your internal feelings. When and how do you feel anxious? Shy? Eager? Confident?

Conclusion

The ideas and exercises presented in this chapter focused on some of the aspects of nonverbal communication that are constantly operating in our environments. We have focused more on developing your awareness of the existence and description of your behaviors than on your levels of comfort or discomfort. In order to sensitize yourself to the elements of nonverbal communication that you find comfortable, review all the exercises and begin to pay attention to elements that were either annoyingly uncomfortable or very comfortable. Throughout the remainder of this book, you will be encouraged to become aware of your own comfort levels and of the behavior of the people around you as it relates to both your level of comfort and discomfort and theirs.

As you become more skilled at noticing the nonverbal elements in your environment, you will become more efficient at understanding your own behavior in cross-cultural situations. If you are getting to know a person from a culture where direct eye contact is considered rude, you will be more likely to take responsibility for your own discomfort in reacting to that person's downcast eyes, than you will be to blaming her or him for being "shifty" or "sneaky." For example, if you are a North American male being introduced to a middle-eastern Muslim female, you will understand why she either refuses to shake your hand or does so with extreme discomfort. Previously, you may have interpreted this behavior to mean that the woman was afraid of you or found you personally unacceptable. Now you will be able to focus on the particular element of nonverbal behavior that caused the discomfort and view the process from a cultural, rather than a personal, perspective. Finally, you will have a better or clearer idea of the nonverbal elements of communication in the dominant United States culture.

If you are a native-born North American member of the dominant, white, Christian, heterosexual, able-bodied culture, whatever makes you comfortable is probably a characteristic of the dominant culture. If you tend to think about your behavior as being particularly representative of you as a unique individual, and as being shaped by your own values and beliefs, that also is typical of North Americans. Our individuality is culturally shaped, defined, and emphasized. As a result, our resistance to acknowledging this is an important signal to all of us.

PART TWO

Developing Awareness of Others

From the Outside In

4

Emotions: Their Permissibility and Expression

Emotions are a natural phenomenon. They are not, as one might assume from our use of the term in English, equivalent to feelings. Feelings are biological responses to both internal and external stimuli. Emotions involve four basic components: *stimuli* (situations or events that cause a reaction); *reaction* to internal and external stimuli; *interpretation* of the situation; and the resulting *behavior.* There is a biological, and hence universal, aspect to emotions, and also a cultural, and hence learned, aspect. Our biology, to some extent, determines the physiological responses we will have to a given situation. A threatening situation can produce a racing heart, sweaty palms, or a facial grimace, maybe all three. Our culture teaches us to label these sensations as fear. It then teaches us to interpret the situation and to evaluate appropriate reactions or behaviors. In other words, emotions are social constructs. How we identify, label, display, or react to an emotion is culturally determined (Abu-Lughod & Lutz, 1990; Matsumoto, 1996a; Lynch, 1990; Carlson & Hatfield, 1992).

Emotions make a statement about our relation to other people, our role in society, or our interpretation of a specific situation. Because some aspects of emotions are culturally specific, the potential for misunderstandings between people is great. For that reason, it is important to recognize which aspects of emotions are universal and shared by all, and which aspects are not. We cannot assume that everyone will feel about a given situation as we do, or will react to it as we do. Neither can we assume that others will correctly interpret our reactions. Because emotions, or rather, the expression and interpretation of emotions, are culturally shaped, we need to recognize the potential for miscommunication and deal with it in a constructive manner.

In this chapter, we discuss the biological and cultural influences on emotion. We examine how cultural and individual differences affect our perceptions, interpretations, and expressions of emotions, paying particular attention to the effects of gender, class, religion, race, and ethnicity. We consider intimate, professional, and public interpersonal relationships, as well as those based on friendship. The exercises in this chapter are designed to allow you to become more self-aware of your ingrained assumptions about emotional expression and to help you develop your sensitivity to others' display rules about emotional expression. (Display rules define the acceptable and appropriate expression of emotions in a given culture.)

Perceptions of Emotions

The first step in interpreting emotions is recognizing the dualistic nature of mainstream perceptions of emotions in the United States. On one hand, the experience or display of emotions is considered a sign of weakness, something to be controlled or, better yet, not felt. At the same time, emotions are seen as a force of nature, dangerous and powerful and beyond our control. The contradictory nature of these viewpoints is obvious. For example, "emotional people" often are viewed as being weak or flawed. In this country, women are seen as being more emotional than men, and they have been disadvantaged by this perception (Lutz, 1990). At the same time, many people use their emotions as an excuse for their behavior. "I was so angry that I just had to hit him!" "He killed her in a jealous rage." "She is hysterical and out of control." All of these statements reflect the perception that emotions are a force of nature, beyond our control.

Emotions are complex experiences. There are several components to consider. The first involves *emotional elicitors,* the antecedents of emotions. These are the situations or events that cause an emotion. The second component involves the *physiological responses.* These are the ways one responds physiologically—for example, with clenched fists, a quickening of the heartbeat, a tightening of the jaw, a curving of the mouth. The third component involves *emotional interpretations.* The physiological reactions and the situational events leading to these reactions must be interpreted and evaluated. These interpretations and evaluations are shaped by our past personal experiences as well as by sociocultural factors. How we interpret and evaluate emotion-producing situations (emotion elicitors), physiological changes, and possible reactions influences what we react to and how we respond (Lewis & Saarni, 1985). In the case of fear, for example, the elicitor is a frightening act, and our interpretation of the act—as well as our physiological response to it—is the fear. This third component of emotions, interpretation, is closely linked to the fourth component, the unique *emotional* experiences that are the result of the other three components.

Although the focus in this chapter will be on how we express emotions, it is important to consider how we label emotions. In doing so, we must remember that people of various ethnicities, as well as people from different parts of the country, different social classes, or different types of communities, may not have identical verbal languages.

Consensus as to how we label emotions is necessary if people are to reach complete agreement concerning emotions. Even though two people share a language, if they do not share a culture, misunderstandings may result due to differences in the labels that are applied to various feelings and situations.

Studies of emotional labels suggest that terms in one language are not always easily translated into another language. In fact, some languages appear to include some emotional categories that are not found in English and also to lack some categories that are found in English (Russell, 1994). For example, the French word *formidable* connotes a sense of awesomeness, whereas in English it means forbidding or intimidating. What the listener hears is not necessarily what the speaker intends because each participant is influenced by past experience. To further complicate things, emotions are not material entities with fixed, intrinsic values. Emotions tend to be products of intentionality. The way we experience emotions is the result of past and current events (Kagan, 1984).

EXERCISE 4.1 • The Vocabulary of Emotions

The purpose of this exercise is to consider the hidden values associated with words and terms of emotion.

1. Refer to the list of emotions that you constructed in Exercise 3.5.
2. Next, think about situations in which you have felt strong emotions, such as anger, happiness, sadness, fear, and so on. With these situations in mind, make a list of all the words you use when discussing emotions or situations that might elicit emotions.
3. Sort the words into these four categories: (1) power/weakness, (2) control/out of control, (3) desirability/nondesirability, (4) and permissibility/nonpermissibility.

Compare your lists with other people's lists and see how much consensus there is as to the words that have been assigned to each category. If possible, compare your list with those of people who have a different first language. Do they have terms in their language that are direct translations (word for word) of your terms, or are the translations inexact? Do they have emotion terms that cannot be translated directly into English? Into which category do these emotions fall?

EXERCISE 4.2 • Emotional Labeling

The purpose of this exercise is to identify how you recognize the emotional aspects of certain situations.

Label the most appropriate emotion referred to or elicited by the following statements and scenarios. How do you interpret the emotional message of each statement or scenario?

- A mother picks up her crying child. She hugs him and gently rocks back and forth while telling him that it is okay.
  emotion: _______________
- "You never listen to me. You don't care about what I want!"
  emotion: _______________
- "The report is due the day after tomorrow, George. Have Frank go over it before the meeting for any problems."
  emotion: _______________
- A friend tells you that she does not want to go to the movies, or out for a drink, or anything. She just doesn't feel up to going out.
  emotion: _______________
- You are walking along and a bird defecates on your head.
  emotion: _______________
- You have to be someplace in 15 minutes and you have enough time to get there, but when you get to your car you find that you have a flat tire.
  emotion: _______________
- A subordinate asks you to do a menial task.
  emotion: _______________
- A superior asks you to do a menial task.
  emotion: _______________

Feel free to add to this list or modify it. Next, compare your labels with a partner's. If you differed on some, discuss how you each interpreted the situation, and try to identify the source of your differences. Do this with several people, such as family members, colleagues, friends, or acquaintances. Notice the types of people with whom you had a higher degree of agreement. In what ways were you similar or different? What types of situations or emotions did you tend to agree on?

Emotions: Biological and Cultural Determinants

Different societies have different ways of viewing emotions. All of these views are influenced by the cultures that produce them. Our society views emotions as a natural phenomenon. It views emotions as occurring within the individual. These values have been translated into theories that regard emotions as unlearned and biological. Accordingly, emotions are viewed as automatic physiological responses to stimuli. They are passive, irrational, and one of the lower faculties of the body. This biological view of emotions is evident in our society's tendency to use drugs such as anti-depressants and anti-anxiety medications to control or alter our emotions. This view also suggests that emotions are universal, that what and how one would feel in a situation is exactly how someone else should feel.

At the same time, our society believes that people are unique and discrete individuals. Hence, emotions also are seen as being unique to the individual. They are valued as individual human characteristics. It follows, then, that emotions cannot be fully explained by biology. Common sense suggests that the truth is more complex. Recent cross-cultural works have produced theories that view emotions as both influencing social structures and norms and being determined by those structures and norms. Among these theories is the cognitive theory, which views emotions as the product of the mind, a consequence of our thinking. In other words, emotions are "cognitively based appraisals of situations" and "are often socially negotiable experiences." (Lynch, 1990, p. 10)

Thus, emotion is a complex socially constructed phenomenon, as well as a natural phenomenon. When broken down into parts, we can begin to understand what is biologically determined (and hence universal) and what is culturally determined. First, Let us consider the stimuli or emotional elicitor(s), something, usually an event, that triggers a biological change. An example might be a member of your family recounting a story about some foolish behavior that you engaged in as a child. This emotional elicitor causes changes in your emotional receptors (basically, the central nervous system), resulting in biological changes (physiological responses). You may feel your muscles tighten up, your breathing become sharper.

Up to this point, all reactions seem to be based in biology. What you think about the event or the emotional elicitors—your emotional interpretation—is the next step in the chain of emotions. If you say to yourself something like "How could he tell everyone about how stupid I was?" "He is deliberately out to get me and make me look bad in front of others" or "Now everyone will see how bad I am," you will become acutely aware of feeling resentful, angry, and ashamed. Thus, what we *do* with emotional elicitors—how we interpret and experience them cognitively—is determined by social values and personal experiences and history. *Cognitions* can also create physiological responses, which influence your emotions (and the way you feel). The interpretation of the cognitions and the physiological responses constitute emotions. The experience is not unidirectional; rather, it is reciprocal.

Any observable changes in your face, voice, body, or movement can be seen as your *emotional expression*—the display of any emotion. Your *emotional state* (including, but not limited to, your physiological condition) refers to your emotional condition at a certain time. Some of your emotions in an emotional state may be expressed; some may be masked. Your *emotional experience* comprises your internal interpretation and evaluation of yourself, your emotional expression, and your emotional state (Lewis & Saarni, 1985). (Your emotional experience includes what you are feeling during an emotional state; it is influenced by personal experiences and history and includes those emotions that are not expressed.) Both emotional expression and emotional experience have been shown to have clear, culturally determined differences.

Universality of Emotions

If emotions are innate, biological phenomena, or if certain aspects of emotions (that is, the physiological responses) are innate, then those aspects must be universal. In other words, if being angry makes one's blood boil in Canada, then an angry person in Greece should also feel that her blood boils. Our physiological responses to feelings should be the same, irrespective of our individual cultures and histories.

Humans have an evolutionary-biological need to be able to communicate some situations accurately and quickly. Emotions can be seen as part of our communications (either verbal or nonverbal communications). For example, the ability to communicate the presence of a *dangerous* situation quickly (and to distinguish it from, say, a *disgusting* situation) could have clear survival significance (Izard, 1977). Victims of street assaults sometimes report that they experienced feelings of disgust about the street people they encountered but did not recognize the danger of the situation. Disgust masked other possible cues.

That there is a definite biological and universal aspect to emotion has been demonstrated by research identifying universal facial expressions (Ekman, 1994; Izard, 1994). As mentioned earlier, we use our faces to communicate nonverbally. By analyzing facial expressions identified by people from a variety of literate and nonliterate cultures, Ekman & Friesen (1975) and Izard (1977), as well as others, have determined that there are six universal emotions. These emotions are expressed in standardized facial expressions, irrespective of one's individual culture. These expressions are: *happiness, sadness, surprise, fear, anger,* and *disgust* (Ekman & Friesen, 1975; Wallbott, Ricci-Bitti, & Banninger-Huber, 1986; Izard, 1994). Ekman (1994) added *contempt* as a seventh universal emotion. One can fairly accurately identify another person's emotions from facial expressions, without resorting to verbal communication.

EXERCISE 4.3 • Facial Expressions

The purpose of this exercise is to determine how we visualize the facial expressions of the universal emotions and whether or not our visualization matches our own facial expressions of these emotions.

Ekman and Friesen have identified three regions of the face that are involved in facial expressions: the brow/forehead; the eyes/lids and top of the nose; and the lower face, mouth, cheeks, nose, and chin (Ekman and Friesen, 1975, p. 28). Draw a picture or describe in detail what someone experiencing each of the following emotions would look like: happiness, sadness, surprise, fear, anger, disgust, contempt. Be sure to consider what the three regions of the face would look like for each emotion. If you do not want to draw, find examples of these facial expressions in magazines.

Now, look in a mirror that is large enough to allow you to view your entire face. Make faces at yourself. Show each emotion as you drew or described it. Does it look familiar? Does it feel right? Was your idea of the facial expression accurate?

Compare your drawings or descriptions with others'. Do they agree?

EXERCISE 4.4 • Intended and Perceived Emotions

Having understood the fit between the perceived and your own facial expressions, we will now learn how accurately you interpret others' emotional expressions and how accurately they interpret yours.

Work in pairs to see if you can identify someone's emotions from looking at his or her face.

On index cards or on small pieces of paper, have one person write down the 7 emotions (one emotion on each card): happiness, sadness, surprise, fear, anger, disgust, and contempt. Shuffle the cards. Have the other person number two sheets of paper from 1 to 7. Decide who is going to *present* the emotion and who is going to *interpret.* Decide on a signal that the presenter will use later to indicate that he or she is ready to present an emotion.

If you are the presenter, select a card and silently read the emotion on the card. Then, remember a recent instance when you felt that emotion. In detail, review the experience in your mind and try to relive the emotion. Think about what you felt, what you said or did, what the other person(s) said or did, and how that made you feel. When you believe that you are showing the desired emotion, give the "ready" signal. Your partner should then write down what emotion he thinks you are showing. Then, the presenter should tell what emotion was intended, and the interpreter should tell how well that emotion was conveyed.

Repeat this procedure for each emotion. (Some emotions may be harder to enact than others.) Then switch roles and repeat the exercise. Compare the perceived emotions with the intended ones. Were you both accurate on all of them? Some of them? Which were harder to identify? Why might that be? Do you think that your partner portrayed each emotion as you would or did? Discuss your findings. If you have time, repeat the whole exercise with someone else. This time, try someone from a clearly different, gender, race, age, or cultural group.

Cultural and Individual Differences

Up to now, we have considered the biological bases of emotions and the fact that there are seven categories of universal expressions. Emotions cannot be purely biological, however; otherwise, you would have had no trouble with Exercise 4.4. In fact, the different principal expressions of the same emotion are attributed to cultural and individual differences. One's society teaches one how to identify and label emotions. For example, babies and young children, who have not been fully socialized, have the least socially altered emotions. Consider for a moment how children display emotions. A two-year-old is told "no," or is in some other manner denied what she wants. Her response is a completely physical expression of anger. She uses not just her face, but also her voice and her body. She may scream and kick, or even throw herself on the floor. Now consider how adults express anger. No healthy, mature adult would throw herself on the floor kicking and screaming! Neither do most healthy school-aged children. What becomes clear is that, sometime during our early years, we are *taught* that throwing tantrums is not acceptable. Some of us are taught that yelling or crying is okay; some of us are taught that no outward expression is acceptable. In short, although each of us learns the socially acceptable way to express anger or any other emotion, we do not stop feeling the emotion. The anger is still there; only the way in which we show it to others has changed.

These rules that we learn, which tell us how we may express an emotion, have been labeled "display rules." Over time, these rules become so automatic that, as adults, we are not aware that we are following any rules. The rules have become internalized (Matsumoto, 1996a). A display rule may forbid an emotion, may determine what intensity of emotion is appropriate, or may require the expression of a specific emotion that is contrary to the emotion that is being felt. Display rules are determined by our cultures. Who has not heard, or said, the following types of statements: "Boys don't cry," "Shouting is unladylike," "It isn't nice to stare," "Don't get so excited." We also transmit display rules nonverbally, by modeling appropriate behavior or ignoring inappropriate behavior. Without realizing it, each of us helps to maintain and preserve these rules, and each of us judges other people by these rules (Malatesta & Haviland, 1985). The presence of such display rules is evidenced by the fact that what is displayed when one is alone or with members of a group such as a family differs from what is displayed when one is with nongroup members or strangers (Ekman & Friesen, 1975; Matsumoto, 1994; Matsumoto, 1996a).

EXERCISE 4.5 • Social Context for Expression

The purpose of this exercise is to recognize the effect display rules have on our emotional expression in different social situations.

For each of the seven emotions—happiness, sadness, anger, fear, disgust, surprise, contempt—consider in which of the following contexts you would feel able to freely express the emotion, and in which you would try not to show what you are feeling.

you are alone
you are with a small, intimate group, such as your family or best friends

you are with a group of people with whom you share activities and values, such as colleagues, church members, or a team of some sort

you are in a crowd of people, many of whom you do not know

Now, for each of the above situations, make a fuller list of appropriate emotions and inappropriate emotions. Consider such emotions as gratefulness, superiority, confusion, and so on. (You may wish to refer again to the list of emotions that you constructed in Exercise 3.5)

Compare your results with other people's. Do you have the same values concerning what emotions are appropriate to express in each situation?

Research suggests that clear differences exist among people from different cultures as to what they find acceptable in different situations. Some suggest that these differences are a result of our different perceptions of self, perceptions that are strongly determined by the type of culture to which we belong.

The United States shares with other Western cultures the concept of the self as a bounded entity with unique, internal attributes. As a result, our society encourages emotions that separate the self from social relations and that encourage independence. Such emotions include pride, superiority, anger, and frustration (Matsumoto, 1994). This contrasts with the concept of many non-Western cultures, which view the self as an unbounded, or inherently interdependent entity, whose major attributes are inseparable from social contexts (Matsumoto, 1994). In these cultures, the emphasis is not on independence, but on fitting in and maintaining interdependence among individuals. In such societies, emotions that encourage social cohesion and relations are desirable, such as friendly feelings, respect, indebtedness, and guilt (Matsumoto, 1994). What these two contrasting concepts of self suggest is that one's culture determines which emotions are desirable, are to be actively sought, and are to be freely expressed. Recognition of which type of self-concept a person holds can help in understanding that person's emotions.

EXERCISE 4.6 • Self-Concept: Emotional Permissions

The purpose of this exercise is to recognize the link between certain emotions and one's concept of self.

At this point, it would be worthwhile to review the list of statements about self that you made in Exercise 2.1. Given your statements, which concept of self would you say that you possess? What emotions do you positively value? What emotions do you most frequently experience?

To determine this type of information about others, start by asking yourself with whom you feel comfortable discussing emotions. Notice what types of people these are. For example, is it easier for you to discuss emotions with family members? With those of the same gender? With women? With people who are at a similar level?

Now conduct the following exercise with at least five people. If possible, include a few people that you do not know well. Have each person rate the following emotions: *friendly feelings; pride; respect; superiority; indebtedness; anger;* and *guilt.* Each emotion should be rated on a scale of 1 to 5, with 1 being low and 5 being high. Each emotion should be assigned one rating for each of the following three criteria: *frequency* (how often they experience the emotion), *desirability* (how often they want to experience the emotion), and *comfort level* (how comfortable they are with the emotion).

Then, have them make a list of 10 statements about who they are, as you did previously. Do their statements support a concept of self that fits with their evaluations of the above emotions?

One result of differences in self-concepts is a difference of ideas about what types of emotions are desirable. In the United States, Caucasians find the expression of contempt more appropriate than do Asians; the expression of disgust more appropriate than do blacks or Latinos; and, in general, the expression of emotions with acquaintances more acceptable than do blacks, Asians, or Latinos (Matsumoto, 1994).

Situations also determine what is acceptable. In the United States, many feel that negative emotions may be expressed to in-group members, but only positive emotions should be expressed to nongroup members. One explanation is that we are most concerned about preserving our independence with people close to us. This is very different from what Poles and Hungarians find acceptable. The fact that they avoid expressing negative emotions with in-groups suggests an emphasis on preserving social connections. Poles have even reported that expressing negative emotions when alone is undesirable. Our culture influences not only what and how we display emotions, but also where.

Display Rules—Culture

If display rules are cultural creations, then there probably are certain rules or patterns that one can use to interpret how people perceive and react to situations. Knowledge of the individual involved will, of course, increase the ability to perceive patterns and underlying emotions. At the same time, it is important to remember that people belong to more than one culture. Which culture is dominant at any specific point in time is often determined by the situation. No hard and fast rules can be given for knowing which display rules an individual is following in a given situation.

The first step in understanding display rules is to identify an individual's self-concept. Consider what you learned from Exercise 4.5, in which you examined how social context influences emotional expression. Also consider Exercise 4.6, in which you identified which emotions are permissible in your culture. How would you go about determining an individual's self-concept? Consider which cultural groups the person belongs to and values. People tend to identify more with some of the groups to which they belong than with others. For example, a highly placed executive would probably identify strongly with the dominant white, male culture of this country. A foreign exchange student who plans to return home would not. Are their primary cultures individualistic or collective? To review, individualistic cultures tend to view the self as discreet, while collective cultures see the self as interdependent with others. Western cultures are more individualistic, while Asian cultures are more collective, but no culture is absolutely and exclusively one or the other.

Certain universal emotions have been labeled as desirable for people with independent self-concepts. These include anger, pride, and frustration. Others have been labeled as desirable for people from cultures with interdependent ideas about self. These include sympathy, shame, and guilt. In addition, research has found that many culture-specific emotions exist that cannot be directly translated into American English (Markus & Kitayama, 1991). Consider a situation in which an elderly person crosses the street in front of someone who is in a car waiting for the light to change. The light changes while the elderly person is in the middle of the street. In the United States, where the elderly elicit feelings of impatience and disgust, the driver may feel those emotions and may blow the horn. In a culture such as China, where the elderly are revered, the driver might feel pride and empathy and might even get out of the car to help the elderly person cross the street.

EXERCISE 4.7 • Categories of Emotions

Having discussed different concepts of self, consider how emotions are associated with these concepts.

1. List all the emotion terms you can think of that promote the separateness of the person experiencing them.
2. List all the emotion terms you can think of that promote, foster, and maintain social relations.
3. Compare the two lists. Do they overlap? How different are the emotions?
4. Compare your list to those of people from similar and different backgrounds who share your language. Is there a difference in the degree of agreement between lists?

Regardless of our personal self-concept, we experience emotions from all participants in a relationship. Everyone experiences emotions that promote independence and interdependence, but our perception of an emotion as desirable is largely determined by the need to assert our individuality or to maintain social relations. This need is determined by the situation, as well as by our personal history. For example, people who fear alienating a lover or friend would find emotions such as anger and pride dangerous, but emotions such as guilt and compassion desirable. On the other hand, people who feel a need to prove they are grown-up and not tied to their mother's apron strings will find anger and pride desirable, but guilt and compassion threatening.

EXERCISE 4.8 • Situations and Emotions

In contrast to earlier exercises in which we look at the effect of social control on emotions, the purpose of this exercise it to consider how a situation often determines our emotion.

For each of the following situations, decide (a) if it is more important for the people involved to assert independence or promote harmony, (b) if the situation is egalitarian or hierarchical, (c) which emotions are permissible for all participants, (d) which emotions are permissible for the person with a higher status (boss, teacher, parent, and so on), or for the person with a lower status, and (e) how often you find yourself in such a situation, and what your role is in the situation (your status):

- A couple who are in debt need to prioritize spending.
- A project proposal needs to be written within a limited amount of time.
- A hiring committee needs to decide on a timetable and on hiring criteria.
- The same committee needs to make a final decision about which candidate to hire.
- A couple needs to discipline their child for not doing what he or she was told to do.
- A couple needs to discipline their child for lying and stealing.
- An elderly parent falls ill and the children need to decide how to deal with the situation.
- A death in the family results in several issues that need to be dealt with speedily.
- At your job, budget cuts need to be made and implemented.
- In a company, limited resources need to be distributed (1) among departments and (2) within a department.
- A limited number of sale items are available at a department store.
- Only one parking space is available for two or more cars.

Would you expect everyone you know to have evaluated the above situations in the same manner as you did? Check this out. Are there any patterns in terms of the types of situations in which independence or social harmony are desirable? In terms of how different types of people evaluate the situations? Are you surprised by any of your findings?

How can you apply the information you have acquired to real-life situations? The first place to start is to try to recognize how other people perceive a situation. If you know that a person comes from a collective culture, like Japan or China, then you can make certain assumptions in terms of their display rules. For instance, such people are less likely to display openly egocentric emotions like anger. Instead, they are more likely to cover their feelings with a harmony-producing display like a smile. Being the most easily controlled and manipulated facial expression, smiles are often social in function, not expressive (Kraut & Johnston, 1979). In fact, smiles may be used in Asian cultures to cover up discomfort (Matsumoto, 1996b). The presence of a smile on the face of a person from a collective culture should not be interpreted as signifying happiness or pleasure, but rather as reaffirming social relations and hierarchy.

EXERCISE 4.9 • Underlying Emotions

The purpose of this exercise is to try to identify any difference between what people may be feeling and what they actually display.

Watch how people react in different situations, and notice their facial expressions and body language. Be sure to watch people of different gender, age, race, and occupation. At the same time, consider how you would feel if you were they. Do their expressions or actions match with what you would feel? Do they match how you would behave? How can you explain any differences between how you would feel and behave and how those observed behave?

Three possible explanations need to be considered: (1) How honest and self-aware are you? Are you accurately assessing how you would feel and react? Spend some time thinking about times when you have been in similar situations, and what your feelings and actions were during and after those situations. (2) How likely is it that those observed do not feel the same way that you would feel? If possible, ask those observed what their feelings were in the situation. If direct questioning is not possible, come up with some hypothetical situations to determine similarity between you and those observed. Consider how you would feel in those situations, and ask those observed how they would feel. In other words, try to determine how universal certain feelings are for specific types of situations. Recognize that not everyone will feel comfortable being honest about their reactions. (3) It is possible that people feel the same emotions as you, but have been socialized to express them differently and react differently. What do you think? Do we all feel the same emotions but display them differently? Do we actually feel different emotions? Or is it a combination of the two?

Underlying emotions are those that are not expressed but that we infer from what is expressed. For example, some people who do not feel they are allowed to express anger may try to cover up that feeling with incongruent facial expressions, attempting to display a calm and happy face.

Before going further, it is important to recognize the display rules of the dominant culture and the display rules of our personal culture (because the dominant culture is not the only culture to which we belong). In fact, the dominant culture in a country is not everyone's dominant culture.

EXERCISE 4.10 • Display Rules in the United States

At this point, it is necessary to determine what the display rules are for the dominant culture in the United States.

What is the cultural ideal (in terms of emotional display) for an individual in the dominant United States culture? What emotions would such an individual express freely? How would each emotion be expressed verbally and/or nonverbally? Describe how each emotion would be facially displayed. You might find it useful to try to recreate the emotion in yourself and observe your facial expression in a mirror. What emotions cannot be expressed? How are they hidden?

Compare your results with those of at least three others, and come to a consensus about allowable and unallowable emotions and their expression. Can you and your group come up with a few rules or generalizations that explain why these emotions are desirable/undesirable, openly expressed, and so on?

Unfortunately, few studies have been conducted that classify the display rules of specific groups of people. One exception is Matsumoto's work on Japan, *Unmasking Japan* (1996b). By considering several research studies aimed at understanding Japanese culture, emotions, and display rules, Matsumoto was able to come up with a series of rules or explanations for why most Japanese react the way they do. Japanese culture is, on many levels, very different from the mainstream United States cultures. We present these here so that you can compare them to those that you just devised for the dominant United States culture. Consider not only how the rules differ, but also why and how these differences would play themselves out in everyday situations.

The first rule for why most Japanese react the way they do is that *emotions are collective.* They are shared and displayed by all group members, regardless of individual feelings (Matsumoto, 1996b, pp. 51–52). The second rule is that *emotions must maintain group harmony.* As a result, emotions that threaten group cohesion—such as anger, contempt, and disgust—cannot be expressed. Instead, one should pretend to feel positive emotions (p. 53).

The third rule is that *one should differentiate between in- and out-groups.* Some emotions are appropriate to display to in-group members, but not to out-group members, and vice versa (pp. 54–55). The fourth rule is that *one must consider whether future relations with the other person(s) are possible.* If they are possible, be polite. If not, indifference is appropriate (pp. 55–56). The fifth rule is that *one should actively work at status maintenance.* This means that what one displays should maintain status differences. The sixth rule follows from the fifth rule: *One must maintain one's own status.* Given one's status and the status of others, only certain emotions are appropriate. Some emotions, such as anger, can be expressed to people of lower status, but not to people of higher status. Other emotions, such as sadness, cannot be expressed downward. Taken together, these rules explain much about how Japanese behave in certain situations and, more important for us, why there is so much room for misunderstandings.

EXERCISE 4.11 • Consequences for Different Cultural Display Rules (Part 1)

The purpose of this exercise is to learn how another culture's display rules—in this case, Japanese—influence responses to certain situations.

Redo Exercise 4.8 and evaluate the situations in terms of the Japanese display rules as defined by Matsumoto (1996a) and given above. How do they differ from what you said earlier?

EXERCISE 4.12 • Consequences for Different Cultural Display Rules (Part 2)

Using what you have learned about yourself, your culture's display rules, and Japanese display rules, in this exercise you will consider how, when, and why people mask "inappropriate" emotions.

The most commonly used mask for inappropriate emotions is the smile. It is the most easily controlled positive facial expression. List the reasons that you would smile in any given situation. Consider the six Japanese display rules. For what reasons do you believe a Japanese person would smile?

With what groups or types of people would it be permissible for Japanese people to express the following emotions: fear, anger, disgust, happiness, sadness, contempt, surprise?

Compare your answers to those you gave regarding when and how *you* feel and express these emotions. Discuss your conclusions with others.

Was it easy to think of reasons that a Japanese person might smile? Here are some likely ones: to share in positive group emotions or experiences, regardless of personal feelings; to preserve in-group peace and harmony and indicate that anger is not being felt; out of politeness due to possible future relations; so as to avoid giving negative news that would contradict or disappoint a superior; and, only occasionally, to let subordinates know that they are still accepted and valued.

With whom might Japanese people express various emotions? Here's an incomplete list: fear, with superiors, sometimes with in-group; anger, with outgroups or subordinates; disgust, with outgroups and subordinates; happiness, with in-group, peers, and superiors, in limited amounts to subordinates; sadness, with superiors; contempt, with out groups or subordinates; surprise, in some situations with in-groups, with superiors.

Display Rules—Individual

Not all display rules are culturally determined. Some are the result of individual idiosyncrasies or individual families. If someone grew up in a family where one parent was always ill and it was necessary always to be quiet, then that person might never display emotions openly or intensely. If someone grew up in a family with five other children and people had to shout to be heard, then that individual might be more disposed to be loud and expansive in his or her emotional display. At the same time, some people seem to have a predisposition to certain emotional traits. These people tend to express frequently a given emotion over extended periods of time (Izard, 1977). A person might be said to be moody or angry, or to have a sunny disposition and always to see things positively. The best way to recognize these personal display rules is through knowledge of the individual involved.

EXERCISE 4.13 • Emotional Traits and Personality Types

The purpose of this exercise is to consider how different personality types display emotions and react to specific types of situations.

List all the people you know whom you would consider to (a) have a sunny personality, (b) be pessimistic or negative, (c) be angry or aggressive, or (d) be given to emotional outbursts or be generally moody. What are the shared observable characteristics of each category of people? How would you expect each type of person to react to the following types of situations? (a) being put down or embarrassed, (b) making a potentially self-destructive mistake, (c) being lauded and praised, (d) having someone else be put down or embarrassed in front of them, (e) having someone else make a bad mistake, and (f) having someone else be lauded and praised.

How do these reactions relate to how *you* would react in similar situations? How would you define your emotional-personality type?

EXERCISE 4.14 • Families and Individual Rules

Having considered your society's display rules and individual personality types, we will now look at family display rules.

Take a moment to consider the display rules of your family of origin. Write them down. If you have siblings, contact them. Do they agree with you? If possible, ask your parents. Do they agree with you? Talk about the role of emotions and the display of emotions in your family. Compare your family display rules with other people's family display rules. Consider your various cultural backgrounds and evaluate any similarities and differences. Which rules can you label as belonging to just your family? Which belong to a larger cultural group?

How do individual and cultural rules affect each other? Can we determine where one begins and the other ends? How similar is your set of family display rules to that of the dominant culture?

Display Rules—Professional/Occupational

People's professions or occupations also affect their display rules. Certain professions require people to learn to control facial expressions. One obvious example is that of airline flight attendants. They must always be pleasant and congenial, no matter what the passenger says or does. The nature of certain professions may make specific emotional expressions more or less desirable. In emergency situations, a flight attendant cannot allow his or her own fear or worry to show. People in the service industries are required to present positive, relation-promoting emotions. Any profession in which there is contact between people can have its own display rules.

EXERCISE 4.15 • Professional Display Rules

The purpose of this exercise is to consider the effect one's profession has on its display rules.

Consider the following professions: movie making, politics, medicine, teaching, the ministry, counseling. All of these incorporate certain types of unequal, interpersonal relationships. For directors, politicians, doctors, teachers, ministers, and counselors, what degree of control over expression is desirable? What emotions are they expected to project?

Answer the same questions for the following people: computer engineer; basketball player; musician; accountant; contractor. How do the display rules for the different groups of people differ?

A given profession can have several occupations or levels. There are managers, technicians, support staff, and so on. In some positions, people interact only with members of their own profession or company; in others, they must interact with people from "outside." Consider your profession and occupation. What are the general display rules that everyone who wants to be successful must practice? Are there position-specific rules? For example, is it all right for a boss to express the same emotions as a subordinate? Are the rules situation-specific? Is adherence to professional display rules an important factor for success in your profession?

Some professions are more in sync with the rules of the dominant culture than others. Sometimes a culture's display rules are influenced by a specific profession. One example of this is acting. How much of what we consider to be normal, typical, and acceptable displays of emotions is determined by how actors portray these emotions in movies and on television? This is a chicken-and-egg type of question. It cannot be answered here, but it is worth considering. It is also interesting to note that those professions that are considered desirable in a culture—such as attorney or physician—often have display rules similar to the dominant culture's display rules.

EXERCISE 4.16 • The Link Between Professions and Cultures

The purpose of this exercise is to explore the relationship between culture and profession as it plays out in display rules.

Consider Exercise 4.10 where we tried to identify the display rules for the dominant United States culture, and what we have said about our dominant culture and its display rules. What professions in our culture are both desirable and reflective of our dominant culture's display rules? Are these professions the same in other cultures? What happens when someone from a minority culture enters one of these professions?

Which professions, if any, have display rules that contradict our dominant culture's display rules? How are these professions valued? What types of people are considered to practice these professions? What happens if a member of the nondominant culture tries to enter these professions? What do you think might be the potential for misunderstanding when people in the helping professions work with diverse clients who have varying display rules?

Display Rules—Situational

One more category of display rules needs to be considered, and that is situational display rules. Certain situations require or assume certain display rules on the part of the participants. For example, at a funeral, attendees should display grief, sadness, and other similar emotions; elation and gloating would be considered abnormal and disturbing. It is okay to cry or smile at weddings, graduations, and most other ceremonies that mark rites of passage, but not at a job interview or in a business meeting. We all have certain "scripts" that layout what is appropriate behavior in certain situations and what emotions are allowable. These scripts, of course, are cultural constructs. The problem arises when an individual's culture display rules conflict with the dominant situational display rules. A recent event that illustrates such conflict concerned the Japanese hockey team. In a game of hockey (a specific situation), a player must try to take the puck from others and keep control of it. Individual aggressive behavior is desirable. In Japanese culture, however, group harmony is the goal. Young members of the Japanese hockey team would pass the puck to older players to show respect or refrain from making too many goals in order not to stand out from the rest of the team. Clearly, the cultural and situational values were in conflict. Misunderstandings and miscommunications resulted. Therefore, one must always recognize the potential for such conflicts.

EXERCISE 4.17 • Spotting Potential Misunderstandings

At this point, we will take stock and consider how our understanding of others has changed as a result of reading this book.

Consider the following situations. How would you have interpreted each before reading this book? How would you interpret them now? What are some of the potential explanations presented by the book for the behaviors described?

- You confront a member of your team about not having done what he said he would do. During your conversation, you realize that the other person had never understood your original instructions. The other person blushes, averts your gaze, and agrees with everything you say, just as he had when you issued your original instructions.
- The manager of your division publicly chastises a co-worker, who listens and smiles.
- You are a doctor examining a patient. You ask if it hurts when you poke and prod. The patient winces but says that it does not hurt.
- Again, you are a doctor examining a patient. You ask if it hurts when you poke and prod. The patient shows no facial expression but says that something hurts.
- You are interviewing a potential employee. Throughout the interview, the person avoids your gaze and smiles.
- You meet a client for the first time. Although you have important information to present, and you try to be friendly and enthusiastic, he or she appears uninterested and aloof.
- As a professional counselor, you suggest to a client she confront her spouse about perceived put-downs in front of friends. Your client changes the subject and begins to talk about stresses at work.

Remember, sometimes a person will consider it offensive to display an emotion in a given situation, whereas you might consider the display desirable. One emotion may be masked by another because of a person's desire to be respectful, or because the person feels uncomfortable about freely expressing emotions in certain situations. Do not automatically jump to the conclusion that the other person has no feelings or feels different from the way you would feel in a similar situation. Rather, consider the possibility that that person is simply following his or her own cultural or personal emotion display rules.

Interpretations of Emotions

The rest of the chapter will deal with specific interpretations of emotional display. It is important to understand that the focus here is on how the dominant culture *interprets* the emotional displays of certain groups, not on how these people actually *experience* emotions. Current research suggests that actual experience of emotions differs little among these groups, but that our culture expects certain emotional displays and interprets expressions of emotions in view of these expectations (LaFrance & Mahzuin, 1992; Brody & Hall, 1993).

Gender

Women are emotional. This is a commonly held gender-based stereotype in our society. Many stereotypes are based on reality, but a distorted reality. Are women, by nature, more emotional than men? Researchers have recently addressed this preconception. Their conclusions suggest that there is no statistically significant difference between how men and women experience emotions, or what emotions they experience. The differences lie in how these emotions are evaluated and expressed (Lutz, 1990). Such findings are not surprising when one considers that "emotion-related behaviors are influenced by situational and contextual variables, task characteristics, age, and culture" (Brody and Hall, 1993, p. 447). Another way to put this is that different display rules exist for men and for women. It is permissible in our North American society for women to express freely all emotions except anger. The expression of that emotion is seen as being desirable only in men (Lutz, 1990). These display rules color how we perceive and interpret emotional expressions by men and women.

EXERCISE 4.18 • Gender and Emotions

The purpose of this exercise is to recognize the display rules for men and for women.

Compile a list of at least ten emotions. For each emotion, write down a corresponding situation, or context. For example, anger (the emotion) in the presence of your boss (the context). Keep this list on hand for all of the following exercises.

Now, for each emotion and situation, describe what the appropriate emotional display would be for someone of your gender. For example, how would a person of your gender display anger in front of the boss? Consider age and generation. Sometimes extreme youth or seniority makes certain behaviors permissible. Now do the same thing for the opposite gender. For each emotion and situation, how should someone of the opposite gender display emotion?

Test your opinion. Interview members of each gender and ask them how someone of their gender and someone of the opposite gender should act in given situations and in response to given emotions. Share your own responses. Discuss the differences. Your objective is to come up with an understanding of how permissible it is to express emotions, how important context is, and whether rules of display vary by gender depending on what emotion is being expressed. For example, it may be permissible for both genders to cry in certain situations, but not others. Or maybe yelling and shouting are permissible for men, but not for women.

Exercise 4.19 • Gender Effects on Perceived Emotions (Part 1)

The purpose of this exercise is to reflect on how our gender affects the situations in which we find ourselves and how we react to certain situations.

Consider the following situations for your gender first, and then for the opposite gender. Take into account whether you are a "typical" representative of your gender. How likely is it that a member of each gender would find him or herself in the following situations? How would a member of each gender react in these situations?

- You are given a promotion.
- You are told that your work is unacceptable and needs to be redone.
- You are asked to show some people around and make them feel at home.
- You are passed up for promotion.
- You are given an assignment after expressing the desire to work on it.
- You are not given an assignment after expressing the desire to work on it.
- You are given an assignment after asking to do something else.

- You explain something technical to a superior/subordinate/colleague, who listens and asks intelligent questions/walks away/keeps interrupting with irrelevant comments and questions.

Evaluate your conclusions and compare them with those of other people (both your gender and the opposite gender). Is there a great deal of agreement among members of the same gender? Between genders?

EXERCISE 4.20 • Gender Effects on Perceived Emotions (Part 2)

Again, we are considering how gender affects display rules.

Starting with your gender, write a description of an acceptable way to display the following emotions in a business situation, social situation, helping profession situation, or with family: *anger, disgust, sadness, surprise, happiness, fear, contempt.* Compare your descriptions with people of your gender; then compare with people of the opposite gender. Are the expectations similar within or across genders?

EXERCISE 4.21 • Gender Effects on Perceived Emotions (Part 3)

The purpose of this exercise is to make explicit our hidden assumptions about appropriate male and female emotional displays.

Identify the people being described in the following situations as male or female.

- In an angering situation, the person yells and stomps feet/tenses up and stares stonily/looks uncomfortable and smiles tentatively.
- After being given sad news, the person cries uncontrollably/clenches teeth and turns away/gives an exclamation and then assumes a blank expression/looks sad.
- After being given good news, the person reacts calmly and thanks the bearer/smiles broadly/exclaims out loud and laughs or smiles/smiles briefly and then changes the subject.
- In a fear-producing situation, the person screams/yells for help/freezes/looks around wildly and takes action/gets into a defensive stance and looks alert.

Did you associate certain situations with only one gender? Compare your identifications with others of your gender and with those of the opposite gender. Do people tend to agree in their assessments?

Class

Our society also has class-linked stereotypes about emotions. Upper-class people are usually portrayed as poised and refined. "Refined" is taken to mean lacking a loud, excessive emotional display. Poor people, on the other hand, are often portrayed as crass, uncultured, and loud. They are thought to shout, laugh, and generally show a lack of control over their emotions. Although these stereotypes come from books, films, and television, they clearly influence our interpretations and expectations of others.

EXERCISE 4.22 • Class and Emotions

The purpose of this exercise is to see how class, or our perception of class, affects display rules.

Use the list of ten emotions and ten situations that you compiled in Exercise 4.18. Consider what class you identify with. Is it the same one into which you were born? Write down how someone of your class should act in terms of emotional display for the emotions and situations on your list. Consider age and gender. Now do the same thing for the other social-economic classes. Consider the same situations and emotions.

Test your opinion. If possible, interview members of each class and ask them how someone of their gender and someone of the opposite gender should act in given situations and for given emotions. Then share the answers you came up with earlier. Discuss the differences. Your objective is to come up with an understanding of how permissible it is to express emotions, how important context is, and whether rules of display vary by class depending on what emotion is being expressed.

EXERCISE 4.23 • Class Effects on Perceived Emotions (Part 1)

The purpose of this exercise is to reflect on how class affects the situations in which we find ourselves and how we react to certain situations.

Consider the following situations for your social-economic class first, and then for the other classes. Take into account how "typical" a representative you are of your class. If you have changed classes over the course of your life, you probably are not completely typical. How likely is it that a member of each class would find him or herself in the following situations? How would a member of each class react in these situations?

- You are given a promotion.
- You are told that your work is unacceptable and needs to be redone.

- You are asked to show some people around and make them feel at home.
- You are passed up for promotion.
- You are given an assignment after expressing the desire to work on it.
- You are not given an assignment after expressing the desire to work on it.
- You are given an assignment after asking to do something else.
- You explain something technical to a superior/subordinate/colleague, who listens and asks intelligent questions/walks away/keeps interrupting with irrelevant comments and questions.

Evaluate your conclusions and compare them with those of other people. Is there a great deal of agreement among members of different groups?

EXERCISE 4.24 • Class Effects on Perceived Emotions (Part 2)

Again, we are considering how class affects display rules.

Starting with your class, write a description of an acceptable way to display the following emotions in a business situation, social situation, helping profession situations, or with family: *anger, disgust, sadness, surprise, happiness, fear, contempt.* Compare your descriptions with people of your class; then, if possible, compare with people in other classes. Are the expectations similar between or across classes?

EXERCISE 4.25 • Class Effects on Perceived Emotions (Part 3)

The purpose of this exercise is to make explicit our hidden assumptions about appropriate class emotional displays.

Identify the people being described in the following situations as belonging to the upper, middle, or lower class.

- In an angering situation, the person yells and stomps feet/tenses up and stares stonily/looks uncomfortable, and smiles tentatively.
- After being given sad news, the person cries uncontrollably/clenches teeth and turns away/gives an exclamation and then assumes a blank expression/looks sad.
- After being given good news, the person reacts calmly and thanks the bearer/smiles broadly/exclaims out loud and laughs or smiles/smiles briefly and then changes the subject.

- In a fear-producing situation, the person screams/yells for help/ freezes/looks around wildly and takes action/gets into a defensive stance and looks alert.

Did you associate certain situations with only one class? Compare your identifications with others of various social backgrounds. Do people tend to agree in their assessments?

Religion

It is hard to separate religious stereotypes from class, race, and ethnic stereotypes. At the same time, religions have clearly accessible ideals of proper behavior. For example, Muslim women must be modest and submissive, at least in public. It is unlikely that a "good" Muslim woman would publicly scream and yell in frustration, although she certainly might feel frustrated. Good Buddhists are calm and unemotional. They are supposed to have no strong positive or negative emotions. After all, the cessation of desire is one of the main tenets of their religion.

It is not possible to determine a person's religion, or the extent to which that person personifies his religious ideals, without questioning the individual. Nonetheless, it is possible to be aware of how religions affect the expression of emotions. Through this awareness, one can begin to recognize the possible effect of religious beliefs on other people's behavior.

EXERCISE 4.26 • Religion and Emotions

The purpose of this exercise is to recognize the effect of religion on display rules. You will first identify the rules for your religion; then you will consider how people practicing other religions would act. What emotions are permissible? What types of emotional expression is allowed?

What is your religion? Do you consider yourself a prototypical representative of that religion? If you do not, skip this part of the exercise. If you do consider yourself typical of a religion, then make a list of how someone of your religion should act. Consider gender and age. Sometimes extreme youth or seniority makes certain behaviors permissible.

Now consider the following religions in terms of how you think a representative of that religion would act. Again, consider the effects of gender and age: Roman Catholic; Lutheran; Baptist; Methodist; Orthodox Jew; Reform Jew; Shiite Muslim; Sunni Muslim; Taoist; Buddhist; Hindu; Born-Again Christian; Mormon.

Try to interview members of these various religions. Some will be easier to locate than others. At the minimum, interview two people from religions completely different from your own. Ask them to describe how a devout member of their religion would act. Then share your answers with them. Discuss the differences. Your objective is to come up with an understanding of how permissible it is to express emotions, how important context is, and whether rules of display vary by religion depending on what emotion is being expressed. For example, it may be permissible to express happiness in moderation to strangers, but not sadness. Or maybe pride is a desirable emotion to express.

EXERCISE 4.27 • Religious Effects on Perceived Emotions (Part 1)

The purpose of this exercise is to reflect on how our religion affects the situations in which we find ourselves and how we react to certain situations.

Consider the following situations for your religion first, and then for the list of religions given above. Take into account how "typical" and devoted a representative you are of your religion. How likely is it that a member of each religion would find him or herself in the following situations? How would a member of each religion react in these situations?

- You are given a promotion.
- You are told that your work is unacceptable and needs to be redone.
- You are asked to show some people around and make them feel at home.
- You are passed up for promotion.
- You are given an assignment after expressing the desire to work on it.
- You are not given an assignment after expressing the desire to work on it.
- You are given an assignment after asking to do something else.
- You explain something technical to a superior/subordinate/colleague, who listens and asks intelligent questions/walks away/keeps interrupting with irrelevant comments and questions.

Evaluate your conclusions and compare them with others of your religion and with those of a different religion. Is there a great deal of agreement among members of the same religion? Between religions?

EXERCISE 4.28 • Religious Effects on Perceived Emotions (Part 2)

Again, we are considering how religion affects display rules.

Starting with your religion, write a description of an acceptable way to display the following emotions in a business situation, social situation, helping profession situation, or with family: *anger, disgust, sadness, surprise, happiness, fear, contempt.* Compare your descriptions with people of your religion; then compare with people of other religions. Are the expectations similar within or across religions?

EXERCISE 4.29 • Religious Effects on Perceived Emotions (Part 3)

The purpose of this exercise is to make explicit our hidden assumptions about appropriate religious emotional displays.

Identify the religion of the people being described in the following situations.

- In an angering situation, the person yells and stomps feet/tenses up and stares stonily/looks uncomfortable, and smiles tentatively.
- After being given sad news, the person cries uncontrollably/clenches teeth and turns away/gives an exclamation and then assumes a blank expression/looks sad.
- After being given good news, the person reacts calmly and thanks the bearer/smiles broadly/exclaims out loud and laughs or smiles/smiles briefly and then changes the subject.
- In a fear-producing situation, the person screams/yells for help/freezes/looks around wildly and takes action/gets into a defensive stance and looks alert.

Did you associate certain situations with only one religion? Compare your identifications with others of your religion and with those of other religions. Do people tend to agree in their assessments?

Race and Ethnicity

Many people maintain strong stereotypes about the emotional behavior of different racial and ethnic groups. Latinos are considered temperamental and very talkative, while the British are silently stoic (Babad & Wallbutt, 1986). In fact, research concerning people outside the United States suggests that many of these stereotypes are false (Babad & Wallbutt, 1986). Research concerning different ethnic groups within the United States suggests that there are differences in terms of how stimuli are interpreted and evaluated, and, hence, in terms of how intensely emotions are experienced (Matsumoto, 1994). Members of different ethnic groups follow different display rules, and within each ethnic group there is variation of conformity to these rules. As a result, they follow different display rules. The research also suggests that even when the display rules are the same, our perception of how intensely members of other groups are experiencing emotions varies. The situation is similar to that concerning gender.

We have preconceptions about how people experience and express emotions. These preconceptions color our interpretation of others' behaviors. If, for example, we expect a certain group to be emotional, then we will interpret their actions as emotional. It is important to remember that members of minority groups are often placed in certain situations that are likely to elicit the negative emotions of others. In a society that values a strongly bounded, independent sense of self, any threat to one's sense of self tends to produce anger, frustration, or other similar emotions. When a black man walks through a white neighborhood, white people may feel fear because of their expectation that the black man is dangerous. In turn, the black man may feel frustration and rage when he sees the fearfulness in the whites. Therefore, certain groups may actually experience some emotions more frequently because of their cultural and personal treatment and histories. Or, as is often the case, our attributions may become self-fulfilling prophecies. If one is accused of always being angry, aggressive, or defensive, one may, in defense, become angry, aggressive, or defensive.

EXERCISE 4.30 • Race, Ethnicity, or Religion and Emotions

The purpose of this exercise is to consider the effects of race and ethnicity on display rules.

Consider the following list of racial and ethnic groups that are found in the United States. Some can be joined together or divided. It is impossible to provide a complete list of all possible ethnic groups; however, feel free to add to this one: Caucasian, Afro-American, Chinese, Japanese, Korean, Thai, Indian, other Asian, Italian, Portuguese, German, Russian, Polish, Irish, Scottish, French, Italian, African, Indian, Arabic, Israeli, Greek, Turkish, Bengalis, Pakistan, Hispanic, Amer-Indian, Eskimo, Jew, Catholic, Muslim, Buddhist, Mormon, Protestant.

What racial or ethnic group do you identify with? Using your list of ten emotions and ten situations, write down how someone of your race or ethnicity should act in terms of emotional display. For example, how would anger be displayed? Consider age and gender. They may influence what is and is not appropriate. Now do the same thing for the other racial/ethnic groups. Consider the same situations and emotions.

Test your opinion. Interview members of as many of the above groups as possible. Ask them how someone of their group should act in given situations and for given emotions. Ask if there are differences based on age or gender. Then share your own answers. Discuss the differences. Your objective is to come up with an understanding of how permissible it is to express emotions, how important context is, and whether rules of display vary by race, ethnicty, or religion depending on what emotion is being expressed. For example, contempt may be permissible only when it is directed toward nongroup members. Or, perhaps a lack of verbal display indicates a lack of anger.

EXERCISE 4.31 • Race and Ethnicity Effects on Perceived Emotions (Part 1)

The purpose of this exercise is to reflect on how race and ethnicity affect the situations in which we find ourselves and how we react to certain situations.

Consider the following situations for your group first, and then for the other racial and ethnic groups listed above. Take into account how "typical" a representative you are of your group. How likely is it that members of a given group would find themselves in the following situations? How would a member of each group react in these situations?

- You are given a promotion.
- You are told that you work is unacceptable and it needs to be redone.
- You are asked to show some people around and make them feel at home.
- You are passed up for promotion.
- You are given an assignment after expressing the desire to work on it.
- You are not given an assignment after expressing the desire to work on it.
- You are given an assignment after asking to do something else.
- You explain something technical to a superior/subordinate/colleague, who listens and asks intelligent questions/walks away/keeps interrupting with irrelevant comments and questions.

Evaluate your conclusions and compare them with those of people of your group and with others. Is there a great deal of agreement among members of the same group? Between groups?

EXERCISE 4.32 • Race and Ethnicity Effects on Perceived Emotions (Part 2)

Again, we consider how race and ethnicity affect display rules.

Starting with your group, write a description of an acceptable way to display each of the following emotions in a business situation, social situation, helping profession situation, or with family: *anger, disgust, sadness, surprise, happiness, fear, contempt.* Compare your descriptions with people of your group; then compare with people from other groups. Are the expectations similar within or across groups?

EXERCISE 4.33 • Race and Ethnicity Effects on Perceived Emotions (Part 3)

The purpose of this exercise is to make explicit our hidden assumptions about appropriate racial and ethnic emotional displays.

Identify to which racial or ethnic group the people in the following situations belong.

- In an angering situation, the person yells and stomps feet/tenses up and stares stonily/looks uncomfortable and smiles tentatively.
- After being given sad news, the person cries uncontrollably/clenches teeth and turns away/gives an exclamation and then assumes a blank expression/looks sad.
- After being given good news, the person reacts calmly and thanks the bearer/smiles broadly/exclaims out loud and laughs or smiles/smiles briefly and then changes the subject.
- In a fear-producing situation, the person screams/yells for help/freezes/looks around wildly and takes action/gets into a defensive stance and looks alert.

Did you associate certain situations with only some groups? Compare your identifications with others of your group and with those of other groups. Do people tend to agree in their assessments?

Conclusion

The ways we experience and display emotions are shaped by culture. Although some aspects of emotions are universal, we cannot assume that others react to situations the way we would. Nor does everyone express their emotions the same way. How we experience and express our emotions is determined by a combination of cultural, individual, professional, and situational display rules. Context is a critical variable.

How we interpret other people's emotional expressions is largely a result of cultural stereotypes and personal experiences. It is important to keep this in mind when interacting with someone from a different background. We cannot automatically jump to the conclusion, for example, that others are not committed, are not serious, or are being deceptive just because they smile frequently, appear aloof, or seem overly friendly. Their responses may reflect how they were trained to react and respond in given situations. With time and continuous exposure to diverse populations, people can learn the display rules that are appropriate to new situations.

As we become more familiar with our own emotional experiences and expressions—including the physiological, cognitive, and affective components—

we can become more aware of the influences of family of origin, gender, race, ethnicity, class, generation, and geographical region on our development. This can enable us to become more sensitive to the sociocultural variables that shape others' emotional expressions. With this understanding, we can check our perceptions and interpretations of others' emotional expressions in order to respond effectively.

5

Self: Where It Is, Where It Ends

Every culture in the world has some type of self-referencing pronoun (the equivalent of *I* or *me*), a prefix or suffix that indicates a speaker's relationship to the person or situation about which she or he is speaking (Mauss, 1985). As far as we are aware, no culture exists in which differences between people are not acknowledged in some form. Among the terms *self, identity, person, personality,* and *individual, self* often carries a significantly different connotation, especially in cultures outside North America.

Self and *identity* often are used interchangeably in the United States (see Chapter 2). *Person, personality,* and *individual* also tend to be used interchangeably. The reasons for these words having roughly equivalent meanings in the dominant culture are based on a set of philosophical assumptions and beliefs about human nature, family and social organization, God, time, and the interplay of body, mind, spirit, and environment in the human condition.

In this chapter, we look at the differing and overlapping concepts of self, individuality, identity, and personality. We elaborate on the perspective that there is no one, unified self, but that, instead, we all have multiple selves, depending upon context. We pay particular attention to the pervasive influences of gender, class, religion, race, and ethnicity on our senses of self in cultural contexts. We consider universal, cultural, and individual aspects of the self-concept.

Definition of Concepts

Self

Discussions of self as a psychological concept that is differentiated from the concepts of personality and individual have increased dramatically in the past thirty years. It can be helpful, therefore, to relate the concept of self to the concept of identity. Identity is described by Erikson (1968) as a sense of personal coherence through time and changing role requirements, a sense of one's value and consistent contributions to one's social world. It is very difficult to think about identity without referring to the notion of self. In this sense, self refers to a set of ideas about who one is, based on social interaction with and feedback from persons in the individual's social environment (Moore, Britt, & Leary, 1997).

In North American psychological discourse, a distinction is made between self-as-subject (the one who knows) and self-as-object (the one who is known or observed). Have you ever thought about what you mean when you say "I know myself"? Who knows whom? Who is the "I" who knows the self? Is the self the same as the "I"? You, the reader, know that you are one person, but you have the ability to "split" that person into several parts. You may think in terms of your "rational self," your "angry self," your "selfish self," and so forth.

Only in recent years have American psychologists (Schwartz, 1987) begun to talk about multiple selves, the notion that we do not have one, unified, true self, but, rather, depending on the context, different selves, even though there may be some characteristics and traits that appear consistently across contexts. This concept of multiple selves appears to be culture-specific; we cannot assume that psychologists in other cultures accept it as universal.

Person and Personality

The concepts of person and individual also have different connotations. The word *person* is derived from the Greek *persona,* which means mask. The *persona* was the mask that actors wore in Greek plays to signify the presence of a particular character, often a god or goddess, whose characteristics were known in advance by the audience. From this perspective, a person is considered to be a set of characteristics and traits that describe the character's functioning in a particular social context (Mauss, 1985). The self can be considered the animating spirit behind the persona. The self appears to others through the behavior, thought patterns, and feelings expressed through the persona, the outer mask (Erchak, 1992).*

Thus, the notion of person is context-sensitive: A person exists in context, and when the context changes, personality can change. Personality is a metaphoric construct that describes the traits, characteristics, temperament, patterns of meaning-making, and behaviors that constitute an individual. It is thought to be influenced by genetics, sociocultural variables, and life experiences throughout the lifespan. Therefore, personality can be inconsistent, because it is dependent on context.

*Erchak (1992) reverses these definitions slightly, indicating that personality is typically considered a set a stable traits, values, attitudes, and cognitions that result in a pattern of fairly consistent behavior. He states that he is representing a rough consensus among anthropologists, but acknowledges that all these terms overlap considerably and are quite ambiguous.

EXERCISE 5.1 • Your Personality

The purpose of this exercise is to help you identify the ways in which you, as a North American, probably believe that your personality is supposed to remain consistent across time and place.

Have you noticed your personality changing depending on the situation in which you find yourself? Are you the same person in a bar with your friends, at a family dinner, at work, in a rugby match, or on a date? Do you ever think about the ways in which your personality changes according to context? Do you feel guilty about it, because you believe that you should be consistent across time, place, and social context?

Identity

The guilt you may experience when considering how your personality sometimes changes probably comes from the North American belief that one should be "true to oneself" across time, place, and context. That demand for consistency is associated with identity and is a particularly North American belief. Identity means "close likeness" and has the same root as the word *identical.* Therefore, one's identity signifies a consistency and similarity of self-concept, behavior, traits, and so forth over time. North Americans tend to value the maintenance of a consistent set of characteristics that they can use to describe themselves in the abstract, such as loyalty, humor, persistence, intelligence, courage, and so on. In many other cultures, people tend to describe themselves in terms of a specific behavior in a particular setting, or in terms of family, caste membership, or the geographic area from which they originated. In the United States, a person's identity also may be defined by family name or occupation. When we think of a "Kennedy," we associate that person with power and money, and perhaps with competitive sports and political activism. Behavior that is considered friendly in some cultures may be considered rude and intrusive in others. Therefore, a person who is considered friendly in her home culture because she asks many questions about other people's lives may find her sense of identity coming apart when she cannot make friends in a more closed culture where people asking these kinds of questions are considered rude.

An example of this type of identity attribution can be illustrated by considering the experience of one of the authors of this text. As a child, she could describe herself as a Fried (her family name) from north Yonkers, New York. That information was sufficient to establish her credentials as an acceptable playmate for the children of many Jewish families from south Yonkers. Her father was a south-to-north Yonkers immigrant who, along with the rest of his extended family, was well known and respected among the Jewish families from a particular part of the city during his youth. In north Yonkers, Fried could describe herself as Rappaport's granddaughter and achieve the same result, but Rappaport's name meant nothing in the other part of town. Fried had a sense of her "self" that was tied to family history and reputation in specific geographic areas and ethno-religious communities, but not necessarily to any characteristics that were unique to her. As seen in Exercise 5.1, movement through the life span broadens and develops the sense of self and identity in different contexts.

Individual

The term *individual* is critically important to members of the dominant culture in the United States. Being an individual involves a highly prized set of rights and obligations that exist in the liberal democracies of Western Europe and North America. The philosophers Locke, Hobbs, Mill, and others created a set of ideas regarding the nature of government and individual rights. They focused especially on the rights to own property, and the means by which the needs of the community, or general populace, could be balanced against the rights of individuals. Individuals, shaped by these beliefs, tend to focus on maximizing their own freedom to make choices, to remain autonomous, to maximize their personal achievements, and to minimize government intervention in their lives. The role of government in relation to the individual is to maintain maximum freedom for the individual and to maintain a social contract among individual members of society that supports an atmosphere of opportunity and individual freedom (Merelman, 1984; Margolis, 1979). Individual, in this case, has nothing to do with self, personality, or identity. Rather, it refers to "an entity who has legal rights to enter into contracts." According to Locke, each individual has the right to maintain and protect his [sic] property. Individuals surrender their individual rights to society only to preserve better their lives and property (Sabine, 1961).

Self in Mainstream United States Culture

In the United States, self usually refers to an individual, a person for whom autonomy and self-determination are very important. An individual is a separate bounded entity, with a consistent set of traits and characteristics, who engages in relationships with other beings out of a sense of free will and choice. These relationships and choices are unencumbered, for the most part, by the expectations of the person's family, faith, or work. The use of this definition of self makes the United States an extremely unusual culture, because self in the United States is decontextualized: It exists independent of and prior to its relationships with others. It is considered a fairly consistent entity that transcends specific situations or demands. In the United States, we can speak about a person who embezzled a million dollars as an "honest" person who behaved in a way that was "unlike himself." We can say "I don't know what got into him" and understand each other perfectly, even though we do not believe in possession by external spirits. Such statements make it clear that self implies consistency, autonomy, choice, and responsibility.

EXERCISE 5.2 • Me, Myself, and I

The purpose of this exercise is to help you identify the various dimensions of your self in different contexts.

1. For each of the following situations, write a one-paragraph description of your self—your inner, most private self; your self at work or school; your self with your parents; your self with your best friend; and your self on a date.
2. Look over your paragraphs. Make a list of the traits, adjectives, or descriptors that appear in all of the paragraphs. Next make a list of all the traits, adjectives, or descriptors that appear in 3 or more of your paragraphs; that appear in 2 paragraphs; that appear in 1 paragraph. Are your paragraphs more similar or dissimilar? How would you explain this?
3. Give a friend or acquaintance one of the paragraphs that reflects a situation in which the two of you would never find yourselves together. Ask your friend to read it. Then ask whom it describes. Tell your friend it is you and discuss your friend's reaction.

In some settings, self may have spiritual overtones associated with the concept of soul. Particularly for Christians, the ultimate responsibility of soul/self is to understand God's will and reason for placing the soul/self on earth; to do God's will in life; and to make a good reckoning of the value of one's life when one rejoins God in heaven after physical death. This reckoning is an individual endeavor. Each person must be saved from sin by virtue of individual acts or individual faith. God is conceived of as parental or fatherly; the self is conceived of as a child. They are related, but do not merge. Self, in this Christian culture, can also be considered in a completely secular light as being individualistic, materialistic, rational, and analytic, with the capacity to observe its inner states (self-as-subject) and its outer behavior (self-as object) (Johnson, 1985).

Self in Other Cultural Contexts

In other cultures, self is a dramatically different phenomenon. Self always exists in relationship to its context and to the people in that context, never in isolation. Individuality, if it exists at all, is perceived culturally as self-centeredness, as selfishness. For example, self in Hindu India assumes that the personal dimension is derived from the Universal Soul. The personal soul/self, when developed to its highest state, has no separate or independent existence from the Universal Soul. Ideas about who one is are derived from caste, family, and gender roles within the family (Naipaul,1977). In China, Japan, and areas of Southeast Asia, and many parts of Africa, self describes a relationship between a person and his or her family, including ancestors and children yet unborn. In many Native American cultures, self refers to one's spiritual connection to the tribe and often to the tribe's totemic animal or animals. In the case of Zuni pueblos, children are given names that signify body parts of a totem animal, such as "claw" or "wing." These names signify the child's responsibilities and potential powers as part of the clan. The self is seen as an attribute of the clan or tribe. It is the animating spirit, which wears a human body but which can wear other bodies as well (Mauss,1985).

Taoism is a Chinese mystical philosophy founded in the sixth century B.C. In the tradition of Tao (the unknowable source and guiding principle of all reality), self is completely fluid. "Outside is form/Inside is thought/Deepest is the soul. . . . At the core of every person is the soul. This is a pure, virgin self. It does not think in the ordinary sense of the word, has no egotism and is not concerned with maintaining itself in the world. . . . The soul is completely without form or features" (Ming-Dao, 1992, p.154).

Nisba, an Arabic system of self-definition, involves "tribe, kinship status, occupation, religious sect and other relational attributes" (Hoare, 1991, p. 49). It places the person in a matrix of social expectations that must be fulfilled, but that have little or nothing to do with personality or self in the Western sense.

In contrast, the center of awareness that North Americans refer to as "self" becomes a totally private phenomenon in cultures that have strong role expectations. "The Western conception of the person as a bounded, unique, more or less integrated motivational and cognitive universe, a dynamic center of awareness, emotion, judgment and action, organized into a distinctive whole and set contrastively both against other such wholes and against its social and natural background, is, however, incorrigible it may seem to us, a rather peculiar idea within the context of the world's cultures" (Geertz, 1986, p. 126).

EXERCISE 5.3 • The Effect of Self

The purpose of this exercise is to focus your attention on the ways in which you define or construct yourself.

Consider how you define yourself, either as a set of individual, abstract traits, or as a set of situationally determined behaviors. What effect would each of these types of self have on how one interacts in new situations? In threatening situations? In the work place? In public situations? In private? Consider the effect of the construct of self on various aspects of your life, culture, and society. Discuss your thoughts with others. Try to talk to people who construct themselves the way you do, as well as to those who use the other method of construction.

Anthropological Perspectives

In order to understand, however imperfectly, the ways that people from different cultures experience, interpret, and act in the world, one has to begin thinking like an anthropologist. Prior to the 1970s, anthropologists generally were concerned with traveling to distant lands and describing the living patterns of the "natives" as if they were subjects in a scientific set of observations. Most anthropologists were North American or European and considered themselves social scientists. (The whole discipline developed during a period of colonization that was strongly influenced by a belief in colonialism, mercantilism, and European superiority.) From this perspective, the "scientific" approach dehumanized and exploited the people who were being studied, often describing them as if they were objects, using an alien and distorting frame of reference (Brettell, 1993). This perspective reflects the mindset of colonialism, which tended to use colonized people as means to the end of enriching the people of the colonial power. Since that time, cultural (and social) anthropology has experienced a transformation in its own self-definition and has developed a postmodernist consciousness.

In modern life, North Americans (citizens of the United States and Canada) who see and interpret the world through the lenses of the dominant culture often make similar kinds of mistakes. Most of us tend to assume that people who are in the United States—particularly those who speak fluent English—experience, interpret, and act in the world in ways that are similar to those of mainstream North Americans. We seem to believe that learning the language and learning the culture are synonymous. This typically causes problems that are far more serious than just failing to understand the meaning of a particular word or idea. Some typical problems include not understanding what subjects are considered public or private in the adopted culture, the difference between a friend and a colleague or acquaintance, and the different meanings associated with a verbal promise compared to a written promise or contract. A simple but frequently cited problem concerns understanding idiomatic usage and punchlines for jokes. Someone who is not a native might very well understand the literal meanings of the words used in a joke and still have no idea why it is funny.

Similar assumptions exist in other countries. When one of the authors of this text lived in England, the assumption that a shared language meant shared meanings and beliefs led to many awkward and embarrassing situations. When the same author lived in non–English-speaking countries, such situations rarely occurred. In fact, the more foreign the language and culture, the more allowances were made for the presence of misunderstandings.

North Americans seem to have a great deal of difficulty understanding that people from other parts of the world have dramatically different ideas about how the world works and what behaviors, values, goals, and beliefs, including those about self, are appropriate. In fact, some anthropological linguists believe that one of the defining traits of Americans is their inability to imagine the different mentalities that shape perspectives among those from different cultures (Agar, 1994). This is probably due both to the limited exposure that most

Americans have to non-American cultures, and to the extensive exportation of American culture to other parts of the world.

Ethnographic research, which is a method often used by anthropologists, involves writing down preconceived ideas about the people being studied before any interviews are actually conducted. This method also involves making one's own frame of reference and one's beliefs about one's self conscious and articulate. Although the exercise that follows is similar to those in Chapter 2, the fact that you have now read additional material will alter your responses.

EXERCISE 5.4 • Who Are You? (Part 1)

The purpose of the following exercises is to focus your attention on the effect of context on your definition of self.

Write down a series of statements that you believe describe yourself. You may use roles (family, work group, and so on), attributes, preferences, values, or any other identifiers that you believe describe you. Use the following format:

I am a person who ____________.
or
I am __________________.

Complete these sentences as many times as you wish.

Now reread each sentence and ask yourself how you became that way, how you discovered that about yourself, or how you were reinforced for maintaining that aspect of yourself. Does your family care about whether or not each aspect of yourself continues to be evident in your behavior and beliefs? If your family had a negative opinion about some aspect, would you try to eliminate it? Strengthen it? Ignore it? Would you display it only when you were not in their presence?

EXERCISE 5.5 • Who Are You? (Part 2)

Review the statements you made in part 1 of this exercise. Label each statement as either (1) abstract/universal or (2) concrete/contextual. *Abstract* labels are generic, and are presumed to exist as part of yourself regardless of context, such as loyal, honest, hardworking, entertaining. *Concrete* labels refer to activities or behaviors that you perform only in a specific setting, even though you may do them often, for example, playing the trumpet, playing baseball, or spending a lot of time with your family.

If you are a "typical" North American, you probably had more abstract labels than concrete ones. Your abstract labels may be derived from your perception that you tend to perform a particular activity often.

That activity, therefore, became an abstract *quality* that you attributed to yourself, rather than a concrete *activity* that you perform often. Instead of being a person who plays softball, you become an athlete. Instead of a person who spends a lot of time with family, you become a family man or woman. Continue to think about who you are in different contexts.

Exercise 5.6 • Who Are You? (Part 3)

The purpose of this part of the exercise is to compare being with doing—who you are in comparison to what you do.

For example, think about the different meaning conveyed when you are "a musician" as opposed to "a person who plays the trumpet." Focus on your own reaction to the difference (It is a subtle distinction). Articulate what this distinction means to you. If you tried to think about yourself as a person who does many different activities in many different settings, but whose main sense of self is conveyed by your last name, how would that change your idea of who you are?

These initial efforts to understand how you define yourself may be quite frustrating. This is the first step in beginning to understand the way a person from another part of the world—where self is subsumed in family identity and is largely unrelated to personal characteristics—defines him or herself.

Cultural Assumptions of Appropriate Behavior

North Americans experience the self as a twofold process: the process of *knowing* (self-as-subject) and the process of being observed (self-as-object). One can be aware of an experience, reflect on the experience, analyze it, or give directions. All of these are *knowing* experiences and examples of the self-as-subject. In any ambiguous or unfamiliar situation, this process can easily become conscious (just as in cartoons a balloon appears over the head of a cartoon character). For example, you meet a stranger, shake hands, smile, ask about the person's name, place of origin, and so forth. You behave in an appropriately friendly North American way. If the experience proceeds smoothly, you probably do not think about it. However, if it does not "feel" right—for instance, if some of your culturally appropriate behaviors are not eliciting the anticipated response—what you are going through may become a conscious process. Your analytic self-aspect may begin talking: What's the matter with her? Why is she acting like my hand is covered with slime? Is my fly open? Do I have spinach in my teeth? What am I doing wrong? In this case, you are experiencing self-as-object. Your self is responding to the cues of the other who is the subject.

EXERCISE 5.7 • Script

The purpose of this exercise is to focus your awareness on the cultural script that shapes the process of meeting new people in the United States.

Write a script for meeting a new person. Who initiates the contact? What is said? What gestures, if any, are made? Consider how you have met people in the past. Now, put yourself in a situation, such as a party, a large meeting, or new class, where you can meet new people. Introduce yourself to someone, using your script. Did the other person follow your script? Did it "feel" right? Analyze the situation and try repeating it with others. Continue until someone deviates from your script. How did you feel when that person deviated from your script? Who was to blame? Was anyone to blame?

What you experienced in Exercise 5.7, when you encountered someone who deviated from your script, was an interaction with a person who had a different set of assumptions about how to meet a person for the first time, what behavior is appropriate, how close to stand, whether or not to touch, and so forth. It is natural to want to understand what happened, why the encounter did not go as you planned. Rather than trying to understand what you might be doing wrong, try to understand how the other person experienced you—what she or he expected *you* to do. This requires some knowledge of the culture of the other person and some ability to get "behind their eyes" and begin to see yourself from their perspective.

EXERCISE 5.8 • Self-as-Subject and Self-as-Object

The purpose of this exercise is for you to coach yourself through the process of meeting a new person who has a meeting script different from yours.

Remember the last time you were confused by a situation or you did not handle it the way you wanted to. Give yourself some advice about what to do differently next time. Use the following format to write down your ideas:

Situation: ____

What Is Happening: ____________________________________

____

What I Did or Said: ____________________________________

____

What I Should Do or Say Differently: ______________________________

____

What I Need to Learn or Understand: ______________________________

____

Do this for a couple of situations. Now ask yourself where the advice came from. Who is the self-as-subject, and who is the self-as-object? We are differentiating here between self-as-subject, the one who experiences and feels, and self-as-object, the one who is observed, manipulated, and so forth. Self-as-subject feels awkward when things do not go as anticipated. Self becomes object as the inner voice talks to the uncomfortable self-state—for example, "What's the matter with you? You're a friendly person. Why isn't he smiling at you?" The self-as-subject is the friendly person who smiles. The self-as-object is trying to observe the behavior and adjust it to increase comfort. Are the "contents" of the two voices different? Do you see a real self, a stable self, an unchanging self? Or is your idea of self a lot more complicated than you originally thought?

Cultural Values and Ideologies

As mentioned previously, North Americans tend to value a stable idea of self that is bounded, unique, goal-oriented, and expressive. Their idea of self constantly involves an internal assessment of others' opinions of their worth and acceptability (Markus & Kitayama, 1991). As a result of these characteristics, North American boundaries around the self are quite different from the boundaries of people whose cultures define self interdependently. North Americans tend to stand up for their own personal beliefs and to resist conforming to demands that violate their sense of autonomy. "Be true to yourself," a North American maxim, means do not do things or assent to things that contradict your own idea of who you are. People from cultures where self is an interdependent phenomenon may be quite flexible in matters of personal preference, but become quickly offended when norms governing respect for family, gender appropriate behavior, social status or caste, or saving face are concerned.

For example, North Americans tend to value self-expression, the public affirmation of one's personal choices, preferences, beliefs, or goals in life. We often ask children what they want to be when they grow up, and this choice of goals is considered a personal one. The Japanese, on the other hand, generally think of themselves as part of the group—in school, in family, and at work. The expression of individual goals, if indeed people have such goals, is minimized. People are expected to restrain their own interests in order to promote family honor and social and team harmony. Individual promotions are rare to nonexistent. The entire team is promoted together. The family's honor and reputation is always more important than an individual's personal preferences. This is also true in Middle Eastern cultures and in India (Roland, 1988).

EXERCISE 5.9 • Self versus Group Interest

The purpose of this exercise is for you to experience the strength of your commitment to your own, culturally shaped way of doing things and to understand why some people make other choices.

Form a group with two to three other people. Together, make a list of situations in which one has to choose between individual reward and the good of the group. For example, studying for a test by yourself, or studying in a group and helping others to understand the subject, which is easy for you. Having made the list, decide which option you would choose for each situation. Share your decisions and discuss the reasons behind them. Be open-minded and try to hear *why* people chose what they chose.

In our society, we value competition. Our philosophy is "May the best man win." The Japanese, on the other hand, have a folk saying: "The nail that sticks up gets pounded down." In Japanese society, face-to-face confrontations are avoided in order to prevent anyone from being embarrassed and to save face. In the United States, such confrontations are considered the most honest way to minimize difficulties between people. When a North American disagrees with another person, either in private or at the work place, the first question a third party probably would ask would be, "Have you spoken to him/her about it?" Asking a Japanese person to do such a thing would be considered intolerably rude.

The North American approach can be considered a method of readjusting the interpersonal relationship between individuals so that differences of opinion can be resolved openly. The Japanese approach can be seen as a collective willingness to rebalance relationships among members of a group so that the group can function smoothly.

North American society is an egalitarian society. Our national ideology considers all people to be equal, and equal is often considered to be synonymous with "the same." By same, we do not mean identical; we mean of equal value and position within society. The behaviors that emerge from our ideology often are seen as confusing or rude to persons from societies that are structured hierarchically. We may seem to fail to grant respect to someone who expects it from us based on his or her rank in another society. Or, we may act in ways that are very confusing for people who expect to be treated as lower in rank. International students who bow to North American faculty or rise when the faculty enter the classroom often cause disorientation for North American professors who experience this behavior for the first time. International students who are asked to express a point of view that is different from the professor's point of view may be equally confused, until they get used to the behavior. Such expression would not be acceptable in a culture where relationships are shaped by rank, and where students are always lower in rank than faculty.

EXERCISE 5.10 • Egalitarian versus Hierarchical Society

The purpose of this exercise is for you to identify specific differences in behavior between hierarchical and egalitarian societies.

Consider the following situations. How would someone act or react in an egalitarian society? In a hierarchical society? Discuss your conclusions with others. Based on what is said, try to identify the type of society into which each of you was born.

- You enter a class as a new student in the middle of the term.
- Your boss walks by you without acknowledging your presence.
- You enter the school or work cafeteria and there are no empty tables.
- You enter the school or work cafeteria and there are many empty tables.
- You are introduced to a new client.
- You meet a new patient.
- At a professional meeting or talk, you disagree with the speaker.
- You see your colleague using the office computer for personal reasons for a period of several hours.

North Americans have historically been isolated from or dominant over persons from non-European cultures. North Americans also have a cultural tendency to subsume all particularities into abstractions that are considered universally true and accurate. This tendency often results in stereotyping, both negative and positive. As a result of the collective effects of these cultural traits, North Americans often fail to be sensitive to the perceptions, expectations, and self-definitions of persons from other cultures within the dominant United States society, and those from cultures that are dominant in other parts of the world.

Gender

Most cultures consider gender an important factor in structuring relationships and in shaping each person's ideas about self, socially appropriate roles, and behavior. Consequently, to some degree, most cultures assign behavioral and role expectations by sex. Sex and gender are not identical concepts. Sex is typically considered a major factor in one's biology, as indicated by genitalia and chromosomal patterns. Gender, in contrast, refers to the pattern of traits, behavior, responsibilities, and roles that one is assigned according to one's perceived sex. Gender is a socially constructed phenomena based on the physical phenomenon of sex.

Cultures range from having hierarchical sex-role assignments to having more egalitarian assignments. The most egalitarian cultures, for example, seem to be the Scandinavian cultures, where neither work roles, family roles, nor personal traits and behavior patterns are defined rigidly by gender (Hansen, 1997). Arab and Muslim cultures appear to be the most hierarchical. In these cultures, where there are rigid role prescriptions based on sex, women may not appear in public without a head covering, must walk behind their husbands, and so on.

In the United States, gender has traditionally circumscribed each person's identity, sense of self, expected social behavior, emotional expressiveness, family roles, and work roles. Since the second wave of feminism, which began in the 1960s, gender expectations in the United States have been changing, although the changes have been uneven, depending on geographic location, religious frame of reference, age, type of occupation, whether work takes place in the public or private sector, socioeconomic status, and legal precedents regarding specific types of discrimination or harassment. Women are entering occupations held heretofore only by men; men are more actively involved in child-rearing; women manage their own finances and maintain individual credit lines, and so forth. Despite this dramatic shift in sex-role stereotyping in the past 40 years, however, many people are still uncomfortable about expanding their self-concept or sense of identity to include characteristics and behaviors that historically have been typical of (or have been reserved for) members of the opposite sex. For example, women on the fire or police forces or in the military may doubt their physical abilities, probably because they are measuring them against norms created over time by men. Women in management may feel uncomfortable when their conflict resolution styles are viewed as "inadequate" according to aggressive male standards.

EXERCISE 5.11 • Self as Defined by Gender

Gender socialization begins very early in life. The purpose of this exercise is to help you understand how gender socialization has shaped your perceptions of male and female behaviors.

Define the following terms: *real man, real woman.* What do these terms mean to you? Try to remember the first time in your life when an adult told you that something you were doing was not done by people of your gender. It might have been "Big boys don't cry" or "Nice girls don't hit people" or "Don't be a doctor, be a nurse" (or vice-versa).

1. In the first column of the following table, make a list of all such statements that you remember hearing as a child. Try to remember the

rules in your family about being a "good" boy or girl and how they translated into being a good, responsible, desirable man or woman. For example, in the 1950s, girls often were told by mothers who wanted them to be socially successful not to act too smart around boys. Girls could be emotionally expressive, were responsible for keeping boys under control sexually, and were expected to focus more of their energy on dating and marriage than on school and career, in preparation for their future role as homemaker and nurturer. Boys were expected to be sexually aggressive, to be athletic, to pick up all the expenses of dating, and not to show any emotions except anger. Their life focus was expected to emphasize career, achievement, and earning power, in preparation for their future role as family provider.

2. Now, in the second column, write down any questions you remember having about gender roles. Then, in the third column, write down the messages you think were conveyed to you about gender roles, as well as your feelings and reactions to them. You may have been told explicitly how to behave, or you may have absorbed gender expectations from watching and imitating the adults in your life.

After you have filled out the chart, think some more about how people in your family conducted themselves. What tasks did men do? What tasks did women typically do? Were some tasks done by the first person who had the time or noticed the need regardless of that person's gender? Did adults of either gender ever express or manifest discomfort about having to do or say something based on their gender, such as crying, yelling, or inviting another person to participate in a social event?

Statements Made to Me About Gender Roles	**Questions I Had About Gender Roles**	**Messages I Received About Gender Roles, and My Feelings and Reactions to Them**

EXERCISE 5.12 • Gendered Family Scripts

The purpose of this exercise is to identify the particular gender-related expectations that your family communicated to you.

Use the ecomap of your family that you constructed in Exercise 2.13. For each member of your family, write a sentence or statement that explains how each member expected you to act as a male or female. For example, your mother may have said "Ladies don't yell" if you are a girl, or "Don't let them see that it hurts" if you are a boy. Next, write the same kind of statement for each of your siblings. (In other words, write down how your siblings were expected to act, as males or females.) How similar are the messages within gender or across gender? How different? If possible, ask your siblings to complete the same exercise. If you feel comfortable doing so, discuss your findings with family members.

Both girls and boys typically have more adult women in their lives than men (primary parent, teachers, or other caregivers), so boys often are more likely to watch and imitate male role models from television or the movies. Gender expectations have changed since the 1950s, but they are still powerful. In the United States, gender is a core element of self—who one is. One's behavior in life is an expression of self and identity. Violation of gender expectations goes to the heart of one's sense of self. Specific gender expectations may vary, but challenging or changing them is an enormous and risky task for most people.

EXERCISE 5.13 • Gender and Self in Your Life Today

The purpose of this exercise is to identify the role expectations you absorbed as a child and the ways those expectations changed as you matured.

Review the early role expectations you absorbed as a child. How have your ideas of what a man or woman should be within the family changed since then? If you are in a relationship with a member of the opposite sex, what changes have you made in your own behavior or sense of self that you never expected to make as a child? Discuss these changes with your partner. Then discuss them with some same-sex peers and try to identify gender-related norms for your peer group. Is your sense of self different in either of the conversations? Is one more threatening than the other? Are you surprised about anything you are discovering?

The expectations that others have for us early in life tend to become internalized as we grow older. Without realizing the source of our expectations, we adopt those our parents imposed on us until we "outgrow" them. The process of giving up outgrown expectations is often more uncomfortable than giving up outgrown clothes.

If you have children or hope to have children, how do you expect your behavior as a parent to be different from your parents' behavior toward you? How will your behavior toward your spouse or partner be different? If you are gay or lesbian, what do you think about gender expectations? Do you think of yourself as a "real" man or woman? (Refer back to the statements you wrote down in Exercise 5.12.) What early messages did you receive about how to behave that do not now match your own ideas of how a person of your gender should behave?

EXERCISE 5.14 • Gender Norms and Relationships with Cultural Others (Male to Male)

Do this exercise if you are male. If you are a female, go on to Exercise 5.15.

The purpose of this exercise is to compare American ideas about appropriate gender behavior with ideas about appropriate gender behavior in other cultures.

In some cultures, it is normal for men to kiss when they greet each other. If you have a male friend who is willing, kiss him on both cheeks as is often done in greeting in parts of the Middle East and Eastern Europe. If you have no willing friend, find a male friend who would be willing to discuss his feelings about doing such a thing with you. If you can find a man from a culture where men kissing men is normal, ask him how he feels about shaking hands as opposed to kissing, or when he would consider each behavior appropriate.

Now, make a list of the kinds of topics you might discuss with a North American male friend. Show your list to some of your North American male friends and sort the topics into the following categories: (1) "conversation and activities with buddies," (2) "conversation and activities with guys I know fairly well," (3) "conversation and activities with my best friend only."

These categories parallel the following domains: (1) public domain (behavior that is associated with a "normal" male in your culture); (2) semiprivate domain (behavior that is not typically exhibited by men in public because it shows their vulnerability in some aspect of their lives); and (3) private domain (the types of concerns that make men feel very vulnerable because they raise questions about their identity as "real men"—that is, questions about sexual orientation, work competence, parenting, or relationship skills).

Now, make a chart indicating which categories of topics are in domains 1, 2, and 3. Use this chart, and the awareness you have developed, to become conscious of your own cultural frame of reference. Realize that when men from other cultures invite you to do things with them or to discuss topics you are not used to discussing, they are acting from their own cultural frame of reference. Rather than assuming that their ideas about how to spend time and what topics to discuss are strange, ask yourself how their ways compare with your ways and what you can do to reduce your discomfort.

Now reverse roles. When you invite others to do things with you or have a conversation with you, you might elicit discomfort on their part because of where the topic or activity falls within their framework. Male-to-male, nonsexual intimacy is considered quite threatening in the United States and is far more normal in other parts of the world. Becoming aware of one's own cultural norms is the first step in crossing the bridge between cultures.

EXERCISE 5.15 • Gender Norms and Relationships with Cultural Others (Female to Female)

Do this exercise if you are a female. If you are a male, you may skip it.

Like Exercise 5.14, the purpose of this exercise is to compare American ideas about appropriate gender behavior with ideas about appropriate gender behavior in other cultures.

In many Eastern cultures and in parts of Europe, it is normal for adult women to walk down the street holding hands. See if you can convince a friend to do this with you. How do you both feel about it? What does this type of contact tell you about your sense of self and about personal boundaries? How do you feel about kissing your female friend in public?

Make a list of the kinds of topics or activities you might discuss with a North American female friend. Show your list to some of your North American female friends and sort the topics into the following categories: (1) "conversation and activities with buddies," (2) "conversation and activities with friends I know fairly well," (3) "conversation and activities with my best friend only." These categories parallel the following domains: (1) public domain (behavior that is associated with a "normal" female in your culture); (2) semiprivate domain (behavior that is not typically exhibited by women in public because it shows their vulnerability in some aspect of their lives); and (3) private domain (the types of concerns that make women feel very vulnerable because they raise questions about their identity as "real women"—that is, questions about sexual orientation, work competence, parenting, or relationship skills).

Make a chart indicating which categories of topics are in domains 1, 2, and 3. Use this chart, and the awareness you have developed, to become conscious of your own cultural frame of reference. Realize that when women from other cultures invite you to do things with them or to discuss topics you are not used to discussing, they are acting from their own cultural frame of reference. Rather than assuming that their ideas about how to spend time and what topics to discuss are strange, ask yourself how their ways compare with your ways and what you can do to reduce your discomfort.

Now reverse roles. When you invite others to do things with you or have a conversation with you, you might elicit discomfort on their part because of where the topic or activity falls within their framework. Female-to-female, nonsexual, physical intimacy may be considered quite aberrant in the United States and is far more normal in other parts of the world. Becoming aware of one's own cultural norms is the first step in crossing the bridge between cultures.

In both male and female situations, it would be easy for a North American onlooker to assume that same-sex couples kissing or holding hands were gay or lesbian. How do you feel about knowing that someone could observe your behavior and draw this sort of conclusion about you? Have you ever observed this sort of physical contact between people from non-North American cultures and become very uncomfortable? How does your own sense of gender identity shape your total sense of identity? If you changed your behavioral norms about same-sex touching, would it change your sense of self?

In the United States, touching across gender lines is filled with ambiguity. There seem to be no clear guidelines about what constitutes sexual touching, friendly touching, or appropriate/inappropriate touching (see Chapter 3, "Self and Nonverbal Interactions"). Guidelines for touching across gender lines are much clearer in other parts of the world. Guidelines respecting each person's sense of self are twofold. They are based both on your reaction to the experience, and also on your understanding and observation of the other person's reaction.

One place where socially prescribed rituals of touch do exist is in the realm of greetings. In general, people from China and Japan bow in greeting and do not touch. The traditional Indian greeting is to bring one's hands together (in what most North Americans would consider a prayer gesture) and touch the center of the forehead while saying "namaste," a Hindi term that means "I honor the place in you in which the Universe dwells" (Peterson, 1988). Muslims, regardless of country of origin, tend to greet each other with a statement of praise for Allah, by saying "Salaam Aleikem" ("peace be with you"), and by inquiring about one's family. Norms of touching are governed by gender and family relationships. Men may touch only women who are their relatives. Women do not touch unrelated men. For example, one of the authors of this text once asked a guest speaker from Amnesty International to address her students. She extended her hand in greeting but noticed that the woman speaker had her head covered, often a sign that a woman is a devout Muslim or Jew. The woman hesitantly shook hands, but clearly was unwilling to do so with a senior male colleague. It was necessary to inform him that the guest, being Muslim, did not shake hands with men.

Other greetings also are based on ethnicity. Men from Europe may or may not kiss in greeting, although in France it is common for men and women to kiss and be kissed by one another on both cheeks. In both Europe and Latin America, women may extend their hands to men for a kiss or a shake, depending on previous relationships (business, family, or personal), social context, and status. In most other parts of the world, greetings between people involve mandatory inquiries about family that often extend to grandparents, cousins, and the family of one's spouse, as well as one's immediate family of spouse, children, and parents. In some parts of Western Africa, even the order in which the components of the greeting occur is prescribed. The greeting itself may take five to ten minutes to complete. Attention to family is considered important and, therefore, worthy of time.

EXERCISE 5.16 • Scripts Revisited

Culture is a fluid process. The purpose of this exercise is to identify the ways in which the information you are learning from this book may influence your ideas about meeting people for the first time.

Look at the script that you wrote for meeting a new person (Exercise 5.7). Revise the script in consideration of what you have learned. Add questions or information about family, one's present situation, and so on. At what points in the script should you be extra careful to monitor the other's response? What are possible alternative actions on your part? For example, if you extend your hand in greeting and the other person seems hesitant or uncomfortable, how might you respond? Try to take your cues from the other person. Remember, if you are unsure how to react, it is always best to ask the other person what he or she expects.

It is impossible to memorize the appropriate greeting for every person you might meet. If you are unsure, let the other person initiate. Wait for him or her to extend a hand, bow, or make some other gesture. Remember that, in other parts of the world, a person's family is an integral part of his or her self, and the person's marital status is necessary information that guides interactions. People are seen as members of a group, not as individuals, so discussion of the state of the group is considered polite and evidence of concern. A somewhat extended inquiry into family welfare is often appropriate, and "getting down to business" or "not wasting time" is considered rude.

One of the authors of this text once picked up a female hitchhiker in the rural area where she lives. The hitchhiker was Cambodian, and the author assumed that the woman probably did not know that hitchhiking for women alone can be dangerous in the United States. As soon as the woman got into the car and the two women began speaking, the hitchhiker asked the author about her marital status and the number of children she had, and then expressed her sympathy that the author was single and without children. The author was so taken aback (having spent most of her adult life trying to define herself by the work that she does, not by intimate relationships and childbearing) that she was temporarily speechless. She did not have the presence of mind to ask the hitchhiker about her family, but asked instead about her work, which clearly was less significant to the hitchhiker than the author's work is to her. The hitchhiker came from an interdependent culture, however, and understood the need to fit into her hostess's world, so she told the author about her current job and her future educational plans in great detail. In retrospect, the author imagined that the woman probably thought her to be very strange and typically North American.

Assumptions about gender relationships vary dramatically from culture to culture. If you sense discomfort between you and the person you are speaking with, stop doing whatever you are doing. Express respect for the person's normal ways of interacting and ask whether a conversation of this type would be conducted at home, or whether it would be conducted somewhere else or in a different way. If something another person is doing makes you uncomfortable, pay attention to your own discomfort—try not to make a judgment about the other person.

EXERCISE 5.17 • Opposite Gender Relationships

Gender often functions as subculture. The purpose of this exercise is to identify the differences between men and women when it comes to feeling uncomfortable with members of the opposite gender.

1. Consider your nonintimate interactions with members of the opposite gender. Make a list of the types of situations that make you uncomfortable. Compare your list and discuss it with members of the same gender. Then discuss it with members of the opposite gender. What do they find surprising about your list? What did they already know or suspect?
2. If possible, have someone of the opposite gender make a similar list and discuss it. What do you find surprising? What did you already know?

Finally, consider that many people in the United States from other parts of the world have learned to interact in ways that are considered culturally appropriate for North Americans. However, they may not be comfortable doing so. Asian people shake hands and hug when expected to do so, but it may not be comfortable for them. Latin Americans may "get down to business" but may feel slightly off-balance in the process, preferring a more leisurely style of conversation. Remember that the dominant North American culture is one of the most noncontextual, nonrelational cultures in the world. We do what we think we need to do as autonomously as possible, and often fail to notice the reactions of others. They, on the other hand, have been raised in cultures, whether abroad or within the United States, where noticing the expectations and needs of others is a prime social value. Increased reciprocity inevitably smoothes relationships.

Class

The title of this section betrays a North American myth that must be addressed. The myth has several components: (1) North American society is classless; (2) if we have a significant class, it is the middle class; (3) class is defined by economic status alone; and (4) everybody has an equal chance to move upward and thus to change class or socioeconomic status (Mantsios, 1995). Since Europeans first began immigrating to North America in the seventeenth century, one of their prime motivations has been economic. Many people have come to this part of the world to seek or increase their personal fortunes. The Chinese, who came to the western United States in the nineteenth century, called the country "The Golden Mountain." The eastern Europeans, who began arriving on the east coast at the end of the nineteenth century, called it "The Golden Land" ("Die Goldene Medina") or the "Land of Opportunity." Each group saw North America as a place to start clean, fresh, without the limitations of one's native social standing.

Wealth and class are tied together in the United States in a fashion that is not typical of other societies around the world. In many cultures, class status is inherited, and high-class status can be associated with "genteel poverty." This phenomenon occurs in countries where class standing is connected to the family's relationship to royalty and often goes back to late feudal times. For example, knights in medieval Europe were given estates, and the right to administer the land as they saw fit, by lords in exchange for military service and financial fees and rents. These knights were called vassals. Family wealth typically went to the oldest son, under the laws of primogeniture. Daughters did not usually inherit. Younger sons became landless knights with hopes of earning or winning an estate or entering the priesthood in order to provide for themselves. Over time, a middle class developed based on the ability of individuals to earn their own money rather than inherit it from their fathers. Wealth began to be considered separate from inherited status, particularly for the merchant class. In contrast, a lord might be impoverished and still retain his inherited status. In order to restore the family fortune, the lord and his entire family might move to North America where economic opportunity flourished. Status did not automatically confer wealth, nor did wealth confer status. This situation is operative in England now, where many noble families have found it necessary to sell the family castle or turn it into a tourist attraction in order to pay the family bills.

In all countries where class or caste are significant, family affiliation, not wealth, is the major determinant of status. In India, which has the most extensive caste system in the modern world, status is inherited and is based on categories established by the Hindu religion. Brahmins are the highest, or priestly, caste. Their relationships with members of other castes are strictly governed by religious principles and rules. Brahmins have the highest status in Hinduism, regardless of the financial status of their families. The same is true for all the other castes.

Historically, China has had a class system based on a combination of feudal status and scholarly achievement, which was often correlated with government service under the Confucian system. The Japanese feudal system has persisted to the present time in a modified form, with huge family systems such as Suzuki, Mitsubishi, and others dominating certain types of industries. Status in Islamic and Jewish societies is associated with piety and religious scholarship. In many Latin American countries, family status goes back to the original conquistadors who acquired wealth and status simultaneously and who continued to build the family fortunes.

In the United States, there is an inevitable connection between wealth and status. In other countries, this connection is far weaker. The difference is important to understand in order to avoid imposing North American cultural assumptions on people from other cultures. For example, few North Americans would challenge Donald Trump's high status in this culture, despite his questionable business dealings, his highly visible, acrimonious divorces, and his frequent self-serving comments in the press. No one asks "So, who were his parents?" "Where does his family come from?" Trump's status is based on Trump's financial success, not on his family heritage.

Our popular maxim, "Nothing succeeds like success," is understood to refer to financial success rather than any other kind. The worth of achievements in other domains of human activity is typically determined by the financial consequences of those activities. A list of the "best" movies reflects the amount of money people paid to see each one. The best movies of the year usually are the ones that make the most money. It is very important for North Americans, who are used to associating status with wealth, to realize that, in dealing with people from other cultures, this association may be misleading.

EXERCISE 5.18 • Class Definitions

The purpose of this exercise is to make you aware of your assumptions about class.

Before reading any further, write down your definition of the following terms:

status
class
upper class
middle class
lower class
working class

Reconsider these definitions as you continue reading.

"Class [in the United States] is more than the amount of money you have" (Langston,1995, p. 100). It is a whole set of behaviors, values, and ideas about life's possibilities that shape a worldview. We tend to divide our society into three classes: upper, middle, and lower. Members of a class share certain worldviews, outlooks, and expectations, which translate into certain lifestyles, career choices, and behaviors. Middle-class people tend to have more economic security than working-class people. Even when their financial situations are temporarily difficult, they tend to believe that things will improve and that they will return to their former way of life. Middle-class people plan for the future and assume that they can control a great deal of what happens to them. They expect their children to go to college, to have economic and career choices, and to move comfortably among successful business and professional people. They assume that work should bring personal satisfaction and that they should be well paid for their efforts. "Middle class is a matter of status as well as income and is signaled by subtler cues: how we live, what we spend our money on, what expectations we have for the future. Since the post-war period middle-class status has been defined by home ownership, college education (at least for the children) and the ability to afford such amenities as a second car and family vacations" (Ehrenreich, 1986, p. 50).

The socioeconomic factor in self-definition may be a stronger consideration among North Americans than it is among people from other cultures. This is not to say that others do not expect to be treated according to their appropriate status, but rather that status of self and others is less related to wealth than to caste or class or family reputation.

How does socioeconomic status contribute to self-definition of those living in the United States? It affects an individual's hope for the future and his or her sense of the possibilities that life offers. It affects a person's "choice" of work or career. Indeed, it determines whether the person thinks about choosing a career or gratefully takes the best-paying job available. Socioeconomic status also affects ideas about marriage and family—when and whom to marry, when to have children, and also how much economic independence a person should achieve before marriage, during marriage, or outside marriage. Finally, socioeconomic status affects one's ability to see him or herself as an individual and to be preoccupied with personal problems (Langston, 1995). When people believe that they have choices and possibilities, the details involved in making those choices become very important. When survival is the issue, anything that contributes to achieving that goal is enough.

EXERCISE 5.19 • Your Self as a Socioeconomic Being

The purpose of this exercise is to help you identify which kinds of class-related values shape your perspective at this time in your life.

1. When was the first time you thought about opening a savings account? If you did this as a child, who suggested it to you? What was the purpose of saving money? Was saving money considered either desirable or possible in your family? Do you have a savings account (or some other form of savings) now?
2. When was the first time you worked for money in or out of your family? What did you do? Who paid you? How did your family react when you did this? What did you do with the money?
3. What were/are your mother's and father's occupations? What have they told you about working? About getting along at work? About what kinds of work to explore?
4. Did you feel you had a choice about attending college or some other educational institution after high school? Did you have a choice about which college to attend, how to pay for attending, whether or not to work while in school, or whether it was okay to borrow money?
5. Do you feel that you will have to choose (or have had to choose) your work according to what opportunities are available near your home?
6. Do you believe that you can change careers if you want to?
7. Do you believe that the main reward for work is money, personal satisfaction, the ability to improve the world, or some combination of these?
8. Has someone in your family been downsized? Laid off? Is there a difference? Did the person receive a severance package or just a week or two's notice? Is getting laid off routine in your family? (In working-class families, lay-offs have been routine in all seasonal industries. In business and professional families, downsizing is a phenomenon of the past decade.)
9. To which class does your family consider itself to belong?
10. Review your answers to all of the above questions and draw some conclusions about your values, based on the sense of economic security and possibilities that you and your family of origin share. Consider the degree of choices and the degree of control. How much is self related to a job? To relationships? To lifestyle?

11. Compare your conclusions and the values with which you were raised with those of friends or others in your class or work group. Talk about family norms and about favorite sayings about money and work ("Put some away for a rainy day" or "How did your trust fund do last quarter?"). Discuss the amount of food available at most meals, and how it was shared. Talk about whether or not you ever had bill collectors come to your door or call on the phone.

EXERCISE 5.20 • Class Values and Behaviors

The purpose of this exercise is to place yourself into a socioeconomic class based on your beliefs and values about money and possibilities for satisfaction in life.

Based on the conversations you had in Exercise 5.18, create a list of so-called middle-class values and behaviors, lower-class values and behaviors, and upper-class values and behaviors. Determine which class you belong to, and identify characteristics of the other classes that make you uncomfortable.

Religion

Religion and faith are enormously important in shaping self-image throughout the world. Perhaps the most important thing for North Americans to take into account when considering how to relate to people of different cultures is the intensely secular nature of life in the United States. Freedom of religion is guaranteed in the United States Bill of Rights, which mandates separation of church and state, and which prohibits the state from establishing or officially supporting a specific religion. This condition, which native-born North Americans take for granted, is extremely unusual. In Germany and in several other European countries, the state collects taxes for the churches and distributes the money according to the wishes of the taxpayers. For example, Lutherans register their religious affiliation on the tax form, and the monies collected from the various Lutheran denominations are given to the Church administration proportionately. In most countries, there is a preferred or mandated religion, and in a few countries, such as Iran, the clergy of the dominant or mandated religion control the government. In many countries, such as England and Denmark, the head of state is also the head of the Church.

Monotheistic Religions

In the United States, religious identity is typically seen as a matter of individual choice. Historically, religions in the United States have been monotheistic. The United States is overwhelmingly Christian, with a minority of Jews and

Muslims. Judaism and Christianity have rather different ideas about the relationship between self and God. A large number of Christian denominations exist in the United States, including Roman Catholic, Orthodox, Baptist, Methodist, Episcopalian, Presbyterian, and others. Although each has a different form of worship, some fundamental beliefs are shared. Christianity asserts that each person is born with a soul, and it is the soul's obligation to live a life that is pleasing to God, to become consecrated to God through a variety of ceremonies at various times in life, and to achieve salvation through either belief, action, or both, so that the soul can return to God after the death of the body.

Judaism also views God as "an external, transcendent reality" (Armstrong, 1993, p. 57) Who is extremely demanding. In Judaism, God speaks to the entire community via the commandments, laws, and prophets. Judaism exists in many forms in the United States today, and its members range from the totally observant ultra orthodox Jews, whose entire lives are governed by conformity to the 613 sacred commandments, to the very Americanized and secular reform Jews. The interpretation of the relationship between God and the Jewish individual also varies, from focusing completely on observing the commandments, to focusing on observing the ethical tenets without paying specific attention to the details of traditional law. In all cases, the Jewish God assumes that Jews live together as a community and that Jewish obligations are communal and sacred obligations. There is little or no discussion of heaven, salvation, or the ultimate fate of the individual. In the words of an old Jewish woman, "A Jew is what a Jew does."

Islam, the third major monotheistic religion, and a growing presence in the United States due to both immigration and conversion, has a great deal in common with Judaism and Christianity. Many beliefs and important figures are shared, such as belief in a holy book and consideration of Moses and Jesus as prophets. Islam is a legalistic faith that provides a complete set of rules by which the faithful must live. These laws are found in the holy book, the Koran. There are five major pillars that all Muslims observe. They are: (1) complete submission to the Will of Allah and acknowledgment that "There is no God but Allah and Mohammed is His Prophet" (Smith, 1994, p. 160); (2) prayer five times daily; (3) charity; (4) observance of the Holy Month of Ramadan, which includes fasting from sunup to sundown; and (5) a pilgrimage to Mecca (called the Haj) at least once during one's life. Islam is a community religion. The religion prescribes many aspects of relationships within families and between men and women, within and outside the family.

EXERCISE 5.21 • Jewish-Christian-Islam Contrasts (Part 1)

Because religion is considered a private preference in the United States, most of us typically avoid discussing religious differences. This is your chance to open a conversation.

Go to a religious service of another faith with a member of that faith. When the service is over, discuss anything that you found interesting, different, confusing, pleasing, or in any way notable with your companion. If you have time and are welcome, go to two services, one in a liberal congregation and one in a conservative or traditional one. For example, go to a reform Jewish service as well as an orthodox Jewish service. Repeat this for different denominations and different faiths.

EXERCISE 5.22 • Jewish-Christian-Islam Contrasts (Part 2)

The purpose of this exercise is to focus your attention on the influence that your religious upbringing has had on your development.

Make a list of the ways in which your religious upbringing has shaped your ideas about yourself. Discuss the list with both a member of your faith and a member of a contrasting faith. Decide if any beliefs or commandments are so basic to your sense of self that you would not be who you are if you violated or ignored them.

EXERCISE 5.23 • Holiday and Values

The purpose of this exercise is to identify the values that are embedded in religious holidays and your own level of comfort with the holidays of your faith.

Identify your favorite religious holiday. List the aspects of the holiday that you enjoy the most and the aspects with which you are most uncomfortable. Try to identify the values that are embedded in the practices associated with that holiday. What do those beliefs and practices tell you about who you are or "should" be? Discuss the holiday with a friend and listen to his or her holiday practices and beliefs. Now, do the same for your least favorite religious holiday. Consider the same questions. In what ways do these holidays give the same messages? In what ways do they give different messages?

Pantheistic Religions

Until the past twenty years or so, monotheism was historically the only approach to religion that was represented in mainstream North American culture. Native Americans, who have a very different belief system, were either ignored, considered pagans, or converted. Native Americans have a wholistic vision of the universe, in which two-legged creatures live with four-legged creatures, and with creatures that fly and creatures that swim, in the Mother Earth, beneath the Father Sky. All are part of a complete system, which is totally integrated and in which harm to any specific element harms all. Native beliefs around the world refer to an experience that monotheistic people would call "God," but there is simply no way to translate Wakantanka, or any of the other native terms for the Great Spirit, into a EuroAmerican frame of reference. In pantheistic religions, "God" is a way of describing all the forces and powers in the universe and is present everywhere, all the time, in all events, objects, persons, and relationships. Divinity is totally integrated into the belief systems of native peoples, and the self/community/spirit is One. Rituals are intended to help participants become one with the Spirit.

One widely practiced and very powerful ritual used by many Native American groups is the sweat lodge. A sweat lodge is a small hut consisting of a wooden frame usually covered by skins. It is low and completely dark inside. In the center is a pit filled with very hot stones. Participants in a "sweat" enter the hut and sit around the pit, often in silence, sometimes chanting and praying together for the welfare of themselves and others. The heat is very intense, leading to the English term for this experience, the "sweat lodge."

> When you are part of a sweat, you are connecting with the living laws of the Creator. . . . All the symbols—earth, air, fire and water—are sacred to us. When you go in there it must be dark—we think of it as going into a spiritual womb of the Great Mother. . . . We humans are linked together by the spirit of life. People say they're from different nations and put different labels on, but when I look, I see just another human being. There's an energy in the universe that links us to all other life forms. We are all children of the Earth. We have these earthquakes and other natural disasters because people are poisoning her bloodstreams and cutting off her hair. They're not following the living laws about caring for the earth (McCloud, 1995, p. 282).

EXERCISE 5.24 • Spirit in the Earth

The purpose of this exercise is to personally experience solitude in nature, which will heighten your understanding and appreciation of Native American culture.

Spend an entire day in the woods alone. If you cannot go alone, do not talk to your companions. Listen to the silence. Spend the entire day looking, listening, and trying not to think. Look at the sky, the birds, the trees, flowers, and other vegetation. Try to go to a place that has a body of water. Sit next to the water and listen. Go to a mountain and watch it all day. Ask yourself who you would be without that mountain. If this question makes no sense to you, you probably will not be able to communicate very effectively with a Native American.

EXERCISE 5.25 • Native American Books, Films, and Events

The purpose of this exercise is to familiarize yourself with Native American books, films, and events.

Some popular films are reasonably accurate in their portrayal of Native American life, particularly *Dances with Wolves.* Many educational films and public television offerings are also available. More and more accurate biographies of older Native Americans are being published, including *Mabel Mckay* (Sarris,1994), *American Indian Women: Telling Their Lives* (Bataille & Sands,1984) and *Messengers in the Wind* (Katz,1995). *Black Elk Speaks* (Neihardt,1972) was the first widely read book to explain the integrated worldview of native peoples to white, monotheistic Americans. In addition, Powwows, which are seasonal, and dance rituals, often are open to the general public for at least part of the ceremony.

Attend one film, read one book, and/or attend one event, and then compare your reactions with those of others who have done the same. Discuss what seems to be universal among Native American tribes and what seems to be characteristic of a particular tribe.

EXERCISE 5.26 • Conversations with Native Americans

The purpose of this exercise is to help you compare your own worldview with that of a person raised in a Native American context.

If you can find a native person, speak with him or her and ask what elements of life in mainstream American society he or she finds most difficult. Ask about values and family history. Ask yourself how the Biblical injunction to "Have dominion over the fish of the sea and over the birds of the air and over the cattle and over all the earth" (Genesis 1:26) has shaped your sense of self. Contrast this with the experience of a native person who shares the planet with brothers and sisters in all forms. If native tribes reside in your area, and if they hold public educational gatherings or dance ceremonies, attend. Scan your local newspapers for opportunities that may present themselves. You cannot learn about native people only by reading about them. You have to be in the settings of ceremonies, rituals, and family life. This often is not possible without establishing a high level of trust and respect.

Syncretistic Religions

In addition to monotheistic and pantheistic forms of spirituality, the United States has recently experienced an influx of people from parts of the world where syncretistic religions prevail. These religions share a common belief that the world is sacred; divinity exists in all life forms; and the "gods," for the most part, represent different aspects of Divinity. There is no polytheistic system of gods who are responsible for different dimensions of life and the cosmos. Most gods in syncretistic systems resemble Christian saints: They represent embodiments of concern for, or power over, some particular area of life that concerns people.

Hinduism, the religion of most people from India, is the parent faith of Buddhism. It can be seen as polytheistic, because it has many gods. Each god or goddess is an aspect of the Brahman, the universal, all-powerful soul or spirit. It also can be seen as a Trinitarian faith whose God is represented in three major aspects: Brahma (Creator); Vishnu (Preserver); and Shiva (Destroyer). Hinduism refers to the divine through an endless number of names, some of which refer to gods and goddesses and others to disembodied spirits. Each god has its devotees. One particularly popular god is Ganesh, who is typically depicted as having a human body with the head of an elephant. He is widely beloved because he is considered the remover of all obstacles (Smith, 1994). In Hinduism, living things never completely die; rather, they are continually reborn or reincarnated, and death is understood as a transition. The goal of Hinduism is Moksha, or reunion with the Brahman; the self disappears, and the cycle of reincarnation ends. In Hinduism, every person is a soul, a spark of the Divine spirit called Atman, which has a body, or many bodies through various incarnations. Progressing spiritually toward reunion with the Divine, and treating every person with respect because of his or her innate divinity, are essential tenets of Hinduism. At the same time, some souls are closer to Moksha than others. They are, therefore, born into higher castes. One's caste is determined by all of one's past behaviors, good or bad, throughout all of one's incarnations. Although some castes are better than others, all share in the divine spirit or Atman. The traditional Hindu greeting, "Namaste," is a greeting from the divine aspect of one person to the divine aspect of another, in which we are all One.

Many religions have been brought to the United States through immigration. Others, as in the case of Native Americans, have always been here. Each has a different worldview and concept of the relationship between the individual and the divine. Unlike Judaism and Islam and like Christianity, Buddhism is concerned with the individual and with individual salvation. A Buddhist spends a great deal of time in meditation, trying to achieve self-awareness and self-knowledge. Thich Nhat Hanh, a widely respected Vietnamese Buddhist monk, believes that Buddhism is compatible with the monotheistic religions, because it can deepen any form of spiritual practice without contradicting it.

Buddhism is similar to Hinduism in some ways. It was founded in India by a man known as the Buddha, or "enlightened one." It is also a growing religion in the United States. Buddhism does not encompass belief in a god or gods, although some branches worship the Buddha as a god. Like Hinduism, there is a belief in reincarnation and the presence of a universal soul. The individual's goal is to return to this soul and leave the cycle of reincarnation. The basic Buddhist beliefs are known as the four noble truths: (1) All existence is sorrowful;

(2) Sorrow is caused by cravings or desires; (3) The way to end sorrow is to end cravings or wanting; (4) This can be done through the observance of the eight-fold noble path, which can be summarized as meditation or mindfulness in all things.

In the syncretic faiths, the self or the individual represents a very different phenomenon from the one represented in Judaism or Christianity. If you consider self as a separate person (on one end of a continuum) and as a small part of the group (on the other end of the continuum), members of syncretic faiths are very far toward the "group" end. People who are concerned about the evolution of their soul and their relationship with all living beings have a very different idea of who they are than people who believe that you only live once, and that one's work in life is to dominate the earth or act as steward of its resources in the service of human life.

If you are concerned about reunion with God or Brahman, you probably will spend more time in prayer or meditation than a North American, and you will be somewhat less concerned about acquiring material possessions or competing with other people for those resources. If you believe that family is the most important group of people in your life, you will be less concerned about asserting your independence and living out your personal choices about career, spouse, friendships, and so forth. You will be more concerned with maintaining harmonious relationships. You will focus a small portion of your life on yourself and your enjoyment as long as that does not interfere with the rest of your family responsibilities. If you are conscious of your faith, your family, and perhaps your personal spirit, extending back into timelessness and forward into infinity, you will be more likely to fit into an established system that has existed in your culture for as long as anyone can remember.

On the other hand, if your family has moved to the United States recently and is no longer living in a homogenous society, surrounded by a community of people whose beliefs are similar, you probably will be torn between spirituality and materialism; between faith and pragmatism; between believing in forward progress and believing in an endless cycle of seasons, births, deaths, and rebirths; and, finally, between respect for the elders and the ancient ways, and the excitement of youth, change, and apparently limitless possibilities. There has been an enormous influx of people from Asia over the past thirty years; they certainly have experienced these conflicts.

The gap between North American ideas about self-as-secular-individual and predominant Asian ideas about self-as-embodied-spiritual-being-in-family-context cannot be overemphasized. In addition, this Asian belief system, which is so powerful in Eastern cultures, is challenged dramatically when people immigrate from East to West. The Asian North American population increased by 79.5% in the 1980s (Atkinson, Morten & Sue, 1993). When you, as a North American of Jewish or Christian ancestry, interact with people from Asia or with Native Americans, do not assume anything about those people's values, priorities, or worldview. If, in the daily course of conversation, profound differences in values emerge (these may relate to who has the right to make decisions for an individual, how important a particular current event is, who is in charge of the children, whether or not to challenge an authority figure, or whether death is preferable to life), do not *assume* anything. Ask questions. Be sure you understand how the other person understands the world and his or her place in it. Strive to understand, not to evaluate. Understanding may be the most difficult task you will face that day.

Race and Ethnicity

Genetically speaking, there is only one race on this planet—the human race. The historical construction of race (as a set of social categories based on physically visible characteristics) is a representation of the beliefs and perceptual systems of the people who created the categories. The perception of race, and the belief systems created to attribute meaning to visible physical differences, have had an enormous effect on people's self-image and on relationships between groups of people since the Europeans arrived on the North American continent. This phenomenon, accompanied by the social stratification that was created to maintain racial categories, is called racism. Racism is real, powerful, and destructive. Race as a genetic phenomenon has no basis in fact. Race as a social phenomenon is but one aspect of our multiple social identities.

Ethnicity is very different from race as a set of social facts, although the two phenomena overlap. Members of particular ethnic groups tend to resemble each other physically. They tend not to resemble people who come from other parts of the globe. In other words, to people who are not from Africa, people from Africa look more like each other than they do like the observers. When people see other people who resemble them in terms of physical characteristics like skin color or shape of nose or eyes, they tend to think of the others as "people." When they observe others who do not share their own physical characteristics, they tend to use a modifier before the reference. Therefore, when an African person sees another African, she or he may think of the other as a person. On seeing a European, the description will shift to "white" person or "Anglo" person. In the United States, the word *person* is typically synonymous with *white person*. All other persons are hyphenated—that is, African-American, Asian-American, Hispanic-American, and so on.

To Africans, those from different African countries are seen as being of the same race, but of different ethnicity. To many Africans, North Americans look like Europeans—white people, hyphenated people. People from Southeast Asia, China, and Japan look more like other Southeast Asians, Chinese, and Japanese than they do like people from Europe. But Asians can easily distinguish among themselves. Ethnocentrism, the belief that one's own "people" are normal, typical, and not hyphenated, is a universal phenomenon.

Ethnicity and race affect one's sense of self in two important ways. The first is the way in which an ethnic group conveys to its members what it means to be in that group. Ogbu's definition of culture—"an understanding that a people have of their universe—social, physical or both—as well as their understanding of their behavior in that universe . . . a guide to interpretations . . . expectations and actions in that universe" (Ogbu, 1990, p. 523)—relates to the ways in which an ethnic group communicates the role of self to its members. In other words, who you are is a function of how you behave, what you believe, and what you expect. Ho adds the dimension of internalized culture. He describes "the cultural influences operating within the individual that shape (not determine) the personality formation" (cited in Ogbu, 1995, p. 5). One's sense of self in an ethnic group is formed partially by the rules, expectations, and beliefs that the group conveys to the person as she or he matures within the group. Mead, an early social psychologist, describes the formation of self as a function of a person's ability to "take the attitude of the group to which he [sic] belongs" (Mead, 1964, p. 33), talk to himself in the common language, and take up responsibilities according to community expectations. In other words, self is a social phenomenon, a dynamic interaction between a person's natural tendencies and the social expectations of the group.

EXERCISE 5.27 • Ethnicity

The purpose of this exercise is to identify some of the ways in which ethnicity influences your perception of the world.

1. List all the ethnic groups that you can think of.
2. Go to a busy public place like a bus station, restaurant, or park. Watch the people. See if you can label their "ethnic" group. What are the criteria that you use? Which types of people or groups do you tend to lump together? Which are difficult to label? Why? What role did race play in your categorization?
3. Repeat this with a partner, one who belongs to the same ethnic group as you. Do you tend to agree on your categorizations or not? Discuss why. Try the exercise with another partner—this time, someone from a completely different ethnic group. How much do you agree on now?

The preceding exercise deals just with ethnicity, not race. The second way in which ethnicity and race shape one's sense of self is via the perceptions and reactions of people who are not members of one's racial or ethnic group. This effect—especially as it pertains to race—is very powerful in the United States. African Americans are North Americans who are usually perceived as a distinct group because of the meaning assigned to their skin color. As we have discussed, individualism and the belief that one is in control of one's own destiny is fundamental to North American culture (Fried, 1995). African Americans, however, can never ignore the fact that they are perceived both as individuals and as members of a group. They are perceived as representing a group to a degree that other members of society are not. For example, a teacher might ask an African American student, "So, how do your people view the situation?" or a similar question that assumes that all African Americans belong to a homogeneous group.

EXERCISE 5.28 • Group Identification

The purpose of this exercise is to explore the ways in which imposed group identity affects feelings and behavior.

Have you ever been perceived as a representative of your group? What was the group? Family? Gender? Religion? Ethnicity? Race? Sexual orientation? How did it make you feel? Did it seem fair or appropriate? Did you feel comfortable in the position of representative? Why or why not?

Have you ever put other people in this situation? Under what conditions and for what reasons? Which group of people?

Given what you have learned so far, do you think that this practice is acceptable? Discuss your conclusions with others of similar or different groups.

Skin color is typically one of the first things a North American notices about other people. Along with the perception of skin color comes the meaning attributed to it—for example, very dark skin is considered evidence of African ancestry and is often associated with a range of behavioral characteristics that are related to stereotypes about African Americans. People of African ancestry in the United States, whether they are from Jamaica, St. Kitts, Trinidad, Haiti, Cape Verde, or any of the countries or ethnic groups on the continent of Africa, tend to be perceived in the United States as African Americans. Although they are perceived as North Americans of a particular racial group, they are considered nondominant. Members of these groups tend to feel less in control of their individual destinies, because their own sense of self is subsumed by the perception of the dominant white North Americans.

People of African ancestry in the United States, whether they are African Americans or members of other ethnic groups, evolve a sense of self from (1) the culture of their primary group, and (2) the ways in which they are treated by members of the dominant group. The two influences interact. Members of other visibly non-European groups deal with the same phenomenon. North Americans of Japanese descent are treated as belonging to the same group as North Americans of Chinese, Korean, Cambodian, Laotian, Indonesian, or Vietnamese descent. They are lumped together as "Asians." Members of nondominant groups perceive self through dominant group norms, leading to their own internalized racism, homophobia, anti-Semitism, and so forth.

Members of non-European ethnic groups must contend with and challenge the sense of self imposed on them constantly by the dominant culture. In the case of African Americans, many images in the dominant culture are negative. African Americans are often presented in the popular media as criminals, welfare recipients, or drug users. They are portrayed as being lazy, incapable of having stable families, unintelligent, unmotivated, and uneducated. Asian Americans often are presented as criminals or as members of organized crime families. They are portrayed as shy, inexpressive or nonassertive, or, at the other extreme, as extremely intelligent, hardworking, or family-oriented. Latinos are viewed as sharing many characteristics with African Americans: They always have large families, they live in poverty, and they often are unable to speak standard English. They also are presented as criminals, welfare recipients, or drug users.

It is easier for North Americans to perceive specific ethnic differences in those who come from Europe. We do not lump all Caucasians or Europeans together. Instead, people are Italian, Portuguese, English, Swedish, Russian, Greek, Irish, German, Polish, or some other group associated with the familial place of origin. Therefore, the effect of ethnicity on self is most apparent to North Americans of the dominant culture when they are attempting to understand or relate to, for example, Italians, Portuguese, English, Swedish, Russians, Greeks, Irish, Germans, or Poles.

To make a sweeping generalization, the effect of visible, physical differences on sense of self in the United States is most evident in the way all members of the "different" group become conscious of both their group identification and the individual self simultaneously. Members of the *dominant* group in the United States are far less often aware of their own group identification. Most whites, when thinking about race, think of people of color, and do not view themselves as a white race. For them, race is not an issue! In truth, being a member of the white "race" is positive in the United States. White people are not continually made aware of their race in the way that nonwhite members of society are continually reminded of their race. Frankenberg (1993) argues that we need to view whiteness as constructed and dominant rather than as the norm. Her research shows convincingly that race is as significant in shaping white identity and experience as it is in shaping the identities of people of color. Carter (1990) and Helms (1990) have demonstrated that awareness of the role of race in shaping identity is a factor in the ability of white people to relate positively to African Americans.

Therefore, in interactions with people who are visibly different from those of European ancestry, the Euro-American must remain aware that such people have what W. E. B. DuBois (1961/1903) called "double vision" and what Frantz Fanon (1967) called "black skin, white masks." Their sense of self incorporates their own integrity with regard to their primary community, as well as their sense of who they are and who they must be in the dominant society in order to accomplish their goals. If a North American of European ancestry wants to understand the differences between him or herself and a European colleague, all she or he must do is find a time and place to discuss beliefs, aspirations, relationships with family, hopes for the future, and so forth. If the same person wants to understand the differences between his or her sense of self and that of a person from a group that is a target of racism, a legacy of shame, mistrust, exploitation and fear must be overcome. The survival of the nondominant groups has depended on their ability to maintain double vision, a "self" for the community and a self for the outsiders.

EXERCISE 5.29 • Awareness of Your Ethnicity-Self Interactions

The purpose of this exercise is to help you trace your personality characteristics and values back to your ethnic roots.

Make a list of anything you can remember your parents, grandparents, relatives, or other members of your ancestral ethnic community telling you about the way "their people" are. What do "their people" do for work? What are the main personality traits "they" are supposed to have? For example, a father considers himself Hungarian and Jewish. Jews are supposed to be ethical, responsible and smart; Hungarians are stubborn and creative. Both groups take care of those less fortunate. They have a strong sense of caring for family and community. This is one man's interpretation of his received personality traits.

EXERCISE 5.30 • Awareness of Your Stereotypes

The purpose of this exercise is to differentiate between stereotypes based on vicariously acquired information and stereotypes based on personal experience.

Make a list of everything you have ever heard, seen, or been told about the "typical" member of a group of "hyphenated" Americans (African Americans, Latinos, Asian Americans, Native Americans, and so on). Review the list and underline information that is a result of any personal experiences you have had with members of these groups. Does your personal experience confirm or deny information that you have acquired vicariously? Which type of information is dominant?

EXERCISE 5.31 • The Ideal North American Self

The purpose of this exercise is to identify characteristics of self that North Americans prize.

List all the characteristics that North Americans have considered commendable over the history of European occupancy on this continent. Think of myths and stories that are told to children to convey ideas about character, such as George Washington's affirmation that he "could not tell a lie" after he chopped down the cherry tree, Sojourner Truth's proclamation "Ain't I a woman" that asserted that women could do anything men could do, and Davy Crockett's injunction "Be sure you're right, then go ahead." Also think about the values and character traits presented in the media, through advertising and articles about sports figures and other current cultural icons. All of these represent aspects of the "ideal" American character. What are these traits and characteristics?

EXERCISE 5.32 • Your Personal Traits

The purpose of this exercise is to compare your idea of who you are with the culture that helped to shape your idea.

Examine all three lists from the previous three exercises. Draw up a list of personal traits that you believe make up your sense of self. How much of you is an "individual"? How much of you reflects the dominant North American belief system of who North Americans ought to be? How much do you have in common with members of historically oppressed groups? Where are the conflicts between who you believe yourself to be "naturally," who you have been socialized to be, and who you are when you are being oppressed either individually or as a member of a group?

EXERCISE 5.33 • Your Comfort Zone

The purpose of this exercise is to become more aware of your comfort with behaviors of people outside your own culture group.

Review the lists that describe alleged personality traits of people outside your own group. Make an additional list of behaviors that you tend to associate with people from other groups, and that make you uncomfortable. Make four columns as follows:

Behavior/Group	Source of My Discomfort	Belief About What Is "Normal"	Source of My Belief

After you complete this chart, try to identify the value judgments you make about "normal" behavior and the connections between your ideas of "abnormal" or "strange" and your personal level of discomfort.

EXERCISE 5.34 • Beliefs About Self-Family Connections

This exercise will help you compare the effects of different cultural worldviews on some very practical day-to-day behaviors and beliefs.

With a friend who is a member of another ethnic/racial group, answer the following incomplete sentences. Then, discuss the reasons for your beliefs.

1. If my cousin needed money, I would ____________________.
2. My sister's child ____________________.
3. Money ____________________.
4. In the future, I really hope ____________________.
5. When my father (or uncle or other adult male in the family) tells me to do something, I ____________________.
6. School ____________________.
7. White people ____________________.
8. Black people ____________________.
9. Asian North Americans ____________________.
10. The most important part of my life is ____________________.
11. Work is ____________________.
12. Religion is ____________________.
13. Respect is ____________________.
14. My mother ____________________.
15. If you were my friend you would ____________________.

Make up more of these sentences as you begin to glimpse some of the key differences between your ideas about self and your friend's ideas about it.

Conclusion

In this chapter, we have studied self as a sociocultural construction that is influenced by history, gender, race, ethnicity, religion, and class. As we increase our self-awareness, we become more attuned to the considerable (specifically, negative) information we have absorbed about people who were different from the family in which we were raised. Because racism, sexism, classism, anti-Semitism, and homophobia, as well as other forms of oppression, are so prevalent in our society, each of us has been imprinted with prejudices and stereotypes about groups of people we barely know.

Likewise, many of us are confused by our own self-concept: Are we who we have been taught to believe we are? Are we who we want to be? Recent psychological literature purports that we each have multiple selves, depending on the context. Certainly there is our inner core sense of self, the self that relates to family members, the self that interacts with close friends, the work self, the public self, the relational self, the achieving self, and so on. In each context, we may feel and behave differently, depending on our degree of comfort, power, degree of freedom, and so on. As we become accustomed to the multiplexity of our own self-identities, we can then become more open to the multiplexity of others' experiences of self. As we go through the life span, our sense of self changes; there are both continuities and discontinuities. At all ages, people's self-concept and psychological functioning tend to be influenced by maturational, genetic, or environmental factors.

Most developmental research (Rutter & Rutter, 1993) emphasizes the importance of social experiences on personal development. Intellectual understanding must be accompanied by real-life interactions in order for us to understand and communicate effectively with diverse populations. When we begin to understand how our own gender, race, ethnicity, religion, socioeconomic class, generation, and geographical region shape our sense of self, we are better able to appreciate how others are shaped by the same variables.

6

Relationships: Rules, Roles, and Scripts

By the time a child enters school, he or she already has developed assumptions and expectations about how people are supposed to behave. By the time a person enters the work force, he or she has had a variety of experiences with people in different settings and has learned how to act and react in certain situations. Thus, in childhood and adolescence, individuals learn certain rules and roles for dealing with specific types of social situations. The *explicit* rules and roles are usually not a problem; the *implicit* ones may present more of a challenge for family members and outsiders.

What complicates interpersonal relationships is that these rules and roles are not the same for everyone. They are determined largely by the assumptions about needs, values, interests, and expectations that one learns from family and culture. We must become aware of the rules and roles presented in the dominant culture of our own society, and we also must become aware of how they play out in social interactions, as well as in nondominant cultures. We must become more sensitive to rules and roles that are shaped by different cultural assumptions about people and relationships. This awareness can enable us to anticipate and respond more effectively and appropriately to different people in different situations.

Human beings are dynamic, multidimensional beings who function on multiple levels, as discussed in Chapter 1. Each level has its own relationship implications. Thus, from an ecological perspective, we need to consider individuals not only at their individual/self core level, but also within their primary groups (family, work, school, community, and so on) and at a universal level. It is the middle level, the cultural groups with which individuals primarily identify, that we will address. This middle level encompasses intimate relationships, social (nonintimate) relationships, and public relationships.

It is important to reiterate that, although similarities and dissimilarities exist between cultural groups, similarities and dissimilarities also exist within any one cultural group. Different cultural groups have different values, priorities, sense of self, and family identities. One must always consider individuals, situational circumstances, and sociocultural context before inferring the meaning of a particular behavior. One must always acknowledge, appreciate, and consider the intersecting influences on individuals and families of class, race, gender, ethnicity, politics, generation, religion, and geography, as well as individual uniqueness, including disposition, temperament, physical and mental capacities, and other personality characteristics.

The purpose of this chapter is to enhance relationship building across cultures. We will focus on how cultures construct intimate, social, and public relationships. Because adult relationships are so strongly influenced by our experiences in our family of origin, we begin the study of relations from our own family systems perspective. We will consider the variation that exists among cultures and within cultural groups in terms of how families understand who they are, the ways they communicate, and the diverse family structures and organizations that determine entitlements, obligations, boundaries, and communications processes. We then will consider how the assumptions we develop in our families lead to expectations of our own and others' power, rules, roles, and scripts in relationships, whether they be with family, with friends, at school, at work, in the community, or in other small groups.

Power in Relationships

Relationships always involve power. This power may be manifested in hidden messages that are expressed through games and manipulation, or it may be overt and explicit. For example, a teenager may express affection to a parent so that the parent will relax and grant permission to use the car. Or, a parent may tell a teenager, "I'm in charge in this house. While you're here, you will do as I say." To catch on to the games and manipulation, we need to be able to discern the hidden messages in both verbal and nonverbal language. Verbal language may range from direct to indirect, dominant to submissive, formal to informal. We will learn more about hidden messages later in the chapter.

The typical power struggle in a relationship is not for dominance; rather, it is for the power to determine the nature of the relationship—the rules, roles, and scripts (Haley, 1963). In some cultures, relational power differentials are more obvious than in other cultures. In mainstream United States culture, relational power differences are masked in order to maintain the North American ethos of egalitarianism.

While there are indeed variations in the use and meaning of language, personal relationships are about individuals in contexts. For example, deference denotes inequality in status between members of a relationship. The deferent person, whether truly believing this inequality or complying with cultural prescriptions, formally acknowledges the dominance of others by using deferent behavior. An individual may accept the need for deference in a work setting, but not in a family setting. Or, an individual may appear to be deferent with his or her spouse in public, but behave quite differently at home, just as children typically behave differently at school than they do at home.

Rules

The term *rules* refers to the ingrained assumptions one has about *how* people are supposed to be in relation to each other. This was illustrated in the communication rules that were described in Chapter 2. In a traditional Western family, a wife may assume that she can make social plans for herself and her husband as a couple without consulting her husband, given that her role clearly is to organize their social life. In an egalitarian Western family, she may even choose whether or not to make a social engagement for them as a couple without consulting her husband. In a traditional Muslim family, the husband may determine how and when his socialization activities occur. His wife may be expected to confine her socialization to relatives within her home or compound. Gudykunst and Kim (1992, p. 60) infer that rules are more specific and have more range in collective, high-context cultures than they do in individual, low-context cultures. The more rigidly social roles are defined in a culture, the more specific the rules tend to be.

Roles and Scripts

Roles are the predominant patterns of behavior that are determined by rules. Rules evolve into scripts—the codes or recipes for playing one's roles in different relationships. Different roles and scripts may exist for intimate, social, and public relationships. In addition, different rules and, hence, roles, may depend on setting. Social relationships at work may differ from social relationships in your neighborhood. In fact, you may self-disclose more to your friends at work than you do to your friends at home. This may have to do with spending more time at work than at home, or with the safety of the contained work environment.

In many patriarchal cultures, rules are based on the primary assumption that within a family, the male is the major breadwinner. He also has the ultimate power (whether or not he chooses to delegate some or all) both within and without the home. The female is delegated to be the major caregiver and domestic manager. Even in the United States, where women often work outside the home for as many hours as their husbands and sometimes earn more, women are still assumed to be the major caregivers and domestic managers. Many work two shifts, one at the workplace and one at home, compared with their husbands' one and one-half shifts—one at the workplace and one-half on the home front (Hochschild, 1997).

In the work setting, however, a man may be in a less powerful position than at home, and he may behave more compliantly. In comparison to traditional cultures, the rules in more egalitarian cultures, such as the middle-class United States, may be more flexible, enabling the provider and caregiver roles to be more shared or to be exchangeable between husband and wife. One or both may work, in however, hierarchical organizations where power and tasks are more fixed.

Role relationships across cultures differ, depending on the degree of personalness, formality, hierarchy, and allowed deviation from cultural norms.

There is a continuum from flexible to rigid cultural role construction (Triandis, 1994, p. 159). Some factors to be considered in understanding cross-cultural role relationships include:

1. amount of intimacy and conflict allowed
2. direct and indirect forms of verbal behavior
3. face management and nonverbal behavior
4. attitudes towards the development of interpersonal relationships with strangers
5. approach and avoidance
6. similarity versus perceived similarity
7. amount of self-disclosure and social penetration

We will examine all of these factors in this chapter.

Face and Facework

The term *facework* refers to facial expressions and nonverbal messages. Facework is a concept of communication and a notion of self-presentation developed by Brown and Levinson (1987) as a way to understand identity management. As defined by Goffman (1967), facework is preventive and corrective communication designed to counteract face threats to self and others. Face threats occur when one's desired identity in a particular interaction is challenged. A face threat, then, is any kind of insult. One example is when someone in a culture that values bowing does not bow deeply enough in accord with somebody's status. Another example might be in Southeast Asia, where how you sit is important. Your feet need to be under you; if you sit with your soles exposed in front of you (as many in the United States do when sitting on the floor), it is an insult to the hostess.

Positive face involves being liked and respected by significant others; negative face occurs when someone has insulted you. In the latter situation, there are no rules, so you have more freedom from constraint and imposition, but you lose honor and credibility. As pointed out by Cupach and Metts (1994), positive and negative face often are paradoxical in that it is difficult to satisfy one type of face without threatening another type. In collective societies, positive face is always the preferred value because saving face is important and the consequences of failing to save face are serious. Thus, one tries to avoid losing face or intruding on someone else's space. In individualistic cultures, people care less about what others think, so there are fewer constraints in facework.

One purpose of facework is to give a politeness message to the other person, while simultaneously giving them room to maneuver so that they can give you back a politeness message (Ting-Toomey, 1994). Communication and morality are both aspects of facework. As noted, there are two fundamental types of face: positive and negative. The desire to maintain identity through face in interactions is presumed to be cross-culturally universal. However, interpretation and management of facework varies across cultural groups in terms of (1) the relative value placed on various aspects of face, (2) behaviors construed to threaten face, and (3) behaviors preferred to minimize or rectify face threats (Wiseman & Koester, 1973).

EXERCISE 6.1 • Observation of Facework

The purpose of this exercise is to become aware of your interpretations of facework.

Go to a restaurant, bus or train station, park, or some other place where people congregate or pass by. Sit in one place and just observe people's faces, whether they are engaged in conversation with others or not. Some may be alone; others may be sitting in pairs or in small groups. What can you infer from their facework? Does facework vary according to gender, ethnic, racial, or age differences? If possible, repeat your observations with a group that speaks a language that you do not understand. Based on facework, how would you describe people's relationships? What do you think the script is? What can you tell about people's social identities and characters from your observations?

Intimate Relationships

We learn how to develop and maintain intimate relationships in our family of origin. Across cultures, some universals seem to exist with regard to families. All families share the overarching values and objectives of ensuring safety, raising healthy, well-adjusted children, and maintaining loyal connectedness or kinship in a community. (The community may be based on familial, racial, ethnic, religious, generational, or regional identification.) Across cultures, an intimate connection or attachment exists between the major caregivers (biological mothers or surrogates) and the children. Attachment studies (Ainsworth, Bell, & Stayton, 1974) have shown universal mother–child attachment behaviors in animal as well as human behavior.

However, just as the *length* of childhood and childhood attachments to parents differs between cultures, different cultures have different primary bonds. In the West, marital attachment (intimacy between spouses) is considered primary, along with parents' attachment to children. We cannot assume, however, a universal value of intimacy between husband and wife, or among siblings. That is more culture-specific. For example, there seems to be an inverse relationship between intimacy of marriage partners and freedom of choice in premarital arrangements. In cultures where marriages are arranged (for example, some parts of India and Arab countries), each spouse tends to be more intimate with his or her birth family than with the marriage partner. Relationships to spouse and spouse's family contain obligatory responsibilities, but intimacy is generally not desirable. The primary purpose of marriage is to propagate in order to preserve and strengthen the family. In such cases, nobody wants to know what a wife feels about her mother-in-law, but people do want to know that she will honor and care for the mother-in-law according to her husband's obligations to his mother or hers as a daughter-in-law (Broude, 1994).

Family loyalty and cohesiveness also vary between cultures and may be manifested in a variety of ways. Family boundaries—the distance between family members—may range from being disengaged to being distant, close, or enmeshed. They may be clear, blurry, rigid, or flexible. For example, in some cultures, the norm of family loyalty and cohesiveness involves multiple generations living together in one house. One of the authors of this text treated an immigrant Cambodian family who were devastated when their daughter and son-in-law moved three houses down the street. The parents claimed, "This is the death of our family." This attitude might be viewed as pathological by a member of the dominant culture in the United States, where individual autonomy and separation from one's family-of-origin is an accepted part of mature adulthood. Another example of culture-specific family loyalty involves a Jewish Russian immigrant who was appalled when he read about the unibomber's brother turning him in. In his culture, with its history of persecution and distrust of government, family loyalty would preclude such an act regardless of the nature of the crime.

Relationships vary over time, as do the levels of intimacy that are expressed through verbal and nonverbal communication. Many Western families become more distant geographically and/or emotionally over the years, even to the point of losing a sense of family identity. Arab, Muslim, and Asian families, on the other hand, typically remain connected geographically and retain a strong family identity, even though conflicts may exist within the group.

As discussed in Chapter 3, nonverbal expression is more influential across cultures than is verbal expression (Brown, Werner, & Altman, 1994). For example, a man from Japan reported that he became a doctor because his father wanted him to. When asked how he knew that his father wanted such a career for his son, the man replied that his father had once left a book about great physicians out on a table in the sitting room. The son and the father never discussed the son's career choice. A woman from India reported that her parents let her know without a spoken word whom they expected her to marry. Her father gave her a certain look and her mother pinched her shoulder every time the prospect's family was mentioned.

In all cultures, the transmission of cultural values to children is viewed as the responsibility of the parents, although religious and educational institutions can provide structured input. How families define their values and what strategies they may select to teach them to their offspring differ among and between cultural groups.

Who Make Up a Family?

As we know, in the United States, the dominant white middle-class culture is an individualistic culture. As a result, it views "the primary family" as consisting of a mother, father, and children. Although in some southern or upper-class families a "nanny" or other surrogate figure may be included in the definition of family, the prevailing view is that membership in a family depends on blood or legal relatedness (Okun, 1996). This group is popularly called the "nuclear" family. In most cases, grandparents, cousins, aunts, and uncles are considered extended family, with less power and involvement than the actual parents. In collective cultures found in the United States, such as Asian, Latino, and African American cultures, grandparents, cousins, aunts, uncles, and godparents are considered part of "the primary family," whether or not they reside in the same domicile. In traditional societies, families lived in one domicile, a complex, or some other architecturally and discrete unit. Fictive kin—friends who may be given the title of "aunt," "uncle," "mama," or "papa"—also are viewed as family in many cultural groups. A great deal of variability exists in terms of how a family unit is defined.

Most cultures determine family groups patrilineally. One is born into and is a part of one's father's family, not one's mother's family. Many cultures also practice patrilocality, where the wife moves in with her husband's family. As a result, the man's parents have more status and power than the husband and wife, and the wife may become isolated from her family (Broude, 1994). This practice is not widespread in this country, but the effects of it still can be seen in family power structures.

Many wedding ceremonies reflect the fact that women's identities include lesser power vis-à-vis men. The traditional Christian European wedding still contains the symbolism of a business transaction, where one family sells a commodity (their daughter) to another family. With this transfer goes responsibilities, duties, and rights, which pass from father to groom. This is indicated by the question asked by the clergyperson: "Who gives this woman in marriage?" Typically, the bride's father answers "I do" and places the bride's hand in the hand of her husband-to-be. Similar transference of power can be seen in other cultures, such as in New Guinea, China, and Java (Brown, Werner, & Altman, 1994, p. 348). Sometimes it is the father-in-law who assumes the responsibilities, duties, and rights that had belonged to the bride's father. In cases where the married children live with their parents, the grandparents may have more power with regard to child-rearing than do the actual biological parents. In these families, whether the family is matrifochal or patrifochal, the oldest generation maintains the power and status throughout life.

As Broude (1994, p. 34) notes, a number of cultures establish avoidance rules to control relationships that have the potential to be disruptive. For example, a man and his mother-in-law or a woman and her father-in-law may avoid each other on a day-to-day basis. Kuschel (1992) points out that within traditional China, because of the social structure, adopted and natural-born daughters are natural enemies, as are mothers-in-law and daughters-in-law and sisters-in-law.

Thus, the very definition of who is considered family differs within cultural groups as well as between cultural groups. White middle-class North American families may feel a closeness toward grandparents, aunts, and uncles, but a boundary still exists around the primary nuclear family, and society expects all parenting power to reside with the parents. Couples who abdicate this parental responsibility to others are viewed by society's agents as irresponsible. Not all family systems are so centralized. In many traditional cultures, all family members—not just the biological parents—are responsible for parenting all of the children. Children in other cultural communities within the United States may have multiple parental figures in their homes and/or communities and may tolerate and expect discipline from a multitude of adults. In other words, child-rearing is the responsibility of the "extended" family or community.

EXERCISE 6.2 • Definition of a Family

The purpose of this exercise is to become aware of the definition of a family and how similar or different your definition is to others' definitions.

Define a "family" from your point of view. What are the boundaries? What qualities must people share in order to qualify as members of a family? Extend the diagram of your family that you constructed in Exercises 2.13 and 5.12. Put yourself in the middle, and look at preceding and succeeding generations, with all members of a generation on one line. Use one geometric shape for male and another for female. Now, given your definition of family, draw a line around *your* family. Who is included? Who is excluded? Does it look right to you? Discuss your findings with others. Did people use similar criteria for their borders? Did people from different ethnic or cultural backgrounds within your friendship system define family differently?

People in nondominant groups, such as gays and lesbians, single parents by choice, unmarried couples with or without children, and multiracial or interfaith families, often create their own nontraditional definitions of family, including their significant other(s), children, and close friends who share their values and beliefs in a communal context (Okun, 1996). They may celebrate holidays together, and make legal arrangements guardianship or for property transfer. Many, feeling disconnected from their disapproving or rejecting blood-related families, may consider their created family to be their primary groups, recipients of their loyalty and allegiance.

In most parts of the world, "family" refers to a larger group of people than what commonly is considered family in the dominant culture of the United States. Refugees and immigrants, often involuntarily cut off from their kinfolk, may band together in their host country with sponsors and other refugees and immigrants of similar race and/or ethnicity to form new "families" who share language, customs, traditions, and history. A multicultural definition of families includes groupings of people who have formed primary bonds and are committed to sharing mutual care and well-being, regardless of legal or blood-related status.

Exercise 6.3 • Primary Family Composition

The purpose of this exercise is to expand your notions of family composition and meaning.

In the next week, survey a minimum of ten people in different settings (at work, at school, on the bus, in a restaurant, or in your neighborhood). Ask whom they include as primary family members and what family means to them. Can you attribute any of these differences to ethnicity? Race? Class? Length of time residing in this country? Compare these findings with your own definition of who comprises your family and what family means to you. If possible, discuss your findings with others who have completed the same assignment.

Choice in Intimate Relationships

Some cultures afford more choices to individuals and families than do other cultures. Families may differ in forms of marriage (such as polygamy or polyandry), methods by which a mate is chosen, kinship and descent groups, and structure of household. The degree to which one can select a mate, choose an occupation or lifestyle, decide whether or not to have children, or determine the number of children varies across cultures. In addition, values and criteria have changed within the dominant culture in recent history.

Some groups, such as Hassidic Jews and Mormons in the United States, and traditional eastern and middle eastern cultures, select mates for their children based on social, economic, and familial viability. Some upper-class or royal families in Western cultures have strong input into mate selection, thinking more in terms of mergers (financial or property) than love matches. Some families in certain ethnic and racial groups within the United States not only dictate educational and occupational opportunities for their offspring, but also control enough of the affectional, social, and economic resources to have final veto power over their offspring's choices. Some families in certain cultural groups, such as Mennonites, Mormons, or orthodox Jews, cut off family members who marry out of their group or who choose a lifestyle that is prohibited by the cultural group's belief system. Other families within these cultural groups, however, discover that their family loyalties transcend the cultural rules, and they find a way to stay connected to errant members despite the disapproval of their larger culture (McGoldrick, Giordano, & Pearce, 1996).

The choice as to whether or not to have a child is ever present in today's high technology era. The development of cheaper, safer birth control and modern reproductive technology has opened up choices heretofore unimagined. In some parts of the world, for example, Israel, couples are encouraged and given financial incentives to have as many children as possible in order to boost the population rate. In China, where overpopulation is a serious concern, couples are allowed to have only one child. In many cultures where males are more highly valued than females, it is not uncommon for families to abort a female fetus or to dispose of a female infant and try again for a male. A common Chinese blessing is "May you be the mother of 100 sons!"

Mobility is another choice that affects families. Within the United States, people migrate in order to obtain broader economic opportunities. This results in families being fragmented and disrupts the continuity of community. Some families accept and tolerate geographical distance, finding other ways to remain close; others find it difficult to remain close when there is such distance. Still others feel bereft about "family loss" when family members relocate and avoid relocation themselves. Internationally, able-bodied people from war-torn or impoverished countries often attempt to immigrate to friendlier societies. Although this may seem to be an inevitable decision, it still remains a choice that splinters families. Migration and immigration can have a profound effect on families, creating conflict between generations—conflict between acculturation and the preservation of cultural rules and roles (Espin, 1995). For example, families from the Azores who have immigrated to urban areas in the northeast openly mourn and grieve their loss when an adult offspring moves out of the family home, even if the move is just down the street (McGill, 1997).

The Meaning of Family

As we have discussed, cultures can be viewed along several continua: low-context/high context; doing/being; individualistic/collectivist; and involvement/independent. Hofstede (1984) amplifies four dimensions of culture that help us to understand and clarify the different cultural meanings assigned to the values, attitudes, and behaviors that we see in different families. These dimensions are masculine/feminine, uncertainty/avoidance, power/distance, and individualist/collectivist. Let us look at each of these dimensions.

1. *Masculine/feminine:* In masculine cultures such as Japan and Latin America, the value is on assertiveness, independence, task-orientation, and self-achievement—characteristics that have traditionally are thought of as being male. Masculine cultures have rigid gender roles and "live to work" values. In feminine cultures such as Scandanavia, the value is on cooperation, nurturing, relationship solidarity with the less fortunate, modesty, quality of life, and a "work to live" ethic—values that traditionally are thought of as feminine. In considering this dimension of culture, it is important to remember that attributes of gender vary widely across cultures so that elements that are masculine in one culture can become feminine in another.

2. *Uncertainty/avoidance:* In high-uncertainty/avoidance cultures, such as Arab, Muslim, and traditional African countries, value is on conformity and safe behavior, avoidance of risk, reliance on formal rules, rituals, and stan-

dards, certainty of data/information, and trust only in parents and friends. These cultures are closed systems whose members are suspicious of strangers, change, and unfamiliarity. In low-uncertainty/avoidance cultures, such as the United States, Singapore, and Scandinavia, the value is on risk taking, tolerance of ambiguity, fluidity of rules and roles, and a problem-solving orientation. Low-uncertainty/avoidance people typically dislike hierarchy and bureaucracy and, therefore, are able to make innovative decisions more quickly and easily.

3. *Power/distance:* This cultural dimension refers to the acceptance of difference between those who hold power and those who are affected by power. In high-power/distance cultures, such as Latin American, South Asian, and Arab cultures, there is an acceptance of hierarchical authority and status consciousness, and a respect for age and achievement. In other words, rank has privilege. Protocol and formality are important. Thus, superiors view subordinates as less adequate than themselves; consequently, subordinates are expected to act deferentially. In low-power/distance cultures, such as Anglo-American, Scandinavian, and Germanic cultures, competence is valued more highly than seniority. The emphasis is on sharing information, consultation, cooperation, and creativity. People from the low-power/distance cultures believe that legitimate power is established by competence and expertise, rather than by status or age.

4. *Individualistic/collectivistic:* In individualistic cultures, such as the dominant groups in North America and Anglo countries, one puts the task before the relationship. Independence is highly valued. The needs of the individual take precedence over the needs of the group, community, or society. Individuals in these cultures strive for self-actualization and autonomy. Relationships are defined by self-interest. In more collectivistic cultures, such as those in Asia, Africa, and the Mideast, the emphasis is on saving face, in-group solidarity, loyalty, and strong interdependence. Relationships are based on mutual self-interest and are dependent on the success of the group. In other words, the needs and welfare of the group take precedence over an individual's interests.

EXERCISE 6.4 • The Dominant United States Culture

The purpose of this exercise is to evaluate the United States dominant culture in terms of Hofstede's four dimensions: masculine/feminine, uncertainty/avoidance, power/distance, and individualistic/collectivistic.

Using Hofstede's four dimensions of culture, describe the dominant United States culture. How would you characterize it is terms of each dimension, and why? Compare your decision with others'. Do you all agree on your interpretations of the dominant culture? Where do differences lie? What might be the causes of these differences? Consider people's "individual" cultures. Do they influence how they view and interpret the dominant culture?

Within the United States, family, work, educational, health, social, and community systems vary in terms of each of these dimensions. Each of these systems can fall anywhere along the continua of the four dimensions. The United States is a unique country in that it was founded by immigrants who were seeking the freedom of choice that goes along with independence. Although indigenous and slave populations have been exploited in order for the dominant immigrant group to develop in this society, the United States always has had a more diverse population than most other countries. Despite the oppression of indigenous and slave populations, the United States has retained an ideology of opportunity, has provided opportunity for a large percentage of its residents, and has maintained more fluid class and citizenship boundaries than many other countries. As a result of this fluidity and value of progress and change, the term *family* has many different meanings, and definitions of family continue to change and evolve.

EXERCISE 6.5 • Family Preservation Values

The purpose of this exercise is to consider the broad spectrum of family values regarding preservation.

Consider the following scenario. You learn that your brother was involved in the holdup of a neighborhood store, which resulted in the killing of a young clerk, who leaves behind a wife and baby. Do you turn in your brother or do you go to any lengths (legal or illegal, moral or immoral) to protect him? What do you think someone from African American, Native American, Anglo American, Asian-American, Latino-American, Mideastern, African, Arab, or European cultural groups might think and do? Why do you think so? What elements of the culture did you consider when answering the question? Are these elements based on stereotype? Are they based on personal contact? What elements in each culture suggest the course of action that members of that culture might take under these circumstances?

Family System Types

A model of family system types proposed by Kantor and Lehr (1975) allows us to look at relationship systems in the United States, particularly families. This model enables us to look at family systems on a continuum that cuts across cultural groups. There are three dimensions to every family system—public, interpersonal, and personal. The *public* dimension is the "face" that a family as a unit presents to the outside world, the image it wants to project in accordance with its professed cultural value system. This is where an outsider initially interfaces with a family, through an external boundary. Then, there are the ways each person relates, as spouse, parent, child, or sibling. These ways of interacting make up the *interpersonal* systems within a family. In contrast, the *personal* system comprises the way an individual behaves outside of the family. (One's way of behaving may or may not be consistent in each of the three dimensions of the family system.)

Kantor and Lehr (1975) describe three models of structural family arrangement that cut across the dimensions developed by Hofstede (1984). These models are:

1. *closed system:* a traditional family system, characterized by fixed space; regular time clock; steady energy; hierarchical power; reliance on rationality and tradition; earnest, sincere affect (emotional expression) with control of public demonstrations; and strong loyalty to the family. This type of family maintains stereotypical gender roles—*the Father Knows Best* model—where the rules for roles and scripts are clear and based on tradition, "the way It has always been."
2. *open system:* a less traditional family system, characterized by movable space; variable time clock; flexible energy; shared, lateral power with consensus and universal participation; shared, open expression of affect; acceptance of differences; and loyalty to family members' individualistic and collective ideals. This type of family is based on collaborative, democratic principles in that everyone has input into the development of the family script. The rules and subsequent roles are flexible and adaptive.
3. *random system:* a loose family organization, characterized by dispersed space; irregular time clock; fluctuating energy; experimental, "laissez-faire" power based on a particular person's charisma and personal ability at a particular moment; expression of passionate, rapt affect; and acceptance of paradox and ambiguity. Although this family system is disorganized and sometimes chaotic, it has a wide range of fluidity, high levels of spontaneity and creativity, and extremes of emotions and productivity.

Although these models are descriptive rather than evaluative, we all have personal values about which is "best." There is no evidence to indicate that any one style is better than another as long as there is consistency and adaptability within a system type. Nonetheless, it is important for you to become more aware of the ingrained biases and stereotypes you learned growing up in your family. And, it is important to recognize that in the United States, variations of the family system types exist within cultural groups, even though some cultural groups may have a prevailing style.

EXERCISE 6.6 • Stereotypes of Families

The purpose of this exercise is to examine your ingrained assumptions about ethnic and religious influences on family styles.

Let us examine your global stereotypes. How do you think the following cultural groups should be rated with regard to predominant family style, according to Kantor and Lehr's model? What characteristics of each culture and/or religion do you take into account as you rate them?

	Open Family	Closed Family	Random Family
Asian-American			
Latino-American			
Traditional African			
European			
Native American			
Anglo/American			
Arab			
Jewish			
Muslim			
Catholic			
Protestant			
Buddhist			
Hindu			

Elaborate on your classifications by jotting down the characteristics that influenced your ratings. Remember that these are very broad groupings and that there are many subgroupings within each one.

EXERCISE 6.7 • Your Family Systems

The purpose of this exercise is to learn which of Hofstede's cultural dimensions and Kantor's system types apply to the family in which you were raised.

Using both Hofstede's four cultural dimensions (masculine/feminine; uncertainty/avoidance; power/distance; individualistic/collectivistic) and Kantor's system types (open, closed, random), how would you assess the family system in which you were raised? What about your spouse's or your significant other's? Look around and see how the families you know and interact with might fall into this model. Discuss your findings with other members of the system. Do you all agree on your analysis?

The rules, roles, and scripts within a family depends on its system type. A range of open and closed family systems exist within both individualistic and collectivistic cultures. Individualistic cultures, such as the United States, utilize direct face-negotiation skills, autonomy-preserving strategies, and self-face maintenance. Collectivistic cultures, such as Japan, are more mutually interdependent, utilizing indirect face-negotiation skills, approval-seeking strategies, and other-face maintenance. (The "face" they are concerned with is the group's face rather than the individual's face.) An example of the differences between Western and Japanese family cultures is described by White and LeVine (1986) in their article about "sunao," a characteristic that Japanese parents value in children:

> Cooperation does not suggest giving up self, as it may in the West; it implies that working with others is the appropriate way of expressing and enhancing the self. Engagement and harmony with others is, then, a positively valued goal and the bridge—to openhearted cooperation as in sunaeo—is through sensitivity." (White & LeVine, 1986, p. 58)

In contrast, white middle- and upper-middle-class North American children are taught to be independent, separate from others, unique, and direct, and to strive for one's own goals. Achievement, rather than relationships, is the major objective.

EXERCISE 6.8 • Family Differences

The purpose of this exercise is to begin to note similarities and dissimilarities of family interactions.

Go to a playground or some other gathering place for young families in your own neighborhood, such as a family gym, the YMCA, a beach, or community center. Observe the interactions of different families for at least one hour. Use the table on the following page to write down what you see as the major similarities and differences in the rules, roles, and scripts that determine the way family members interact with one another. You probably will focus on parenting strategies. Note any obvious cultural and class diversity among the families you are observing.

For example, at the beach, it is interesting to note who plays with the children, how children's requests or demands are met, how discipline is exhibited, and how the parents interact with regard to the children. Do they pay more attention to the children than to other adults?

EXERCISE 6.9 • Observations of Different-Culture Families

The purpose of this exercise is to note similarities and dissimilarities among families from cultural backgrounds different from your own. If you live in a homogeneous community, you may want to observe at a playground or community center in a different ethnic or more heterogeneous community. Again, observe the similarities and differences in family interactions. Now compare and contrast what you observed in this exercise with what you observed in Exercise 6.8. What universals can you discern? What differences might you ascribe to culture?

A. Forms of Interaction

	Socializing		Play		Discipline		Teaching	
	Verbal	*Nonverbal*	*Verbal*	*Nonverbal*	*Verbal*	*Nonverbal*	*Verbal*	*Nonverbal*
Between Adults:	______	______	______	______	______	______	______	______
Rate level of each form of interaction from low 1 to high 5.								
	______	______	______	______	______	______	______	______
Rate effect of each from negative 1 to positive 5.								
Between Adult(s) and Children	______	______	______	______	______	______	______	______
Rate level of each form of interaction from low 1 to high 5.								
	______	______	______	______	______	______	______	______
Rate effect of each from negative 1 to positive 5.								
Between Children	______	______	______	______	______	______	______	______
Rate level of each form of interaction from low 1 to high 5.								
	______	______	______	______	______	______	______	______
Rate effect of each from negative 1 to positive 5.								

B. Degrees of Similarity Among Families

Rate each from dissimilar 1 to similar 5.

Socializing	______	______	______	______	______	______	______	______
Play	______	______	______	______	______	______	______	______
Discipline	______	______	______	______	______	______	______	______
Teaching	______	______	______	______	______	______	______	______

EXERCISE 6.10 • Cultural Stereotypes

The purpose of this exercise is to expand your awareness of cultural stereotypes.

For each of the lifestyle attributes listed in the lefthand column, check the ethnic family group(s) that you think applies:

	African American	Latino American	Asian American	Native American	Anglo American
Autonomy					
Harmony					
Uniformity					
Interdependence					
Oral traditions					
Collectivism					
Obligations					
Cooperation					
Spirituality					
Avoidance of conflict					
Challenging authority					
Compliance					
Independence					
Achievement					
Loyalty					
Support to elders					
Past-time orientation					
Present-time orientation					
Future-time orientation					
Clearly defined gender roles					
Fluid gender roles					
Uniformity					
Improvisation					
Cooperation					

You will note that many of these characteristics cut across cultural groups and are, in fact, a matter of degree. Now ask as many people as you can in your own and other cultural groups what these lifestyle attributes mean to them and how they affect relationships. What do you think the implications are for the way people handle relationships?

EXERCISE 6.11 • Meaning According to Family Cultural Group

The purpose of this exercise is to understand different meaning systems. For each of the cultural groups below, write down the meaning that you think is assigned to each of the concepts in the lefthand column.

	African American	Latino American	Asian American	Native American	Anglo American
Life/death					
Expression of pain, suffering, grief					
Acceptance of outside help					
Expectations of family responsibility					
Acceptance of outside authority					

Check your answers with others and do some library research to confirm or disconfirm your assumptions.

Parent-Child Intimacy

Another controversial area of sexuality and physical affection is the notion of the "family bed." In many cultures, families sleep together in one bed or room and children may or may not be aware of their parents' couplings. The cultural assumption is that parent/child physical and emotional togetherness while sleeping promotes the well-being of both parents and children. In the dominant middle class of the United States, this type of togetherness often is viewed as problematic. Heated debates on the pros and cons of the family bed can be found in most parenting magazines. Readers of these magazines seem to be equally divided in the practice. The age of the child is a contributing factor. More people seem to find it appropriate with babies than with toddlers or older children. In fact, families that practice a family bed with older children may be reported for inappropriate behavior, and the couple's relationships may be seen as "disturbed."

The assumption that parents should not relate sexually while their children are sleeping in the same room is culture-specific. Sleeping patterns also have an economic basis. Members of larger, poor families often share beds and rooms. For example, in the movie *My Left Foot,* all of the sons slept in one room in one bed and all of the daughters in another. Where heating bills are high and winters cold, children often sleep with their parents, a way of ensuring that the children do not succumb to the cold.

Sexuality and Affection

The oppression and control of public and private sexuality is based on centuries of tradition and practice established by religious and governmental laws. These laws determine who may marry whom, what the duties and responsibilities of one spouse are to another, the political and financial status of members of each gender, and numerous other practices and behaviors that affect how people act both publicly and privately. In Massachusetts, a law prohibiting conjugal relations on Sundays still remains on the books from Puritan times. As a result of such laws, in many societies the husband has the societally sanctioned power to force his will on his wife and children. In past times, and even in some societies today, this has included the right to punish or kill as he sees fit. It also has included the right to coerce one's wife to satisfy one's sexual appetite.

These rights have influenced and been influenced by various cultures' gender roles. In some cultures, men are permitted, even expected, to freely express sexual desire and interest. It is not uncommon for a woman walking in a Mediterranean country to find herself the object of lewd stares, pinches, or sexual comments by both men and boys. In the United States, such behavior increasingly has been labeled as "sexual harassment" (Pryor & DeSouza et al., 1997). Similar behavior is less frequently found in women, although cultures do exist in which women are expected to display sexual desire publicly (Kochman, 1981).

How we tend to behave with members of the opposite sex, whether publicly or privately, is culturally prescribed. For example, in many cultures, husbands and wives do not show affection publicly. In others, couples display their intimacy publicly (Broude, 1994, p. 4). One only has to walk down a high school corridor or onto a college campus in the United States to see examples of this display. Culture also affects whether or not sex is an acceptable topic of conversation and what form of conversation can take place. In the United

States, sex often is spoken of openly in technical terms, whereas in Russia, the topic is suitable only for private discussion, and the cultural preference is that it be discussed in a relational, sensuous way (Wiseman & Koester, 1973).

EXERCISE 6.12 • Sexuality Comfort and Discomfort

Discuss with one or two members of your group how you think about heterosexual and homosexual relationships and what kinds of behaviors you have observed. What behaviors are you comfortable observing? What behaviors are you comfortable displaying in public? Does the setting matter? Does the age and gender of the couples matter? What topics are you comfortable talking about? What topics are you uncomfortable discussing in public settings? How do you communicate your discomfort? By averting your gaze? Changing the subject? Boasting? Turning your attention to someone else?

Some cultures, such as those in Latin American and Mediterranean countries, are known for *machismo.* This term relates to male roles and involves pride, responsibility, honor, and courage, as well as innate aggression, uncontrolled sexuality, and superiority to women (McGoldrick, Giordano, & Pearce, 1996). The concept of *marianismo* also is related to Latino cultures. It refers to the qualities of the Virgin Mary, and dictates the nurturing, homemaking, caretaking, submissive, and dependent roles and behaviors of women. This exemplifies how cultural frames support female–male power inequities in some societies.

In many cultures, wives are obliged to show public deference to their husbands. This does not mean that wives have no influence. In those cultures with public deference, provocative verbal and nonverbal gestures between men and women are accepted as harmless flirtation and may be experienced as flattering. In other cultures, such as Anglo/American, these same gestures might be viewed as offensive. Chivalry, which often has been given lip service in Anglo/American cultures, indicates male deference to women's supposedly frailer status. Touching and sexual expressiveness in intimate relationships is considered by most cultures to be private. If it occurs in public, it usually is viewed as exhibitionistic and provocative behavior. For example, in the United States and many other Western cultures, public sexual expressiveness is associated with lack of class, manners, and knowledge of the correct behaviors.

EXERCISE 6.13 • Sexual Gestures

The purpose of this exercise is to become aware of the range of sexual gestures and how they are used and interpreted.

In a small group, list all of the gestures you can think of that might contain sexual innuendoes. What differences might gender, ethnicity, race, region, generation, or sexual orientation make in terms of how these gestures are used or interpreted? Over the next few weeks, check out your group's list by observing people as you go about your daily activities.

Sexual Orientation

Across cultures, heterosexual behavior is considered the norm for mature adults. Heterosexism, the assumption that homosexual behavior should be suppressed, often accompanies the heterosexual norm. Particularly in collectivist cultures where the good of the group is far more important than the desire of the individual, heterosexual behavior within the context of marriage is considered an obligation. Sexual behavior itself rarely is discussed as long as a person marries and produces children. Sexual behavior typically is not subject to scrutiny, although homosexual and "deviant" behavior must be hidden.

In most societies, marriage and childbearing are more important than individual desire or sexual behavior. However, in modern societies such as the United States, as sexual activity has become divorced from reproductive activity, sexual orientation as a component of identity has become particularly important. Lesbians and gays from collectivist cultures in the modern world who cannot tolerate a charade of marriage and who choose to identify themselves via sexual orientation often flee to more progressive, individualistic cultures.

Sexual behavior (heterosexual or homosexual) outside marriage may be acceptable as long as it is discrete and kept separate from the marriage. For example, in Brazil, thousands of men regularly leave home for extended periods of time to work on construction sites, and they are housed in all-male dormitories. Brazilian men justify their homosexual behavior, if they discuss it at all, on the basis of their own powerful sexual drives and their need not to be unfaithful to their wives. They do not consider themselves homosexual people. They think of themselves as men who need to take care of their sexual urges without violating their marriage vows (Del Castillo, 1993). Another example concerns an upper-class, dominant-culture United States family who urged their adult son to stay married to a mentally ill woman and "to have discrete sexual liaisons on the outside" in order to avoid divorce and shaming the family.

Physical Contact

Another way to consider the sexual practices of various cultures is to view them on a continuum of contact/noncontact. Sexuality includes many forms of affectionate communication, such as touching, verbal and nonverbal flirting, and seduction. For example, around the world, physical contact between people of the same sex is commonplace (Broude, 1994). Men hug and kiss men, women hug and kiss women. In some cultures, however, such as Anglo/American cultures, it is not permissible for men to have physical contact, such as hugging, kissing, or holding hands (Broude, 1994, p. 7). The degree to which physical contact between same-gender people, particularly males, is permissible may change with age or in special circumstances, such as festivals and holidays.

EXERCISE 6.14 • Observing Touch

The purpose of this exercise is to develop awareness of how people use touch in relationships.

Use the following form for each step in this exercise.

Person Touching	Person Touched	Area of Body Touched	Apparent Purpose of Touch
1.			
2.			
3.			
4.			
5.			

1. Go to a mall, restaurant, movie theater lobby, or, weather permitting, shopping area. Watch the people walking around, focusing on adults. Who touches whom? Is the contact accepted? What are the genders, ages, possible relationships? Use the chart to write down your observations.
2. Observe the people around you—family, friends, and colleagues. Ask yourself the same questions: Who touches whom? Is the contact accepted? What are the genders, ages, possible relationships? Use the chart to write down your observations.
3. Now take some time to look at yourself. Whom do you touch? How? In what context? How are you touched? By whom?

Many of the cultural rules about touch and open displays of physical affection apply to premarital couples. There also are cultural rules for marital couples, but they are not as explicit. In many cultures, it is feared that couples might engage in sexual acts prior to marriage. Although prohibitions against premarital sex have loosened up in many parts of the Western world, in many cultural groups they have not. Many cultures keep the genders segregated, even after marriage. Latino immigrant families, for example, may seem to be overly restrictive about their daughters' whereabouts, fearing contamination by looser North American customs.

Argyle (1988) reviewed studies of cross-cultural touching and illustrated cultural differences in public displays of affection in three urban areas: San Juan, Puerto Rico; Paris, France; and London, England. Puerto Rican couples in San Juan touch each other publicly (in cafes) almost twice as much as Parisians, who are much more demonstrative than couples in London. In his review of other cultures, Argyle (1988) found that Japanese couples reported much less public touching than North American couples. "In public places in Japan there is very little bodily contact, not even hand-shaking. But, in crowded trains and buses, it is accepted. In private, there is a great deal of touching—there is less privacy so sleeping in the same room and bathing together do not have the sexual implications they have elsewhere" (Argyle, 1988, p. 60). Argyle's review found that the high-contact areas are in South American, Mediterranean, and Arab countries, and that touch occurs largely between people of the same sex. Low-contact cultures include European and North American groups, where touch is more formal and constrained.

EXERCISE 6.15 • Touching in Public

The purpose of this exercise is to observe how people respond to touch in crowded situations.

Go on a bus or train during rush hour. How do people hold themselves? What happens when you lean into someone? What happens if someone leans into you? If you have ever been to another country, try to recall similar situations and how people acted. Otherwise, find someone who has lived abroad and ask him or her about crowded situations.

Gibson, Harris, & Werner (1993, p. 180) point out that misinterpretations may occur due to cultural differences. A person from a contact culture may view his or her noncontact culture acquaintance as distant and aloof, whereas the individual from the noncontact culture may see his or her opposite as being overly assertive or intimate. Understanding that both high-contact and low-contact cultures are present in the United States can sensitize us to these differences to avoid misunderstanding and embarrassment.

Other examples of different contact preferences are noted by Poyatos (1983). If an American man were to shake hands with an Indian man, he might be surprised to find that the Indian kept holding his hands for several minutes while conversing. This might be uncomfortable for someone from a low-contact culture, who would fear some sexual meaning associated with this physical contact. In the United States, fathers and sons usually greet each other by shaking hands; in Russian, Latin, and Arab cultures, they hug and kiss. Women in some cultures kiss on the lips; in others, they brush cheeks. Same-sex displays of affection can arouse stronger homophobic anxieties in members of noncontact cultures than they do in members of contact cultures. Displays of affection have different meanings in different cultures. In some cultures, the physical display of affection between males and females is a precursor to sexual intercourse; in other cultures, it is part of the courtship or flirting process. Even within the United States, varying meanings can be attributed to different behaviors.

EXERCISE 6.16 • Self-Awareness: Contact

The purpose of this exercise is to learn more about your and others' comfort with contact.

Would you label yourself as high- or low-contact? Which feels more comfortable? Now consider your friends and colleagues. Which ones are high- or low-contact? Test your conclusions. Try making contact with them, such as a hand on their arm, a brief touch, or even a hug. Do they pull away or tense up? Alternatively, keep yourself physically apart from them. Do they try to make contact or ask you if something is wrong? Which behavior felt more normal for you? Consider what you have learned. How would you identify low- or high-contact people? What physical or verbal clues should you be looking for when interacting with them? Make a list of each type of clue. Add to it as you recognize more clues, and keep it at hand until you are familiar with it.

Many different kinds of friendship exist. Some friendships are personal and intimate; others are less personal and are based on sharing activities, work, or social life within a community. Still others are more acquaintanceships than they are friendships. Most cultural groups accept nonsexual same-gender intimate friendships. At the same time, opposite-gender friendships are prohibited, particularly in non-Western cultures where there often is segregation of the sexes. Such relationships often are viewed as precursors to sexual relationships. In other words, many cultures cannot conceive of the possibility of a nonsexual intimate relationship between males and females. In the Western world, suspicion about sexual relations between male and female work colleagues still abounds. Office romances are frequently frowned upon. The United States military and many business companies have formal nonfraternization policies. Often, the people involved in such relationships will try to keep their romances a secret. It is not unusual for husbands and wives to be uneasy about their spouses' business meetings and travel with colleagues of the opposite gender. This unease relates to the belief expressed more openly in other cultures that people, specifically men, cannot control their sex drives and that, given the opportunity, when two people of opposite genders are alone, sex will occur.

EXERCISE 6.17 • Comfort Levels with Public Displays of Affection

The purpose of this exercise is to further enhance your awareness of your comfort level with public displays of affection in certain situations.

Rate your comfort level with the following behaviors from 1 to 5. A high comfort level is 1; a high comfort level is 5.

	Comfort Rating				
Holding hands with same-sex friend	1	2	3	4	5
Holding hands with opposite-sex friend	1	2	3	4	5
Kissing opposite-sex friend on cheek	1	2	3	4	5
Kissing same-sex friend on cheek	1	2	3	4	5
Kissing opposite-sex friend on lips	1	2	3	4	5
Kissing same-sex friend on lips	1	2	3	4	5
Hugging same-sex friend	1	2	3	4	5
Hugging opposite-sex friend	1	2	3	4	5

Compare your list with those of others. Discuss what kinds of messages about sex and sexuality you received in your family. How comfortable are you talking about sex? Are you more comfortable with same-sex or opposite-sex friends? How do you know when someone is coming on to you? How do you let people know you are interested or not interested in them sexually? How do you get your needs met? How do you feel when others are not sensitive to your needs and wishes?

Gendered Sexual Behaviors

Cultures have different rules and roles for males and females with regard to sexual behaviors. For example, sexual boasting is characteristic of macho societies. If this type of verbal aggressive behavior is common and expected for men, it is condemned for women, although it may be tolerated with prostitutes (Desouza, 1997). Societies do exist where women can and do boast, although it usually occurs with other women, not with men. However, in most cultures, public aggressive behavior of women is frowned upon, whereas it is tolerated and sometimes encouraged for men.

Some cultures place more value on "feminine" qualities. Cultures high in spirituality, such as the Native American culture, place a high value on femininity, because they view many aspects of nature as feminine ("Mother Nature"). They regard the sky, wind, and mountains as having both masculine and feminine elements. In these cultures, women's sexuality seems to be more respected than in machoistic societies (Quintero, 1995). In these cases, femininity is synonymous with the expression of the female principles of nurturance and life-giving receptivity. These principles are considered to be as strong as the male principles of dominance, achievement, and intrusiveness and are thought to exist in balance and rhythm. The Yin Yang symbol associated with Buddhism expresses this idea. (The Yin Yang symbol, which appears on the Korean flag, is a circle with a wavy line through the middle, with a dark fish with a light eye chasing a white fish with a dark eye in an endless circle. It is intended to represent the total balance of things.)

In the history of the West, women have traditionally been considered to progress through three stages in life and to control life in at least two of these stages. The stages are maiden, mother, and crone. The maiden is the virgin, she who has yet to mature and give birth. The mother has given birth, a manifestation of the greatest earthly power. The crone controls death and wisdom (Hall, 1980; Harding, 1970). In Hindu mythology, the same god/goddess who creates also destroys, and male-female power is balanced in this way.

Social Relationships

Social relations are composed of relationships between individuals, family members, and others—neighbors, friends, work colleagues, and so on. One's social relationships depend on one's status in any given relationship system. We form a notion of who we are not just in relationship to our family, but also in relationship to those outside of our family. In most societies, the rules, roles, and scripts pertaining to social relationships are different from those pertaining to intimate relationships.

In the dominant United States culture, social relationships are more formal and distant, particularly for males, who tend to bond around activities and work. Just as with intimate relationships, in social relationships men tend to use more joking and humor and may seem to jockey for power and status more than women do. Women tend to seek and give approval, and emotional support and conversation are likely to revolve around feelings and family (Tannen, 1990). Individuals have expectations about the relationships they define as friendships, about correct and incorrect ways of doing things, about kinds and values of a variety of social relationships. These expectations vary across cultures.

The potential for misunderstanding exists among intercultural social relations. For example, the topics that are considered suitable for a new relationship may differ across cultures. The Chinese, for instance, when introduced to another, infer more information about the character of that person from nonverbal behaviors than do North Americans. There are many topics of conversation that they categorize as prohibitive. Chinese people may regulate relationship distancing in specific ways—either through the way they introduce themselves by family position or marriage status, or through some other indicators of social placement. North Americans, on the other hand, have a reputation for wanting to achieve "instant" intimacy. They do this by categorizing more topics as obligatory, believing that open self-disclosure fosters close relationships (Alexander, Cronen, Kang, Tsou, & Banks, 1986). As a result, Americans frequently are considered insincere and intrusive by members of other cultures.

Suspicion about different race and ethnicity may be masked in politeness, especially in cultures that avoid direct conflict or disruptions. For example, the Japanese often use a smile to mask negative comments or feelings (Triandis, 1994; Matsumoto, 1996b). Americans might misread this politeness as encouragement for them to be more open and forthcoming. This is likely to result in a pursuer/distancer relationship dynamic, whereby the more one person pursues, the more the other person distances. This, in turn, intensifies the pursuer's efforts and, likewise, intensifies the distancer's retreat, which is expressed by an even higher degree of masked politeness. Understanding and negotiation can occur only when this pursuer/distancer cycle is interrupted. Therefore, do not automatically equate a smile or the answer "yes" with an invitation for greater intimacy. Consider the potential of different cultural rules and expectations.

Politeness is expressed both verbally and nonverbally. It is not itself culture-specific, but the situations that call for politeness, the degree of politeness, and the form of expression are culture-specific. A smile is just one aspect of one possible polite expression (Ekman & Friesen, 1975; Ekman, 1994; Izard, 1994; Ekman, 1972; Izard, 1977). As discussed in Chapter 4, some aspects of facial expression are universal, and some emotions have universally recognized expressions, but cultural variations do exist. Many expressions, such as those associated with politeness, are not direct expressions of emotions, but are, rather, culturally coded expressions that involve emotions. What is allowable in specific situations is determined, as we saw in Chapter 4, by a society's "display rules." A given expression, or movement, or sign may be interpreted differently by members of different cultures. De Jongh (1991) notes that in Brazil, the Anglo-American "OK" sign of circled thumb and forefinger is considered to be obscene. It also is considered impolite in Greece and in the Soviet Union. The V-sign, shown with the back of the hand, is a rude gesture in Britain, but in Greece it simply indicates "two." Twirling the index finger around the ear, a gesture used in the United States to mean "crazy," is used in the Netherlands to indicate that someone is wanted on the telephone (Morris, 1994).

EXERCISE 6.18 • Politeness

The purpose of this exercise is to expand your awareness of expressions and gestures of politeness.

1. Make a list of all polite statements, such as "I am sorry" and "Would it be okay if." Think about the situations in which these statements arise. How would you view someone who used these statements in *all* situations or never used them? Discuss your ideas with others.
2. Make a list of polite expressions and gestures, such as smiles, nods, and so on. Again, consider the situations in which they are used. What happens when you see these expressions and gestures "out of context"? What if they are missing? Which expressions and gestures have multiple meanings? In other words, which are only polite in certain situations? What happens when someone else has a different idea of "polite" situations? Discuss your ideas and observations with others.
3. When is avoidance considered politeness? Think of situations and settings where you would avoid verbal and nonverbal communication because of your views about politeness. Again, discuss this with others.

EXERCISE 6.19 • Nonverbal Social Gestures

The purpose of this exercise is to become more aware of nonverbal social gestures in social situations.

For the next week, observe the nonverbal gestures and the distances people exhibit in social situations. For example, at a party, a meeting, in the cafeteria, or in a restaurant, become aware of how you draw inferences from others' nonverbal behaviors. Note who maintains eye contact, who averts his or her gaze, who fidgets, who paces, touches, gestures, nods, smiles, scowls, and what the circumstances are. Talk with others in your group about their observations and see whether you can develop a list of nonverbal gestures and their meanings used by people in different cultural groups. You may also observe television programs and movies.

The nature, level, and extent of social relationships is influenced by families as well as by the larger culture. Closed-system families exert a great control over social relationships, monitoring one's associations outside the family carefully. More open-system families have permeable boundaries, respecting and trusting family members to develop satisfactory social relations, and valuing intercultural friendships, although this permissibility does not always extend into love affairs or marriage.

Ethnicity also moderates social networks. One study by Cantor, Brennan, & Sainz (1994) compared white, African American and Latino American New Yorkers, age 65 and older, and found that the whites had the most inclusive social networks, although, geographically, they were widely dispersed. Latino elderly had narrow, family-centered networks, with kin living nearby. The networks of older African Americans were intermediate to those of Latinos and whites, being less inclusive than whites and Latinos, but with kin living nearby. The researchers found that, in addition to ethnicity, other factors, such as income level, gender, and functional ability, also influence social relationship networks. In countries such as the United States, Great Britain, and France, where the demographics are becoming more multicultural, there is increasing contact between members of different cultural groups in schools and the workplace, leading to the development of more intercultural social relationships regardless of the family's or culture's proscriptions (Okun, 1996).

Public Relationships

Public relationships refer to those we maintain at work or at school. They are the relationships over which we exert the most control, and in which we are most aware of status and power differentials. They also are likely to be least congruent with our internal values and beliefs. Most of us attempt to conform to the dominant culture in our public relationships in order to avoid censure. Thus, the rules, roles, and scripts in these relationships may be strikingly different from those in our social and personal relationships. Certainly, distance is greater, contact is less, and we are more careful to mask our true feelings.

One of the difficulties that women and minority groups have faced in public relationships is that they are not as familiar with nor as practiced at the rules, roles, and scripts as are the dominant white male players. This is because their personal cultures often have different values and practices. Their socialization does not prepare them for participation in the dominant culture. For example, as women entered management levels and professions previously dominated by men, they tended, at first, to adopt male-determined styles of leadership and professional behavior. As more women moved into these levels and positions, they pioneered ways of being that were more congruent with their feminine styles and values.

Unless one has a mentor, one often must make one's own way in such situations by trial and error. Over the years, we learn social behaviors through observation of others. We need to learn when to be present and visible, when to slip into the background, when to leave a task, when to persist, when to conform, when to resist. The rules for these behaviors may vary, depending on gender, age, or status. Women are learning that employers' attitudes and tolerance for certain behaviors are different for women than they are for men.

Culture-specific factors, such as saving face and keeping face, protecting one's dignity, and avoiding negative or undue attention and conflict, shape the rules of public relationships. In most cultures, aggression and the display of emotion are discouraged in public life, although in the United States this varies drastically by class and gender. From childhood, across cultures, one is taught the rules of one's dominant culture. All parents want their children to be safe and secure, to "fit in."

Gender

Gender affects intimate, social, and public relationships. Gender differences in families are associated with role constraints within the family, and these also may influence our relationships outside the family. We learn our notions, rules, roles, and scripts about gender from our earliest experiences in our family. Although gender ideology shapes our expectations of males and females, the ideology does not always correspond to behavior (Del Castillo, 1993).

In all cultures, women bear the children and are held responsible for the major tasks of early child-rearing, whether these tasks are defined by the fathers, by religion, or by cultural rules. In some cultures, child-rearing is turned over to others, or to the larger community. For example, on a traditional Israeli kibbutz or on some Native American reservations, children may be raised collectively by the entire community or by designated persons of either sex who are not necessarily the biological parents. In the United States, mothers generally are legally accountable for child-rearing, regardless of cultural factors. One result of this is that mothers usually get custody of children in a divorce. Even when women work the same hours as their male partners, they usually end up taking responsibility for most of the child-rearing. They are in charge of day care arrangements or are the ones who miss work when a child is sick.

All of these actions correspond to our stereotypic assumptions and expectations about mothers. In recent years, however, gender rights for men have been spawned in the United States in reaction to the gains achieved by the women's movement. A "men's rights" movement, advocating fatherhood for divorced dads and more equitable child-rearing decisions and practices, has begun. This challenges the cultural assumption that women are by nature the "better parent." The term *Mom,* in fact, is more of a functional label than it is a gender-linked label. In an increasing number of families, the husband stays home with the children while the wife works full time. In one such couple, for example, the husband takes responsibility for primary childcare during the school year while his wife works full-time. In the summer, the couple reverses their roles. The husband works full-time and the wife takes care of the children. As a result, Mom gets called "Dad" and Dad gets called "Mom" after each changeover.

EXERCISE 6.20 • Gender Attributes

The purpose of this exercise is for you to examine your and others' assumptions about male and female characteristics.

Fold a piece of paper in half vertically. In the lefthand column, write down all the attributes that you associate with females. In the righthand column, write down all the attributes that you associate with males. Put a "B" beside those attributes that you think have a biological origin, an "S" beside those that you think are due to socialization, a "+" by those that you feel positive about, and a "–" by those that you feel negative about. Compare your list with others' and see if you can arrive at a consensus.

EXERCISE 6.21 • Gendered Child-rearing

The purpose of this exercise is to check your assumptions about male and female responsibilities and obligations with regard to child-rearing.

In a small group, make a list of child-rearing activities. If you have children, mark which activities the father and/or mother performs. Add a "+" if the activities are frequently performed, a "–" if the activities are performed rarely, and an "=" if the activities are performed equally by both. If you do not have children, ask a friend who has children to fill out who does what. Have your spouse or the spouse of your friend fill out a similar list. Compare your results with those of spouses and other people who have completed the exercise. What expectations are evident? What surprised you? If you want, fill out such a list for your parents and compare their answers to current practices. Are there any changes? You also can expand the list to include people from different cultures. Ask them to fill out a list and compare results.

Distribution of Power

Traditionally, families, work, and education systems expect complementary relationships between genders. This is based on the ingrained cultural assumption that, due to biological differences, males have more power and privilege, and also on the assumption that males are more valued. The degree of this complementarity varies across cultural groups. In patrifocal cultures, there is a myth of male superiority; females tend to protect their men and this mythology by behaving deferentially in public.

The public persona that one learns to play outside the family can be confusing both to the person playing the role and to respondents, in that the boundaries between what is "real" and what is "role playing" become blurred. In some cultures, there is no role playing as both genders are equally valued holistically, although there may be some dimensions where one gender is valued more or less than the other. Interestingly, in the United States, the spiritual power of woman is valued more by the indigenous Navajo culture than by any other cultural group. In Native American cultures, as previously mentioned, everything is conceptualized as having both male and female aspects and qualities (even such things as rain and mountains). Religion is believed to have been brought to the Navajo people by a woman and kept by a man (Quintero, 1995).

Ucko (1994) points to the integration of African and American gender role ideologies as being a possible influence on the high rate of wife abuse in African American families. The African heritage of relative equality, respect, and interdependence between spouses collides with the male dominance/female subservience concept of the dominant North American culture. This collision is exacerbated by the prejudice and socioeconomic deprivation experienced by African Americans, particularly by males, who experience a lack of job opportunities for the working class. This leads to emotional turmoil and is manifested in a cycle of violence and guilt. Just as female slaves achieved higher status by being assigned to housework rather than to menial work in the fields, African American women today have more opportunity to attain higher-status educational and employment possibilities than do African American males (Carter, 1995; Boyd-Franklin, 1989; Comas-Diaz & Greene, 1994). The sequelae of years of slavery results in black women's awareness of the hardship and powerlessness that African American males experience in the world. Black women may be more likely to forgive male aggression and work hard to protect their partner's "face." An example of this is the support O. J. Simpson received from older black women when he was accused of spousal abuse and murder.

Inequalities of power between men and women are not unique to Latino or African American cultures. Disproportional power and gender role expectations have been identified in Filipino cultures (Root, 1997), Appalachian cultures, (Lemon, Newfield, & Dobbins, 1993), Asian cultures (Comas-Diaz & Greene, 1994) and Cambodian cultures (Frye & D'Avanzo, 1994).

In immigrant and refugee families, as well as in other struggling families, women are seen as the "cultural brokers" who facilitate adaptation and acculturation to mainstream society (Espin, 1995). Consider that in many immigrant situations, the men come to the United States alone and work to send money back to their families. When women come to the United States, they are more likely to focus on relatives and family care and may not interact with the society at large as much as men do. Even though overt displays of power and control are traditionally under the purview of males, within the family, the senior women often have the power and control. In many Latino and Asian families, women use less obvious forms of influence in an instrumental manner. They may actively seek jobs for the men in their family by obtaining information, making phone calls, and so on. Likewise, Mexican and Russian women immigrants to the United States, and African American women migrants from the south to the north, are often the family members who take the initiative in the decision making regarding migration, employment, and schooling for themselves and family members.

Traditional male and female authority often is challenged by the younger generations, who are exposed to the more egalitarian mores of the dominant culture. The resulting differences in socialization and values create stress within the family along both generational and gender lines. In traditional, patriarchal societies where the family is the source of decision making, both senior men and women exert a considerable power. As the role of the family becomes diminished through assimilation into our individualistic society, both senior men and women lose status and power. We often see men's needs to cling to tradition or to assert their dwindling authority result in feelings of possessiveness, jealousy, and acts of violence. One way that this is played out is that women may be blamed for children's school difficulties, for men's job failures, or for any other family difficulties. As more and more immigrant and oppressed women are exposed to women's egalitarian roles in the United States, whether through the media or through actual observation, their self-images and interactional behaviors begin to change. This can result in tenacious power struggles between men who are eager to preserve the heretofore status quo and women who are eager for greater assimilation. The same struggle can occur between parents who want to maintain close family systems and children who want to establish open family practices (Espin, 1995).

Women's need to cling to tradition or to assert their dwindling authority is played out between them and their daughters and is expressed in dress, eating habits, and other "domestic" spheres. As immigrants, Muslim or orthodox Jewish women may continue to wear their head coverings when out in the secular world, although their daughters may discard them when they enter public school. Mothers have more difficulty accepting daughters' being different from them than they do accepting their sons' differences, which are present from birth. They are facing a loss of power in relation to both their spouses and their children, and they often are stricter about maintaining tradition.

The influence of the culture in the United States regarding the meaning and practice of open sexuality can create a tremendous dilemma for family cultures with more closed views about sexuality. Changing dress or talking to members of the opposite sex may be viewed as leading to dangerous sexual behavior. This cultural collision can be viewed by male fathers and priests as a "weakness" or "flaw" of the mother rather than as a cultural impasse, thus increasing a need on the part of the mother to maintain traditional practices.

Because women of all cultures have experienced the oppression that results from what the culture says women's roles should be, a certain empathic attunement exists among women, across cultures. However, although there are some shared values and experiences of oppression, most white women have no idea of the marginalization, oppression, and disempowerment of women of color and of women in lower socioeconomic classes. These women are marginalized not just for their gender, but also for their color and cultural practices. Like white men, white women take certain privileges for granted and benefit from the color of their skin.

EXERCISE 6.22 • Entitlements

The purpose of this exercise is to become aware of your and others' assumptions about entitlements and obligations.

This exercise can be done individually or as a group. In your work or class setting, ask at least five people of your own gender and five of the opposite gender what they see as their entitlements and obligations regarding sex, money, decisionmaking, child care, social relations, leisure time, housing, housework, and work life in today's family. What gender differences emerge? What class differences emerge? What ethnic differences emerge? Repeat the exercise, using race or ethnicity as the variable.

EXERCISE 6.23 • Energy Investment

The purpose of this exercise is to see how different people proportion their investments of energy (effort) in different areas of their lives.

How do people balance their investments of energy? How do you and your partner negotiate the differences in your needs and values in order to achieve balance in your relationship? In some relationships, there is *complementarity,* where, for example, one partner puts more energy into the couple's domestic life and the other puts more energy into work in order to provide for the couple. Other relationships may be more *symmetrical,* where each partner is expected to invest the same amount of energy into the different areas of life.

The diagram in Figure 1 shows one's energy investment as being proportional in several different areas—self, spouse, children, family of origin/kin, work, friends, community, and avocation/leisure. Each member of your group should redraw the diagram so that it accurately reflects his or her energy investments in the various areas. Have members ask their significant others to draw the same kind of diagram. How do people negotiate the differences in order to achieve balance?

Gilligan (1982) and others have shown how the pathways of white North American female development differ from those of white North American male development. Although not enough data exist for us to generalize cross-culturally, we do know that women in most cultures function more relationally than do the instrumentality-oriented (achievement- and productivity-oriented) males. When family is very important in a culture, women tend to have defined roles and rights in order to maintain their family honor and economic status. Women's status tends to be high in simple cultivation societies and in places where women work cooperatively with one another or in complementary relationship with their husbands. "There is a curvilinear relationship between societal complexity and sex equality" (Giele & Smock, 1977, p. 9). In agrarian societies, where the descent is through the father (patrilineal), women have the fewest options and are most role-restricted. This was typified in the 1800s, when mail-order brides were sent to farmers in the western United States.

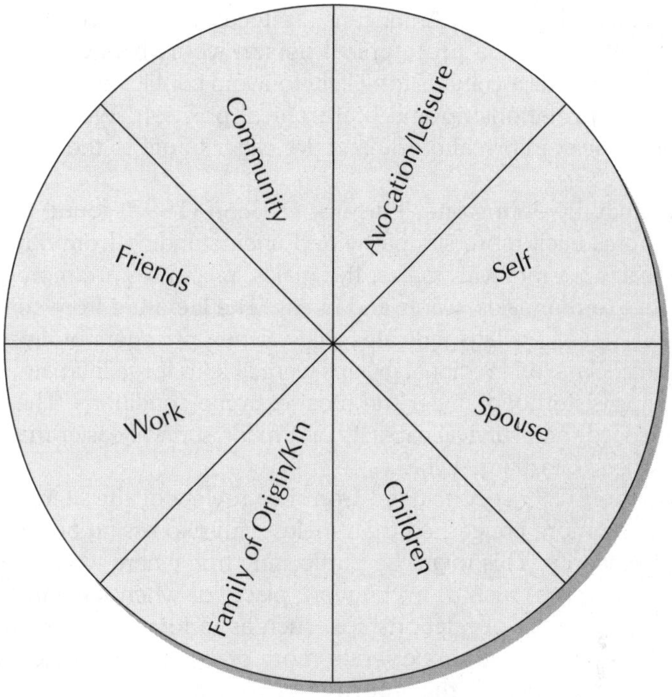

FIGURE 1 • Proportional Investments of Energy

Communication

Several gendered conversation styles have been explicated by Tannen (1990), Cathcart & Samovar (1992), Erber & Gilmour (1994), and others. Women's conversation styles reflect their emphasis on relations. Women tend to self-disclose more than males, believing that this will increase intimacy, a desired end for women who tend to define their self in relation to others. There is more touching among women in most cultures than there is among men or between men and women, except for erotic situations. Women, perhaps because of their relational expertise, express and exhibit more empathic attunement to the needs of others. Valentine (1995) found that women, more so than men, tend to handle conflict with compromise and avoidance; competition was the least-favored strategy. Men are much more likely to engage in debate, argument, and competition.

Even among women, however, there are cultural differences. Chinese women, for example, may regard more topics as unmentionable than do middle-class North American women (Alexander, Cronen, Kang, Tsou, & Banks, 1986). English women tend to withdraw more into themselves and reveal less than North American women (McNeill, 1992). People from eastern cultures, which tend to be collectivistic, are more concerned about how to behave appropriately given one's relationship to specific people in the situation, whereas middle-class North Americans are focused more on changing behavior to conform to how a prototypical person would behave. Thus, women and men from eastern cultures are likely to avoid conflict and focus on the establishment of relationship and hierarchical position. Westerners, on the other hand, speak informationally and are eager to get to the main topic and point.

One study by Johnstone, Ferrara, & Bean (1992) found that females across cultures elicit more sympathy and understanding from other females. When females interact with males, the males' responses are more joking and are attentive to the males' wants and needs. The literature from concentration camps and Stalinist gulags indicates that women prisoners of diverse ethnic, generational, class, and regional groups were able to forge intimate, supportive relationships (sisterhood) under the most extreme conditions. These relationships enhanced their survival capacity and made survival easier than it was for male prisoners (Ginzburg, 1968).

Shimanoff (1994) concluded from her review of the literature that females may be more concerned than males with expressing approval, fellowship, and solidarity. This might be particularly true where women are considered status inferiors, such as in the work place, or when they are considered to be the emphasizer of relationships, such as in female and friendship networks. Males and Westerners operate more on a scientific, objectivist model and focus on getting all the information out on the table. Females and easterners, on the other hand, rely more on a relational, subjective model, using the accumulated wisdom of their elders and groups to establish and ratify relationships before getting "down to business." These gender and cultural differences are critical in business or government negotiations, as well as in professional relationships. They influence all interactions. With an increasingly culturally diverse population, it is important for teachers and business people to take these differences into account when preparing lessons, contracts, or negotiations.

Perhaps even more important, males and females have different assumptions about the purpose of communicating. As you may have noticed, these differences are similar to the differences between individualistic and collectivistic cultures. Western males typically want to solve problems in a focused and direct manner. Women want to express their feelings and have discussions, rather than merely exchange information. Although they may be direct in their relationship negotiating, they are also attuned to the many levels of indirect communication.

Some cultures are more direct than others and, within cultures, certain topics or settings are more prone to directness than others. Directness is a valued attribute in the dominant United States culture. Psychologists tell people to "say what they mean." Business people want to "get down to business." Indirectness is undesirable, and people who are indirect may be labeled as shy, dishonest, insincere, untrustworthy, or as possessing other negative qualities. The situation is very different in other societies. Many cultures regard the avoidance of face-to-face conflict, at *all* costs, as more important than directness—especially (but not exclusively) in collectivistic societies (Triandis, 1994). In Japan, where one must never offend a superior or threaten social relations, indirectness has become an art (Matsumoto, 1996b; Tannen, 1990). In fact, more cultures practice elaborate systems of indirectness than value the direct approach practiced in the United States (Tannen, 1990).

EXERCISE 6.24 • Expression of Conflict

The purpose of this exercise is to become more aware of your comfort level with differing expressions of conflict.

1. How would you write a script telling someone that his or her idea is inappropriate or flawed? Role play it with a partner, taking turns reading each role. Is your approach direct or indirect? Does your partner find the script direct or indirect? How do you feel in each role? Now, role play again, reading your script to each of the persons listed here:
   - a superior; an equal; a subordinate
   - someone of the same gender; someone of the opposite gender
   - a friend; a colleague; a new acquaintance
   - someone from a different cultural group
2. Rewrite your script to be first extremely direct and then extremely indirect. Now complete step number 1 again.
3. What feels comfortable? What would happen if two people met and each had a different script in mind? How can you recognize that the other person is acting out a different script? Mark the points to watch for on your script.

In many cultures, women have learned to understand the values that are reflected in the verbal and nonverbal communication styles of men. Without this learning, it would be difficult to survive in a male-dominated culture. However, males and other members of a dominant culture (for example, whites, as opposed to people of color) can choose whether or not to learn about and understand the values and communication styles of nondominant groups. This is another example of how those with power have more choices than those with less power. The powerful can choose to ignore the less powerful. The less powerful do so at their own risk.

Assimilation and Acculturation

There is a belief within the white dominant culture in the United States that everyone aspires to be like whites—to share the same values, attitudes, beliefs, and expectations. Therefore, minorities are tolerated and accepted as long as they "think and act" like the dominant group. In other words, they are accepted as long as they conform to the dominant cultural pattern. The assumption is that anyone, with the right kind of work ethic, can attain the privileges of the dominant culture. Those who do not are considered "lazy" or "stupid"—flawed in some way. These thoughts are in line with the traditionalist assimilationist contract in this country. This contract embraces English as the national language, liberal democratic principles, and the Protestant work ethic. Schools are the traditional tools of those who promote this form of assimilation. Schools enforce the mastery of a dominant language and culture. How many people whose parents or grandparents are immigrants know their parents' or grandparents' primary language? Although the past model of assimilation has been one of conformity, the myth has been one of a "melting pot," where all cultures contribute part of their unique cultures to the creation of a new, distinct culture. A growing conflict today arises from the multiculturalists' push for a model of partial assimilation, in which cultures retain aspects of their own culture, such as language, certain customs, and beliefs (Levinson, 1996). Many immigrant and minority groups want to maintain their cultural identities. Other groups want the society at large to recognize that the reality is neither conformity nor a "melting pot," that race and classism make assimilation impossible. These groups often simultaneously blame the unassimilated for their lack of conformity and success.

The difficulty for marginalized families, as well as for immigrant and refugee families, is that adaptation to mainstream American society demands modification of and even abandonment of their own cultural traditions and cherished customs. Those families that resist assimilation to the dominant culture may rigidify their customs and traditions, isolating and insulating their families from "others." This reaction can result in future generational splits, pitting the youngsters—whose psychological experiences in this society differ vastly from their parents' experiences growing up—against their elders. The dilemma is whether or not it is possible to preserve one's cultural identity while acculturating to the United States society.

Every cultural group has had a different experience in assimilation, resulting from its members' physical appearance, the reasons for migration or immigration, the generation in which the assimilation occurred, and the skill and educational level of its members. Some refugees or immigrants, such as Haitians, Cambodians, Vietnamese, and Mexicans, are viewed by the dominant society as "intruders," while others, such as Russians, Koreans, Chinese, and Japanese, often are welcomed for their class status and technical expertise. Illegal immigrants receive very different treatment than do legal refugees. The acceptance that migrating African Americans experience from their own community may be different from what they experience from the dominant white community when they migrate to urban areas seeking greater employment. The community into which one moves affects the experience. There are issues of verbal and nonverbal language, communication and relationship patterns, work styles, attitudes toward time, space, energy, and so on.

EXERCISE 6.25 • Immigrant Experiences

The purpose of this exercise is to develop your understanding of the experiences of immigrants to the United States and of migrants to your geographical area.

Think about people you have met in your class, at work, or in your community, or people who are members of your extended family. Select two or three who have immigrated to this country or who have migrated from another area, and talk to them about their assumptions, expectations, and actual experiences. Ask them what their aspirations were before they moved, what they are now, what they want for themselves in this society, what they are willing to give up or change about their traditional expectations in order to meet these goals, what difficulties they are experiencing, who in their family is having the easiest time, and who is having the most difficult time. What can you learn about the different elements involved in acculturation and assimilation? If your family migrated or moved in the last few generations and the people involved are still alive, ask them the same questions. Are there temporal differences? Differences due to origin, religion, skin color, or other factors?

Class

Throughout this text, we have emphasized the ways in which socioeconomic class, whether inherited or attained through achievement, impacts every single one of us. Socioeconomic class refers to more than just level of income. It includes verbal and nonverbal language usage, dress and presentation styles, educational level, acceptable occupations, leisure and social time styles, and a mindset shaped by certain values, attitudes, interests, beliefs, and behaviors. In short, each socioeconomic class can be considered as a distinct culture group.

EXERCISE 6.26 • Your Socioeconomic Class

The purpose of this exercise is to become aware of your definitions of and stereotypes about your socioeconomic class and that of others.

Write down on a piece of paper what socioeconomic class you think you belong to today, what class your parents belong to, and what class your grandparents belong to. What are your reasons for your classification? Now look around the room and write down what socioeconomic class each member of the group belongs to. How did you make those judgments? On the basis of appearance? Language? Setting? If it feels comfortable, check your list with others' lists and discuss the similarities and dissimilarities. Discuss the assumptions that shaped the categories to which you assigned each person.

Lower-class members in the United States struggle with daily living needs such as housing, safety, and food. They do not have access to the same community, educational, health, legal, and social resources as do higher-class, wealthier individuals, nor have they the transportation means to get to certain jobs or school programs. They are at a great disadvantage with regard to dress, educational props, cultural supports, and other advantages when competing with higher-class individuals. Due to these deprivations, they may face more illness, dental decay, risk for substance abuse, and confinement to low-level jobs. Security and upward mobility may not be possible for them under any circumstances. As part of the cultural discrimination, the daily stresses and hassles faced by the underprivileged are overwhelming. Family and intimate relations often become targets for the frustration and rage that results. Consequently, this population is also at severe risk for fragmented families, homelessness, domestic violence.

Although most of what we have been discussing applies to members of the lower, or working, class, the increasing homeless population makes up the lowest rung of our society. People who are homeless come from all segments of society. They are very vulnerable in their current circumstances.

EXERCISE 6.27 • Observation of Homelessness

The purpose of this exercise is to learn more about homelessness and your feelings about it.

Walk around neighborhoods in your community or in nearby communities where the homeless appear. Watch them carefully and note how they relate to each other and how they panhandle. Observe not only their verbal and nonverbal behaviors, but your own verbal and nonverbal reactions as well. You may try to find a homeless person to speak to or go to a shelter and ask for permission to talk to a couple of people. Discuss your experiences with others in your group who have done this exercise and see what you learn about different people's responses. How do you feel about your own privilege? Do you feel any shame or anger?

EXERCISE 6.28 • Fantasy of Loss of Privilege

In this exercise, you will imagine how you would respond to loss of privilege.

Now imagine that you were to lose your source of income, your residence, and all of the assets and privileges you take for granted. What are your worst fears? What do you think will happen to you? On whom do you think you can rely for help? What kind of help would you accept? If this were to happen to a close relative, what would you be willing to do to help? What if this predicament happened to a friend?

EXERCISE 6.29 • Fantasy of Upward Mobility

Now consider how your life and self-concept might change with upward mobility.

Imagine that you were to rise to the next higher socioeconomic class. How do you think your life would be different? What would you have to do to get there, to stay there, and what would you have to give up? What kinds of privileges do you think you might have? What personal behaviors and customs might keep you from actually gaining membership in a higher class?

Social scientists are just beginning to look at the families from which resilient members are able to transcend the effects of deprivation and oppression. Certainly, native intelligence and strong determination on the part of the individual are factors in whether the person's efforts will be successful. More important, however, is the fact that if at least one parent or some type of mentor, neighbor, teacher, clergy, or relative, has been able to create a climate of secure attachment and consistent discipline for a youngster, that relationship can serve as a springboard for finding a way to access more opportunity. Anecdotal data indicates that the role model often has a dream that becomes the inspiration for the youngster. The American dream, however, is not a high probability for most people who contend with the daily struggles of minimal survival (Okun, 1996).

Religion

Religion can have a major influence on intimate relationships and family systems. The more orthodox or fundamentalist religions tend to promote patriarchal family structures and community cohesiveness. As a result, they have the most influence on individuals and families, directing many facets of daily living. Islam, for example, has specific rules for how people interact within the family, and with same-gender and other-gender members outside of the family. It also has specific rules regarding the foods, rituals, and other customs that comprise routine living. The lives of orthodox Jews are similarly influenced by religious rules. The Baptist church determines appropriate behavior for southern Baptists, forbidding them from dancing, playing cards, or drinking.

Fundamentalist religions promote a "we–they" attitude between members of the church and those who are not. This attitude causes splits between family members who invest in religious observance and those who question the authority of the religion (Whipple, 1987). In these groups, guidance is sought only from those with authority in the church who have the responsibility of leadership. Typically, the chain of command places God first, husbands second, and wives last. The focus on "having faith" places the locus of control outside the individual and emphasizes prayer, perseverance, and forgiveness as primary functions of family units.

Castex (1994) points out that there are intercultural religious influences. There is, for example, an increase of conversion to Protestantism among Latino immigrants. Many of these Latino immigrants were practicing Catholics upon their arrival to this country. Smith-Hefner (1994) reports increasing conversion to Christianity among southeast Asian groups who have immigrated to the United States. Their conversion enables them to assimilate more easily, participating in a new array of social habits and American cultural values. In contrast, many previously Protestant African/Americans are converting to Islam (Carter, 1995; Cose, 1992). This may reflect their focus on ethnic pride and social activism. It is important to distinguish between the two kinds of Islam prevalent in the United States: the traditional Sunni, or Shiite, Islam and Farrakhan's Nation of Islam. The latter is more controversial than the former, and both sects are vying for African American members.

EXERCISE 6.30 • Effects of Religion (Part 1)

The purpose of this exercise is to become more aware of the effects of religion on your relationships with others.

Have each person in the group state what his or her religious affiliation is, how important it is in their lives (on a scale of 1 to 5, 1 being low and 5 being high), and what the impact of their religion is on their relationships with others. Because of the traditional separation of church and state in the United States, people often feel uncomfortable talking about the presence or influence of religion in their lives, so this may not be a comfortable exercise. That in itself, however, will be instructive in informing you about the impact of religion on relationships.

EXERCISE 6.31 • Effects of Religion (Part 2)

Now we will focus on the effects of religion on interfaith families.

Think about any couples you know (even in your own family) who are of different religions. How important has this been to them and to their families of origin? Have they ignored, compromised, or accommodated either of their families? What has been the impact on other family members and on their children?

Church participation is, and has been since Reconstruction, very important in rural southern black communities. In urban settings, African Americans have found more secular opportunities to achieve social status. However, in the United States, across cultural groups, there is an increase in religious affiliation in Catholic, Protestant, Jewish, Buddhist, Mormon, and other sects. Perhaps this is in response to the stresses of urbanization and the destruction of community and extended family groups.

Although there seems to be an increasing worldwide polarization between fundamentalist religions and more liberal religions, family rules, roles, and scripts have remained fairly constant. As family members become more orthodox or fundamentalist, strained relations among family members may result in family break-offs. There is an increasing number of interfaith and intercultural marriages. The concept of hemogomy (marrying your own kind) is lessening, not just in the Western world, but also in mideastern and eastern cultures. Much of this is attributable to increased travel and media access, to say nothing of the World Wide Web.

Western and Asian religions depict different styles of religious observance. Western religions promote the individual, who is responsible for him- or herself alone. Asian religions promote the abolishment of the individual, who is just part of the collective whole. Iannaccone (1995) outlines the differences between Western and Asian religions: (1) Western religions focus on collective action, with the congregation as the basic unit of religious production. Membership is expected, and diversification is discouraged. (2) Asian religions are family-based and focus on household rituals, on individuals' exchanges with the gods (that is, purchase of charms), and on encouragement of diversification. Membership is a meaningless construct.

There has been an increased interest by members of Western cultures in the wholistic spirituality of Asian and Native American cultures. Also, Asian immigrants (Plais and Sanders, 1994) are bringing about a revival of Buddhism among second- and third-generation immigrants as well as among a growing number of western converts. These Asian and Native American cultures have traditions of storytelling and view mind, body, and spirit as intertwining elements of the whole. In the United States, eastern medical practices, such as acupuncture, and cultural practices, such as yoga and meditation, are slowly being incorporated into mainstream Western medicine. Religious and spiritual communities provide a basis for connection and well-being among their members. Westerners' fascination with eastern spiritualities and religions is increasing, indicating a yearning for more collectivistic and spiritual values. This, perhaps, accounts for the increase of evangelism, primarily among the white population, throughout the United States.

Race and Ethnicity

As previously discussed, everyone has a racial and/or ethnic identity, although we are not always conscious of it. Both, to various extents, are social constructs. The boundaries for a specific type are defined by society, although there is a biological component to race. The terms need to be defined, since people come at them differently, depending on their history and cultural affiliation.

EXERCISE 6.32 • Defining Race and Ethnicity

The purpose of this exercise is to help you to clarify and become more aware of your definitions and meaning of race and ethnicity.

1. Define *race* and *ethnicity.* Consider the types of attributes associated with each term. Give a few examples.
2. Compare and discuss your definitions with others.
3. Consider as a group where the boundaries are between different races or ethnicities and between the terms *race* and *ethnicity.* For example, some North American Jews are more shaped by their ethnic (Jewish) identity than by their racial (Caucasian, Latino, African, or other) identity. Blacks from the Caribbean experience themselves and others differently than do African Americans. There are overlaps as well as differences between race and ethnicity.

As is apparent from the preceding exercise, people ascribe different attributes to the terms *race* and *ethnicity,* or ascribe different boundaries to them. In the United States, a person with an African American ancestor is considered African American. In Brazil, on the other hand, a person with a Caucasian ancestor is considered white, no matter how dark or African his or her features. The categories, their boundaries, and the attributes that "count" are determined by the dominant culture, not by some objective, scientific set of standards.

Race, in North America, is based on physical features, primarily skin color. These physical features are then assumed to connote attitude, behaviors, interests, and values. In reality, all "racial" groups incorporate several smaller cultural units, as socioeconomic class, religion, gender, and other factors are equally influential.

In some societies, ethnicity and race are synonymous. In the United States, ethnicity tends to reflect national origin, especially for whites. Unlike race, in which society decides whether or not an individual belongs to a particular category, ethnicity is a self-assigned definition in which a group such as Irish-Catholics, Portuguese, or Jews, claims membership to a self-defined cultural group. Again, individual members are assumed to represent the whole, but it is easier for the individual to claim or disclaim membership. As with race, class, religion, and gender are important factors.

For people of color, who have a long history of experiencing marginalization, discrimination, and oppression in the United States, racial self-definition usually predominates over other identities (Carter, 1995). The history of cultural, individual, and institutional racism cannot help but have a profound psychological impact on people's psychological development and well-being. These psychological impacts lead to invisibility, a sense of being in a place where one is not acknowledged or recognized and has no legitimacy or validity. People of color often suffer from internalized racism, believing that white is better and feeling guilty for believing that some of the negative social attitudes about people of color must be true. This, in turn, heightens their negative self-evaluations, the stresses they experience from daily racist hassles, and their feelings of isolation and racial exclusion. As pointed out by Steele (1997), internalized negative stereotyping can have a major impact on learning and job functioning. Other nondominant groups also suffer from internalized negative stereotyping. Gays and lesbians often internalize homophobia, and Jews may internalize anti-Semitism.

Racial socialization explains the phenomenological differences within and between racial groups. One's personality and psychological life are shaped by how one interprets and responds to messages from family, neighborhood, community, school, church, media, and larger social forces about one's attributes, characteristics, qualities, and opportunities, and about the barriers that are associated with one's racial grouping. Since whiteness is a constructed dominant norm in our society, all people of color are subject to devaluing feedback. There is even data to indicate that different racial paths lead toward different achievement-related strategies—that is, strategies that serve as the means for gaining status. For whites, individualism, the Protestant work ethic, and a balance in different aspects of self lead to more achievement-related strategies. For blacks, collectivism, ethnic identity, and low endorsement of individualism lead to achievement-related strategies (Oyserman, Gant, & Ager, 1995). Likewise, McMiller, & Weisz (1996) found that seeking help for students having learning difficulties in school was not the preferred strategy for African Americans, and Latino families, compared to Caucasian families for whom it is the preferred strategy.

EXERCISE 6.33 • Racial Insensitivity (Part 1)

The purpose of this exercise is to become more aware of verbal and nonverbal racial insensitivity.

For one week, write down every racially insensitive comment you hear. Listen carefully. Also write down negative nonverbal behaviors. For example, note when a white person steps back from a person of color on the elevator or avoids sitting next to someone of color on the subway. Be vigilant with this task and become alert to how prevalent racially insensitive verbal and nonverbal behaviors are in daily life. Remember, your personal history and culture will affect what you perceive and identify as racially insensitive. Be open-minded and hypersensitive. What you consider an innocuous comment, someone else might consider an insult.

EXERCISE 6.34 • Racial Insensitivity (Part 2)

Now we will focus on being a token in a different cultural setting.

Go into a restaurant, store, or neighborhood park where your race, ethnicity, or sexual orientation is different from the others in that setting. You may take a partner along if you like. Stay there as long as possible and notice not only how you feel, but the ways others react to your presence.

Even within family systems, racial or ethnic differences may not be talked about or may be glossed over. In some multiracial families or in families of color, people with lighter color skin receive privileges and advantages not given to members with darker skins. This discrimination, called *colorism,* is one of the legacies of racism. The value that white is better has been internalized by people of color. Most often, what happens in public settings is that people of color who mingle with the dominant culture at school, at work, or in the community are ignored by the people they interact with at school, at work, or in the community; they are invisible outside the context of their school, work, or community role interactions. Private, social relationships are often nonexistent. As long as they "play the white man's game" in school, work, or community interactions by observing his rules, roles, and scripts, they are accepted and included. No one refers to their different appearance; everyone expects them to share or aspire to "universal" middle-class values and interests. In short, they are allowed to participate as long as they act as though they are white.

People of color and/or different ethnicity who work or live in mainstream dominant culture systems have learned to "fit in"—to use the same language, food practices, and dress of the dominant culture. When they are with other members of their racial or ethnic group or are in the privacy of their own homes and communities, their language and food practices may become more culture-specific. They can stop role playing and can relax comfortably and practice their own cherished customs with people with whom they feel kinship. As with gender, the boundaries between what is "real" and what is "role playing" can become blurred to the individual, to his or her community, and to society at large.

Racism and ethnocentrism may enhance the intimate relationships of the oppressed. They may take validation from each other and depend on mutual support. Together, they may find a safe harbor against societal oppression. On the other hand, intimate relationships may be destroyed by the substance abuse, unemployment, and futility that are associated with persistent discrimination.

Choice and Privilege

Political, economic, and social resources affect one's ability or capacity to make and implement choices regarding lifestyle, particularly those that violate cultural customs. Frequently, those enjoying the most privileges are least aware of their privileges. It is something that they have always had and, therefore, it is something they take for granted.

Obviously, those with more privilege have more choices. Privilege has to do with the racial, socioeconomic, and dominant cultural group into which one is born. In the United States, the dominant white Protestant male has been born into power. The wealthier ones have automatic privilege to determine the rules, roles, and structures that shape the fabric of our society and livelihoods. Sharing in these privileges also are those who are less wealthy, and also white Protestant women. McIntosh (1989) identifies multiple daily effects of being born into privilege, such as being able to live where one wants, socialize with people of one's race when one wants, go shopping without being followed or harassed, learn about one's history or culture readily, be assured that one's children receive good public education, have no difficulty with financial credit, always be treated as a bonafide cultural insider, take a job without suspicion of having been hired to meet affirmative action quotas, and choose public accommodations without fearing mistreatment.

People who are not born into privilege may have some chance of attaining some degree of privilege through achievements, but they are likely to be more restricted regarding access to resources and opportunities. Furthermore, as will be discussed later, if they belong to marginalized groups, such as those of color, refugee or immigrant status, or minority sexual orientation, they will experience the psychological effects of marginalization, oppression, and discrimination, which further limit their opportunities for growth and development. If they eventually are able to achieve some status and power, they must contend with the loyalty conflicts that are associated with assimilation into the dominant culture and distancing from one's own cultural group.

Valuing choice, however, is an ethnocentric point of view, a value of Euro-Americans. Certainly, the history of the United States is predicated on this value of free choice, as exemplified by our Declaration of Independence and the Bill of Rights. This ethos of prizing the ability to make choices results in a mythology that anyone can achieve status and more choice and privilege in this country. It ignores the realities of discrimination and oppression. Thus, the have-nots become even more discriminated against, because they are viewed as people who chose not to become assimilated into the dominant class—as lazy, or as failures.

Socioeconomic class, whether automatic or earned, is one of the primary indicators of the privilege of choice. The rules, roles, and scripts governing membership in middle- and upper-class strata in this country result in a false assumption that everyone has the same values, attitudes, and expectations. Many people who have struggled for entry into higher socioeconomic classes have learned how to follow these roles, rules, and scripts to maintain and further their status, but they still adhere to or struggle with the cultural values with which they were raised. The transgenerational effects of acculturation and assimilation can create conflict and distance between generations of families.

EXERCISE 6.35 • Privilege

The purpose of this exercise is to help you become aware of your privileges. For the purpose of this exercise, privileges are defined as automatic entitlements, such as education, health care, occupational resources, opportunities, relationships, family style, and so on.

List the privileges you are aware of in your generation for each member of your family. For example, if you are the oldest son, you may have certain privileges that a younger sister does not have, such as pursuing educational opportunities, carrying on the family business, being given a car when you go to college, and so on. Compare these privileges with those of your parents' generation, and those of your grandparents' generation. How did you obtain these privileges? Which groups in our society have the same privileges? If possible, work with a colleague, relative, or classmate to help define both your own and the other person's awareness of privileges.

EXERCISE 6.36 • Cross-Cultural Expectations

The purpose of this exercise is to learn about the expectations of people belonging to different cultural groups.

Interview four people whose race, gender, class, or ethnicity is different from yours. Ask them the following questions:

1. What were their expectations when they were little about what they would be when they grew up and what their life would be like?
2. Did they feel they had a lot of choice in selecting dates? In selecting mates? In finding jobs? In finding housing? In obtaining credit? In obtaining medical care?
3. How did their expectations get met or not met?

Based on these three questions, assess how their expectations differ from yours. Which groups in our society do you think have the most privilege? The least privilege? What experiences, including powerlessness, discrimination, and prejudice, are associated with minority status? How might these differences affect relationships?

Conclusion

In this chapter, we have examined the complexities of understanding and forming relationships with people who have different cultural heritages. We cannot assume that everyone has the same rules, roles, and scripts, and we must respect differences in the meaning of "self-in-relation" in different contexts.

Looking at intimate, social, and public relationships from multiple perspectives, and considering how cultural heritage and current social contexts are intertwined, can teach us to consider possible meanings of what we observe and experience in relationships. This kind of sensitivity allows us to be more self-aware and more other-aware, to be more attentive to our own and others' communicative behaviors, and to be more adaptive in our responsiveness. We need to learn to suspend our assumptions of meaning by listening carefully, questioning others when we are not sure we are understanding, explaining more thoroughly when we feel misunderstood, and reflecting on our experiences and on our interpretations of others' experiences before jumping to conclusions. As stated throughout this text, awareness of our own values, attitudes, and beliefs can enable us to be more open to others' different values, attitudes, and beliefs. This awareness can then lead to appreciating, respecting, and valuing these differences.

7

Time and Space: Hidden Communications

It should be apparent by now that communicating involves a great deal more than just talking. Two aspects of communication that most people are unaware of are time and space. How we use, manipulate, and interpret these dimensions is determined by our personal cultures, the groups that we belong to, and their values. We learn these forms of communication at an early age, and by the time we are adults they have become a part of who we are. As a result, we rarely are aware of them. The purpose of this chapter is to make you aware of the use of time and space in communication, both within the dominant United States culture and in many subdominant cultures.

Culture and Nonverbal Communication

Before discussing the dimensions of time and space, it is important again to consider what we mean by culture. Three aspects of culture need to be restated: (1) Culture is not innate, but learned. (2) The various components of culture are interrelated. (3) Culture is shared within groups and defines the boundaries between groups (Hall, 1971b). As a result, everything is touched by culture.

What we take in with our senses and how we interpret it are shaped by culture. Our senses are capable of taking in an enormous amount of information, but we are not capable of interpreting all of it. Thus, we filter out information at different stages of the perception process. Much of this filtering and interpretation is done at an unconscious level. Accordingly, most of our nonverbal communication is unconscious and is culturally determined. This is the reason for many of the misunderstandings that arise between people. We send messages without being aware of the message or of its interpretation by the receiver. At the same time, we receive and misinterpret messages all the time, or rather we interpret them within *our* cultural system of values and beliefs, which is not how they were meant. Take, for example, the use of eye contact. In the

United States, people who will not make eye contact are viewed as sneaky, insincere, or embarrassed. In other countries, people who do make eye contact are viewed as rude, pushy, and intrusive. The use of time and space has similar diverse interpretations, depending on the people involved, the situation, and the culture(s).

Several aspects of the dominant United States culture have an effect on the manipulation and interpretation of time and space. First is the fact that we live in an individualistic culture in which the individual is seen as a separate and valued entity. This probably is the most important cultural pattern in the United States. Somewhat related is the notion of equality—the cultural value that all people are created equal—which influences our social and business structures and underlies many of our other values. The dominant culture is also based on a pattern of materialism. People are judged by their possessions, and reality is seen as a material reality. Physical comfort is highly valued. Science and technology are two additional aspects of our culture that are highly valued. One result of these patterns and values is that people in the United States believe that reality can be rationally ordered and, hence, is controllable. Related to this idea are the patterns of progress and change, which lead to a future orientation and optimism. Progress and change are seen as positive and moving in a forward direction. Finally, United States culture emphasizes activity and work. Activity and work are also viewed as positive, leading to recognition, money, and power (Samovar and Porter, 1995).

Take a moment to think about how each of these patterns might affect how people in the United States perceive time and space. How would a culture that emphasizes individuality and equality regard time and space?

The Role of Time and Space in Communications

Time is based on physical and biological cycles, like the cycles of the sun and moon, or cycadic rhythms, but it is more than that. Time is also *mechanically* measured—in minutes, hours, days, and so forth. Space also is based on physical and biological cycles. We perceive space through our senses: eyes, ears, nose, skin. A person takes up a certain amount of space, depending on his or her size. However, space refers to more than just the physical occupation of a certain area. Space involves isolation and crowding, small and large areas, and so on. In other words, both time and space are based on physical aspects of the world, but, through culture, they have become much more than that. They are used to mark individual and group status and territories. Without realizing it, we use time and space to indicate what we feel about another person. For example, if a person we are meeting is important, we tend to be on time for the appointment, whereas if the person is unimportant, we tend not to worry about being late. In the United States, white people often will stand farther away from an African American when conversing than they will from another white person (Samovar and Porter, 1995).

It is difficult to separate time and space. In fact, physicists no longer speak of time or space separately (Capra, 1989). The uses of time and space often are intertwined, but for ease of understanding we will deal with them separately in this chapter.

Time

EXERCISE 7.1 • Time Metaphors

The purpose of this exercise is to recognize how the concept of time permeates language.

Think about how time is represented in English (and in your native language if English is not your native language). Make a list of all the terms or metaphors that are used to connote time, whether they are direct, like *moment, minute,* or *second,* or evaluative, like *late, tardy,* or *punctual.* You will be surprised at how many English terms we have that relate to time.

Polychronic and Monochronic Time

As mentioned above, each culture has its own concept of time. Anthropologists, sociologists, and others have devised certain theories of time that divide temporal concepts into manageable categories. One of the most well-known theories was devised by E. T. Hall (Hall, 1971b, p. 82). Hall divides time into polychronic and monochronic time. In *polychronic time,* people engage in many tasks at any given moment. People are highly involved in their tasks. Time is viewed holistically, with the emphasis being on the activity of the moment. Time is cyclical (Gudykunst & Ting-Toomey, 1988). It is not a tangible entity, but is rather unstructured. In polychronic time, people tend to be more spontaneous, and they view appointments as being breakable. One reason for this is that the emphasis is on people, not on schedules (Samovar & Porter, 1995). This is in sharp contrast with *monochronic time,* in which only one task is undertaken at any given moment. Time is viewed as fixed in nature (rather than cyclical), and as a manageable entity. It is linear, not cyclical (Gudykunst & Ting-Toomey, 1988). It is seen as something tangible that can be divided and wasted (Samovar & Porter, 1995). As a result, schedules take on great importance and appointments are sacred (Hall, 1966b, p. 82).

EXERCISE 7.2 • The Importance of Time

Before proceeding further, we need to determine what category of time describes your culture.

To which view of time—polychronic or monochronic—do the majority of North Americans subscribe? Try answering the following true/false questions to determine if you, and your culture, are polychronic or monochronic. Circle T for true or F for false.

T F **1.** Time is cyclical.

T F **2.** Time can be wasted.

T F **3.** A colleague's feelings are more important than getting a job done.

T F **4.** It is best to do one thing at a time.

T F **5.** It is important to spend time on social niceties.

T F **6.** It is best to do one thing at a time and finish it before starting on the next task.

T F **7.** Spontaneity is a desirable trait.

T F **8.** It is insulting to be kept waiting.

T F **9.** A task can always be finished tomorrow.

T F **10.** Time equals money.

If you answered true for most of the odd numbers and false for the rest, then you probably have a polychronic view of time. If you answered true for the even numbers and false for the rest, then you probably have a monochronic view of time. Of course, it is unlikely that every member of a polychronic culture will be completely polychronic, or vice versa. In addition, there probably are some situations in which you are more polychronic or more monochronic.

There tends to be a strong link between the type of time a culture subscribes to and other cultural features. Collectivistic cultures, such as Latin American, Middle Eastern, Mediterranean, Japanese, and French cultures, tend to favor polychronic time. Individualistic cultures, such as German, North European, and North American cultures, tend to favor monochronic time (Samovar & Porter, 1995; Gudykunst & Ting-Toomey, 1988; Hall, 1982). We also have talked about high-context and low-context cultures. In high-context cultures most of the information transmitted is contained in the physical context (the setting) or is internalized in the people who are interacting. (In other words, the context gives the message its meaning.) As a result, very little information needs to be transmitted explicitly. In contrast, low-context cultures put most of their information into the explicit message. Most of the information is stated verbally. The United States tends to be low-context, whereas China, for example, is high-context (Hall, 1971b). There is a strong correlation between high-context cultures and polychronic time and low-context cultures and monochronic time (Hall, 1971b).

Past, Present, and Future Time Orientation

Another way to consider time is in terms of time orientation. Cultures emphasize different types of time: past, present, and future (Samovar & Porter, 1995; Crohn, 1995; Hall, 1966b).

In past-oriented societies, the past, and history, are seen as the most important parts of time. Family and cultural history and traditions are remembered and honored. They serve as a guide for present-day decisions. Cultures with an emphasis on the past have a deeper sense of time and chronology, and they tend to resist change and take a long-range view of events. They do not think in terms of today, or next year, but in terms of hundreds of years. The return of Hong Kong to Chinese jurisdiction exemplifies a long-range view. For the Chinese, one hundred years means little, which is one reason they agreed to cede Hong Kong to the British in 1842. Other past-oriented cultures include Britain, Native American cultures, Greece, France, Japan, and other Asian cultures (Samovar & Porter, 1995; Crohn, 1995).

Present-oriented cultures see the present moment as the most significant. What is real is the here and now. Little importance is attached to traditions, and there is little planning for the future. Instead, a casual, relaxed lifestyle, which may appear impulsive and spontaneous, is pursued. People try to live life to its fullest and enjoy the moment. Traditional, often agricultural, societies tend to have this orientation (Crohn, 1995). Examples of cultures that are present-oriented are the Philippines, Latin America, and many countries with an Islamic tradition. Islam leaves worry about the future to Allah. The past, present, and future are seen to come together and are interwoven (Samovar & Porter, 1995).

Future-oriented cultures focus on the future and believe that it will be better than the present or past. Little importance is placed on tradition and history, and present-day enjoyment is delayed in order to plan for a bigger, brighter future. Continual forward movement occurs, and people always are moving on to the next thing. As a result, there is little tolerance for extensions or postponements. The best example of a future-oriented culture is the United States (Crohn, 1995; Samovar & Porter, 1995).

Our concept of time has been strongly influenced by the invention of the clock. According to Keyes (1991), before a mechanism existed that could divide time into uniform segments, everyone had "soft time." This type of time was not uniform, but vague. It was seasonal and was measured or judged only by what one was doing at a given time. When conditions were optimal for an activity, then the time was right! Since the invention of the clock, which was first devised in Europe in the late thirteenth or early fourteenth century, time has become rigid, uniform, and measured. We now have "hard time," which needs to be filled up with activities in order not to be wasted. A correlation exists between Keyes's concept of hard time and Hall's concept of monochronic time. Both see time as a commodity that can be segmented, managed, and wasted. The advent of the clock gave merchants and churchmen the ability to measure time; with this development, the notion of "schedule" began to gain importance. As the schedule gained influence, it combined with the assembly line to promote the development and industrialization of Western societies. Time also began to equal money. Today, time is one of the dominant organizing principles of North American society. And, although it is a social construct, time is viewed by most people as something that is imposed on them as an outside constraint. How many people have felt anxiety and frustration when trying to meet deadlines and appointments? Why is it that sitting in traffic during the morning commute raises a person's blood pressure?

EXERCISE 7.3 • Time Orientation: Soft and Hard Time

The purpose of this exercise is to determine which concepts of time you hold.

Which of the following statements best reflect your values? Circle the number of the ones that apply.

1. Live each day to the fullest.
2. Do not put off until tomorrow what you can do today.
3. If it was good enough this way for 10 years, then it is good enough this way for another 10 years.
4. Don't fix what isn't broken.
5. Tomorrow is another day.
6. A stitch in time saves nine.
7. This too will pass.
8. Haste makes waste.
9. The early bird gets the worm.
10. With time, everything will get better.

As you look at your choices, determine whether you are predominantly past oriented, present oriented, or future oriented.

Activities and Schedules

Everyone is involved in activities, but the importance one attaches to completing a given activity is dependent on one's concept of time. As previously mentioned, monochronic cultures tend to focus on one activity at a time, whereas polychronic cultures undertake several at a time. People in monochronic cultures tend to want to finish what they have started before beginning something new. At the same time, they are less invested in the activity and more invested in the outcome or product (Hall, 1982). People in polychronic cultures tend toward the opposite. Being multitasked, they are more concerned with the activity itself than they are with the outcome or product. Once involved in an action, however, they are unwilling to let it go. As a result of these different approaches, two people working on the same activity, one with a monochronic concept of time and the other with a polychronic concept of time, will approach the activity very differently. It is important to recognize the fact that people have different concepts of "getting the job done." One person will focus solely on doing the job, while the other will take time to consider the effect of the activity on the people involved and any other activities that might impede his or her progress.

EXERCISE 7.4 • Time Orientation: Family Influences

Now you need to determine the concepts of time your family of origin held.

What were the rules about time in your family of origin? Was time fixed? In other words, were mealtimes and bedtimes always at the same time? Or was time more flexible, allowing for adjustments to be made according to individuals' needs? Perhaps time was a fluctuating concept, and you never knew when meals would be served or when bedtime would occur.

Do you consider yourself to be an "on time" person? How do you feel when you are kept waiting? How do you feel when others' time orientation differs from your own?

EXERCISE 7.5 • Monochronic and Polychronic Tendencies

Your concept of time affects how you approach your work. Therefore, in this exercise, you will determine whether you have monochronic or polychronic tendencies.

1. Take a moment to think about how you approach tasks or activities. Then answer the following questions on a scale of 1 to 5. 1 = extremely important; 2 = somewhat important; 3 = neutral; 4 = important; and 5 = extremely important.

_____a. Once I start something, I have to finish it.

_____b. Coffee breaks and talking when working are wastes of time (or should be avoided).

_____c. I like to stay at work until I am finished with what I am working on.

_____d. I can't get things done at work because of all the interruptions.

_____e. It is easier to work on my own. That way I waste less time.

If you answered 1 or 2 to most of these questions, then you have a predisposition to view work monochronically. If you answered 4 or 5, you tend to be polychronic.

2. Chances are you do not always work alone, but must at times work with others. Consider the people with whom you find it easy to work and those with whom you find it difficult. Ask them to answer the same questions. How do their answers relate to yours?
3. Given what you know about the different approaches to tasks and activities, what actions on your part might make it smoother, more satisfying, and more productive for monochronic and polychronic people to work together?

One consequence of our concept of "hard" time has been the development of schedules. In the United States, people are inculcated with the importance of schedules from the time they start school as children. The day begins at an arbitrary time and is divided into arbitrary blocks of time denoted by a whistle, bell, or buzzer. Each block of time is designated for a specific activity. When the bell rings, the activity stops, regardless of whether an adequate amount of teaching or learning has been accomplished. By the time we have reached adulthood, schedules and their importance are no longer questioned. Neither is the sacredness of appointments. In fact, our lives become regulated by the clock.

EXERCISE 7.6 • Clocks

The purpose of this exercise is to become aware of your dependence on clocks.

1. Take time to notice the importance that is placed on clocks in your work place, in public places, and at home. Notice where clocks are located. Are they prominently displayed? Does everyone at work have his or her own clock? Is there a clock in every room at home? What about in stores or along the street. In Bern, Switzerland, clocks can be seen on many street corners.
2. How important are clocks and time in your life? Do you wear a watch? If so, how often do you look at your watch? How many activities during the day are scheduled for a specific time? Do you tend to schedule one activity at a time, or many?
3. Try going without your watch for one day. Can you still be on time?

Although schedules play an important role in our society, they are not equally important to every culture or in every situation. Everyone has been kept waiting at the doctor's office, where a 3:00 appointment might mean you will be seen at 3:45, or even 4:15! In some offices, activities are multi-scheduled. Activities such as interviewing, talking on the phone, and giving messages occur simultaneously.

What happens when you go to an appointment and the person you have come to see spends half the time on the phone to other people, or people keep popping into the office and interrupting you? The person with whom you have the appointment may have a polychronic concept of time and may not realize that you find it frustrating that you do not have his or her exclusive attention.

EXERCISE 7.7 • Appointments

The purpose of this exercise is to learn about your attitudes regarding appointments.

1. Begin by considering what a typical business appointment should be like. How is the starting time determined? How is the length of the appointment determined? What activities should take place? Now, think of examples that correspond with your prototype. Do appointments with your boss match what you described? What are some examples of appointments that do not fit your description? What causes the misfit? Given what you now know about how people think about time, what are the possible reasons for different appointment scripts?
2. What other scheduled events do you participate in? Consider doctor appointments, concerts, dates, and so on. Evaluate them just as you evaluated your business appointments. Do most of them match up with your prototypes?
3. What clues should you look for in order to determine whether or not the person you are meeting has a different concept of time from the one you have? How can you reconcile the two concepts in an amicable manner? Your strategy will need to vary depending on the status of the other person, his or her culture, the situation, and your objectives. For example, it is not likely that you can ask an important client to refrain from taking phone calls while you are meeting with him, nor can you ask friends to ask their friends *not* to drop in. On the other hand, you can tell a friend that you are uncomfortable with the fact that he or she is spending all of your visit talking to other people. You can tell a colleague at work that you have too many things to do to sit around waiting for him or her to get off the phone.

Pace

In Europe, one can always spot a North American by the way the person walks, even at a great distance. North Americans walk at a different pace from Southern Europeans. Their pace tends to be quick, with the body leaning forward, whereas most Southern Europeans tend to walk slower and more vertically. Different groups of North Americans, of course, have different paces. When we refer to pace, we mean more than just the speed at which a person walks, we also mean the speed at which other activities are pursued. Ralph Keyes (1991) looked at the walking speed of people in Japan, the United States, England, Italy, Taiwan, and Indonesia. People from Japan walked the fastest, followed by England and then the United States. People from Indonesia walked the slowest. Keyes also looked at how fast people got served at the post office. Japan was still the fastest, followed by the United States, with Italy being the slowest. Keyes looked also at the accuracy of bank clocks. Japan's clocks were the most accurate, followed by the United States. Indonesia's clocks were the most inaccurate. Taken all together, Keyes's study suggests that both Japan and the United States have very fast-paced societies.

Besides speed, post office transactions, and clocks, criteria for determining pace include length of meals, duration of other types of transactions, amount of time given to social rituals, and so on. Another factor is the time orientation of the culture. Keyes argues that Japan is faster paced than the United States, based on speed of walking, post office transactions, and bank clocks. What happens when the time orientation of these two societies is considered? The United States is a future-oriented society. It therefore makes sense that North Americans would always be hurrying on to the next item. In fact, many of the metaphors related to time that you came up with in Exercise 7.1, like "fast lane" and "rat race," suggest a fast pace of life. Japan, on the other hand, is a past-oriented society. Decision making, for example, is a slower process in Japan than it is in the United States (Matsumoto, 1996b). People in the United States expect tasks to be accomplished in minutes or hours; the Japanese are willing to spend hours or days (Samovar & Porter, 1995). In other words, how one evaluates pace depends on all the criteria one uses, but in most cases the United States seems to be faster paced than most other societies.

EXERCISE 7.8 • Pace of Life

The purpose of this exercise is to become aware of your and others' pace of life.

1. Before looking at other people, determine your own pace. Take a few days to observe the amount of time you take to perform certain tasks and activities. For example, how long do you spend at meals? Because they often take place in different situations and have different functions, consider all three main meals—breakfast, lunch, and dinner. Breakfast probably takes place at home, with your family or

roommates. Lunch may take place at work, and dinner may be more of a social function that occurs at a restaurant.

Choose from the following list of activities that you perform on a regular basis and clock how long you take to complete each one. At the same time, note how you feel. Do you feel rushed? Impatient? Content?

eating meals	going to a party
buying stamps at the post office	getting dressed
grocery shopping	participating in meetings
getting a cup of coffee	going to the airport
waiting in line for a ticket	taking a walk
talking on the phone with a friend	waiting for a train or bus

2. Compare your times with others who have completed the same exercise. How similar are your times for the different activities? How do you feel about the amount of time it takes to accomplish the various activities? Did you find that the amount of time assigned to work-related activities varied less than the time assigned to social or personal activities?
3. Observe other people's pace and ask them how they feel about the amount of time they spend on various activities. What types of people have a pace that is similar to yours? Can you identify the American subcultures that have a different pace of life from yours?

Lateness and Respect

In a society in which time is equated with money, it stands to reason that "wasting" someone else's time would be viewed as a sign of disrespect. In fact, in the United States, the easiest way to insult people is to keep them waiting. Being punctual is a sign of respect. However, this is not the case in other countries or cultures. In Latin America, being late is actually a sign of respect, whereas in China being early is a sign of respect (Samovar & Porter, 1995). Clearly, if we react to punctuality without considering how people view time, we are likely to misinterpret other people's motives.

EXERCISE 7.9 • Lateness

The purpose of this exercise is to explore your attitudes about lateness in certain situations.

Consider the following questions as they apply to a business situation, a social situation with an acquaintance, and a social situation with a close friend or family member:

Your appointment is for twelve o'clock noon. How much after twelve o'clock would the other person need to come for you to consider him or her late?
At what point in time would you expect an apology?
At what time would you call to see if something had gone wrong?
When would you decide that the person was not coming and leave?
Would you be angered or insulted by the other person's behavior?
If you were late to an appointment, how late would you have to be in order to feel you should apologize?

Clearly, our concept of lateness has to do with the individual situation. People tend to allow more leeway in social situations than they do in business situations. With close acquaintances or with family members whom we know to be habitually late, we allow greater amounts of time to pass before we become annoyed or concerned.

The number of minutes that equal "late" is also culturally determined. Before looking at how different cultures ascribe lateness, it is useful to look at the five intervals of lateness for an appointment that Hall (1966b) proposed. Keep in mind that Hall arrived at these categories after interviewing white, male, middle-class North Americans from the northeastern part of the United States.

1. mumble something time
2. slight apology time
3. mildly insulting time
4. rude time
5. downright insulting time

The times for each interval suggested by Hall (1971b) are 0–5, 5–10, 10–15, 15–30, and more than 30 minutes. In monochronic cultures, the first interval could be as small as 5 minutes, whereas in polychronic time the length might extend to 45 or 60 minutes (Gudykunst & Ting-Toomey, 1988).

EXERCISE 7.10 • Intervals of Lateness

The purpose of this exercise is to apply Hall's intervals of lateness for an appointment in various situations.

For each of the situations described in Exercise 7.9 (business situation, social situation with an acquaintance, and social situation with a friend or family member), assign a period of time to each of the above intervals devised by Hall. Over the next few days, note at what interval you and others arrive for appointments. Do your observations fit the time periods you assigned? Ask people from different cultures how they would assign time to these intervals.

These exercises demonstrate that situation plays a large role in how we ascribe lateness. Another factor is the position of the other person involved. As mentioned earlier, people constantly are kept waiting in doctors' offices for amounts of time that would be considered downright insulting in other situations. In addition, we are more likely to tolerate lateness in a superior than we are in a subordinate.

Culture is another factor involved in how we perceive lateness and other aspects of time. It is perfectly acceptable in the United States and Britain to be 5 minutes late for an appointment, but not 30 minutes, especially for a business appointment. Socially we are more lax. Fifteen minutes late for a social luncheon would be in the "mumble something" interval. This is in sharp contrast to Arab cultures, where people normally are 30 minutes late for business appointments. Italians also allow greater time intervals. One can be up to two hours late for a social function without being insulting. In some third world countries, people often are as late as one day. At the other end of the scale is Japan, where being late might cause loss of face to the host (Hall, 1966b; Samovar & Porter, 1995; Triandis, 1994).

Dominant, white North American time clearly is monochronic. As a result, schedules and punctuality have become very important. This focus on monochronic time has also led to the compartmentalization of time into arbitrary units, as typified by our school systems. Given that this is the dominant perspective, and that it clearly is reflected in public institutions and businesses, how representative is it of the various subcultures that are found in the United States? This question will be dealt with later in the chapter after we have looked at the concept of space.

Space

EXERCISE 7.11 • Space Metaphors

The purpose of this exercise is to recognize how the concept of space permeates language.

Think about how space is represented in English, and in your native language if English is not your native language. Make a list of all the terms or metaphors that are used to connote space, whether they are direct, like *space* or *area,* or structural, like *room* or *building,* or metaphors, like *off our back* or *cold shoulder.* You will be surprised how many terms we have in English that relate to space.

Space Perceptions

As with time, space is based on physical and biological systems. Based on our senses, there are several ways we perceive space. In fact, there are several types of space: visual, auditory, thermal, olfactory, and tactile. Our culture determines what type of spatial information we perceive or screen out and how we interpret the information. For example, the Japanese screen out visual information, but the Germans and Dutch screen out auditory information (Hall, 1982). Culturally, space is used to convey messages about power, status, and dominance. The use of space is further complicated by rules relating to resources and population density (Matsumoto, 1996b). Different occupations take up different amounts of space. What we are primarily concerned with here is how we use space socially.

EXERCISE 7.12 • Perceptions of Space

The purpose of this exercise is to consider the different types of space and how they are perceived by different cultures.

1. *Visual space.* What we consider space or how we define it is also determined by our culture. Look up at whatever is in front of you. How would you describe the space you see? In the West, we see objects and the boundaries or space around them. In the East, the area between the objects is often what is perceived. Try to view the space from both a Western and an Eastern perspective. One way to learn about how other cultures perceive space is to look at their drawings. Take time to go to your local museum and look at paintings from different cultures. How is space delineated? How is depth delineated?
2. *Auditory space.* Close your eyes and listen. What is nearby? What is far away? What level of noise makes a room feel small or crowded? What does open space sound like?
3. *Thermal space.* How far away does someone have to be for you to feel his or her body heat? Do you feel comfortable feeling the heat of another person? Does it depend on how well you know him or her?
4. *Olfactory space.* In the United States, our olfactory space is underdeveloped because we try to eliminate all personal smells or mask them with synthetic smells. Television commercials promote products to reduce or eliminate body odors, or to cover them up with perfumes. Consider the role of smell in your life. What are good smells? One of the authors of this text loves the smell of fresh baked bread. She also loves the smells that she associates with her children. What are bad smells, those that make you wish to distance yourself? The smell of a skunk probably is one! How do you feel about people being able to smell you? How do you feel about smelling them? In Arab cultures, smell is considered an important source of information. People purposely stand close enough to smell each other's breath (Hall, 1982).

5. *Tactile space.* This type of space, which involves touch, is the smallest space that is accessible to our senses. (Visual space and auditory space are the two largest spaces that are accessible to our senses.) One must be within arm's length in order to touch something. What are your feelings about touching or the possibility of touching? Does it depend on the relationship or situation?

Types of Space

We are concerned with two types of space and space usage. The first is *interpersonal* space. This involves how far away we position ourselves from people when conversing, or how close we can get to other people before feeling crowded. The other type of space that we will deal with is *environmental* space. How much room around us do we need in order to feel comfortable? How are our needs expressed by the way we position furniture or the houses in which we live?

EXERCISE 7.13 • Personal Space

The purpose of this exercise is to begin to recognize the existence of personal space.

How much space does an individual need? Go to a public place where people gather in groups or go individually, like a cafeteria, park, or mall. Can you recognize who is in a group and who is there alone? How much space surrounds the people who are alone? How much surrounds those who are in a group? Can you tell anything about the relationships between people by the amount of space between them? Find a bench or a line. How far apart do people sit or stand? What other observations about how people use space can you make?

Contact and Noncontact Species

Much of what we know about the use of space has come from ethologists (anthropologists who specialize in comparative cultures.) Some ethologists study the spatial behavior of animals. One of the things that they have observed is that there are two main categories of animals, contact species and noncontact species. Contact species need to be close to each other and have physical contact. Seals are an example of a contact species. Look at a picture of them on the shore, lying every which way, their bodies overlapping. Noncontact species, on the other hand, avoid physical contact. Most bird species are noncontact. Look at the way they arrange themselves along telephone lines, with almost regular spacing between each one.

Human cultures also can be classified as contact or noncontact cultures (Hall, 1982). Certain cultures, such as Mediterranean, Arab, and Latin American cultures, are more tactile and allow touching. Asian, Native American, and North American cultures discourage touching outside of intimate situations (Triandis, 1996; Gudykunst & Ting-Toomey, 1988). Of course, with humans the situation is further complicated by gender. In some societies, cross-gender touching is permissible, while same-gender touching is not. This is the case in the United States. Other cultures allow same-gender touching but do not allow cross-gender touching and do not have the same degree of permissibility for each gender. In the Mediterranean, it is common to see men holding hands or touching in public, but not women, whereas in Japan, it is common to see women touching, but not men (Gudykunst & Ting-Toomey, 1988). Of course, the amount of touching allowed is also dependent on the social situation and on the position of the participants. It is permissible for a teacher to pat the back of a student as a way of saying congratulations, but it is not permissible for a student to do the same.

EXERCISE 7.14 • To Touch or Not to Touch

The following activities are designed to make you think about whether or not humans are a contact or noncontact species.

1. Find a place where strangers stand in line or sit on benches, such as an airport, a bus station, or some other place. Observe how people space themselves. How close together do they stand in line? When they sit, how close together are they?
2. Go to an outdoor area where a lot of people will pass by in a small amount of time. Notice who touches whom and the type of contact that occurs. Consider the race or ethnicity of the people. Go to another area with a different population and observe how people behave there. What differences or similarities do you observe?
3. In your personal life, who touches whom? What are the circumstances? You probably will notice that the rules are different with children. All children, across species, tend to be high-contact.

Proxemics

The study of proxemics was first proposed by Hall (1966b), who, through his work as an anthropologist, recognized that different cultures use space differently. According to Hall, "the use of interpersonal space or distance helps individuals regulate intimacy by controlling sensory exposure" (Gudykunst & Ting-Toomey, 1988, p. 124). Altman takes a slightly different perspective. He sees proxemics as the claiming of personal territory, including the "personalization or marking of a place or object and communication that it is owned by a person or group" (Gudykunst & Ting-Toomey, 1988, p. 124). The determining variable is a person's need for controlling sensory exposure and contact, something that is culturally programmed.

Before discussing the different types of conversational space that are employed by people, one concept needs to be discussed further—personal space. All individuals have a personal space, an area around their body into which others cannot intrude without causing discomfort. (The original purpose of personal space probably was self-protection.) The dimensions of a person's personal space are controlled by several factors and change depending on the situation. Intimate friends can come closer than strangers without inducing stress. Uncertain situations cause one's personal space to increase (McAndrew, 1993; Freedman, 1975).

EXERCISE 7.15 • Your Personal Space

The purpose of this exercise is to determine the shape of your personal space.

Repeat the following exercise with someone with whom you are intimate, with friends of each sex, and with people of each sex whom you barely know. You can also do this exercise with people of different ages and cultures.

In the middle of a piece of paper, draw a circle to represent you. Draw an arrow to show which direction you are facing. Note the gender, age, race, ethnicity, and religion of the person you are with. Stand in the middle of a large, empty space and have the other person stand in front of you at least six feet away. Have the person slowly move closer. When you feel intruded upon, have the person stop. Take a moment to notice which sense you are using to perceive the other person's presence (eyes, ears, smell, touch, or whatever). Mark on the paper the distance at which the person stopped. Repeat the procedure with the person coming up to you from each side and from behind. Each time, mark where the person stopped on the piece of paper, and notice how you recognized his or her presence.

Compare the drawings for each person you were with. What happened to the size and shape of your personal space? Which approaches were you most comfortable with?

EXERCISE 7.16 • Other People's Personal Space

Now, having determined how close people can get to you, look at how the proximity of strangers affects behavior.

The following is done near a water fountain, but other objects could be substituted.

1. Find a drinking fountain. Stand across the hall from it, as far away as possible while still being able to easily observe people using the fountain. Notice who uses it, for how long, and notice anyone who seems to want to use it but does not. Observe how people line up or take turns. The amount of time you spend observing will depend on how many people come by to use the fountain.
2. Stand along the same wall as the fountain, approximately four feet away from it. Again, observe who uses the fountain, who wants to use it but does not, and so on.
3. Now stand two feet away, then one foot away, then right next to the fountain. Notice any changes in people's use of the fountain, the length of time they stand there drinking, and so on.
4. What changes occurred? What types of people stopped using the fountain as you moved closer? What types of people took shorter or longer drinks? What other changes occurred?

Hall (1966b, 1977, 1982) studied how people converse in different types of situations. He identified four distances of interpersonal space. They are intimate distance, personal distance, social distance, and public distance. *Intimate distance,* as its name suggests, is reserved for intimate relations such as those between parent and child or those between lovers. The other person is allowed within our personal space to the point where touching can occur and nonvisual stimuli and senses are employed. Visually, the focus is on the face and head. For white, male North America, intimate distance is from 0 to 18 inches. *Personal distance* tends still to be within touching distance, but the visual field increases to include most of the upper body. This is the distance for casual conversations between friends. Personal distance is from 18 inches to 4 feet. *Social distance* is the distance we use for formal conversations or with people we do not know well. It is clearly outside touching distance and outside one's personal space. The whole person is visible. At the far end of the range, a raised voice is often required in order to be heard. Social distance is from 4 feet to 12 feet. *Public distance* is the distance used for public speeches and other similar situations. This is the distance for very formal interactions or for communication between strangers. It also is a distance of respect. At this distance, all sensory input is visual or auditory, and the whole person can be seen (Hall, 1971a, 1982; McAndrew, 1993).

The distances given here for the four types of interpersonal space apply to white, male North Americans. The distance probably will be different for people of different cultures, genders, or physical abilities. For example, someone who is hard of hearing might have a closer social distance.

EXERCISE 7.17 • Conversational Distances

In this exercise, you will see whether or not Hall's four types of conversational distance match your experiences.

Observe how far away you stand from people when you talk. For each encounter, take note of the gender of the other person, the person's age, the person's race, how well you know the person, and the situation. Make a table of your observations. Do your conversation patterns relate to Hall's four distances of interpersonal space? How would you explain any discrepancies?

EXERCISE 7.18 • Conflicting Conversation Distances

This exercise explores further the concept of conversational distance by observing how people try to maintain it.

If a person's personal space is invaded, in most cases the person responds by adjusting his or her personal space. The same is true for conversational distances. Find out what other people's limits are by moving toward or away from them. How do they respond? Do you observe any signs of discomfort or stress? Do they move away from or toward you? Experiment in different situations, using different types of moves on your part. Notice how people react. Consider your reactions and the other person's reactions the next time you feel uncomfortable in a conversation, feel intruded upon, or find yourself moving closer to someone in a conversation. Try to adjust your conversation distance so that the other person does *not* move or display any signs of discomfort.

Sociofugal and Sociopetal Space

Sociofugal space occurs where a room is arranged with furniture and objects to keep people apart and to discourage interaction. *Sociopetal space* occurs where the space in the room is arranged to bring people together and to encourage conversation (Hall, 1982).

Our concept of space is strongly influenced by the environment in which we grew up. A person who grew up in the flat plains may feel claustrophobic living in Denver, while someone who grew up in the mountains may find Chicago uncomfortable. Someone who grew up in Seattle will have a different concept of a "typical" house from someone who grew up in New York City. In short, we tend to be most comfortable with what we are used to.

In previous chapters, you considered how space was used in your home, what the various functions of the rooms were, and so on. At this point, we want to focus on the effect of furnishings on communicating.

EXERCISE 7.19 • Seating and Conversations

The purpose of this exercise is to look at how seating arrangements reflect conversational intent.

1. Go to a cafeteria or restaurant. Notice which seats people take and whom they talk to. Do people tend to sit across from each other? Do they sit next to each other? Do they position themselves at angles? Which positions seem to foster more talking?
2. Go to a library or another place where people are *not* supposed to converse. Again, observe the seating patterns. How do they compare to those that you observed in the cafeteria or restaurant?

In general, North Americans tend to talk with people who are seated opposite them or at an angle. In casual social conversations, two North Americans rarely will choose to sit side by side to have a conversation if the furnishings allow another arrangement. In contrast, Chinese people feel alienated and uneasy when sitting across from one another. Seating also may function as a sign of status. In the United States, leaders sit at the head of the table. In fact, studies have shown that the person seated at the head of a table is often the one that a group will choose as its leader (Samovar & Porter, 1995).

How we use furniture and where we choose to sit affects not only with whom we talk, but how we perceive each other. Most people try to arrange their living room so that it is sociopetal, but other locales are purposely arranged to be sociofugal. Waiting rooms are notorious for being sociofugal.

EXERCISE 7.20 • Furniture Placement

Through this exercise, you will begin to recognize if furniture arrangements are sociofugal or sociopetal.

1. In the United States, seats placed side by side tend to inhibit conversation, while seats placed at angles or across from each other promote conversation. Consider the placement of seats and tables in different settings. Visit several offices, waiting rooms, or other places. Are the furniture arrangements sociofugal or sociopetal? What about the typical classroom, where the seats are arranged in rows? What is the hidden objective there?
2. If you wanted to promote communication and put people at ease, how would you arrange the furniture in your office? How would you arrange it in your waiting room, if you had one? If you were a teacher who wanted your students to talk among themselves, how would you arrange the desks or chairs? If you wanted the students to work indi-

vidually and not communicate, how would you change the seating arrangements?

3. The decisions you made in question 2 probably were based on the assumption that other people would agree with your definitions of sociofugal or sociopetal. What if this were not the case? What if people had differing ideas about interpersonal space? How would you arrange the furniture so that the maximum number of people would be comfortable and would feel encouraged to talk? There is, of course, no way to make *everyone* equally comfortable without continually rearranging your furniture!

Territoriality and Dominance

Another way to look at environmental space is to consider the concept of territoriality. A territory is a fixed geographical location. Territories can belong to an individual, group, or nation. Territories can contain smaller territories, be part of larger territories, or transect other territories.

Territoriality is the group of behaviors an individual or group uses to lay claim to a territory and protect it from all transgressions (Hall, 1982; McAndrew, 1993). Although the methods and materials that are used may be different, all societies recognize boundaries. People who transgress boundaries usually are punished, and territorial rights are then negotiated. The study of human territoriality—how people define, mark, and protect territories—is in a sense the study of human behavior (Scheflan & Ashcraft, 1976).

Territoriality has been shown to be closely linked to *dominance,* the need one person has to exert control over another. Dominance is initially determined through aggressive encounters, which establish who is stronger, more powerful. The result is a difference in status or power, which is usually expressed and maintained through ritualized behavior. An example would be the use of an honorific such as "sir" when addressing a superior or expecting someone to give up their seat or place. The existence of such ritualized behaviors eliminates the need to redefine continually who is dominant. As a result, aggressive behavior is unnecessary and tends to subside. In situations where both parties have what they consider to be an adequate amount of territory, dominance is not a factor, but when territory is limited or shared, dominance becomes an issue. One could say that territoriality and dominance are negatively correlated. Both are used to maintain social order (Sommer, 1969). As a result, the behaviors associated with each are culturally determined.

EXERCISE 7.21 • Office Space

The purpose of this exercise is to see how the concepts of power and dominance translate into spatial arrangements of furniture.

1. Go to an office building and notice the allocation of space. How does it correlate with status and power—with dominance? Are all offices the same size? Who gets the largest office? Which people do not have individual offices, but work in public areas such as reception rooms or hallways? Who has to share work space? Who gets their own areas? Who has a window? What type of space does senior management have? What about middle management? New employees? Secretaries?
2. Look at the way office space is allocated in your local town or city hall or at the White House. Where is the mayor's office located? Which people have offices close to the mayor's? Which is more important—to have an office close to the boss, even if it is small, or to have an office that is large, even if it is farther away from the boss?

Territoriality is related not just to an area but also to one's personal space and to the objects that habitually are used by an individual. Chairs, tables, or other objects might be considered someone's territory. Remember the television show *All in the Family*? Archie Bunker had his own chair, which no one else was allowed to sit in. At beer houses in Germany, local patrons often have a *stammtisch*, a table that is reserved for their use. People often become territorial about objects or areas that they have become attached to through repeated use and time (McAndrew, 1993). People who feel a need to defend their personal space often take positions that are easily defended, such as choosing a table in a corner facing the door. People may also use certain body gestures, such as blocking access with their legs, to keep others at a distance.

EXERCISE 7.22 • Territoriality in Public Places

In this series of exercises, you will consider how people work or delineate their territories.

1. If you are going to a cafeteria, library, or some other place where tables could be shared among people and groups, but you wanted to have a table to yourself, what type of table would you pick? Where in the room would it be located? What seat would you take? Would you face the door or would you seat yourself so that you were in a corner? How would you stake out your territory?
2. Go to a cafeteria, library, or some other such place. Observe how people choose their tables, mark them, and defend them.
3. What happens when someone invades a "territory"? How is it done, and by what type of person? How does the original occupant react?

Territories have many functions. They can be used to preserve and regulate privacy (a function that is discussed below), or they can be used to assert personal identity. In an individualistic culture like the dominant United States culture, this second function can be important. Notice how lockers in schools, desks in offices, and bedrooms at home are decorated in order to declare the individual personality of the occupant. It is important to allow people to personalize their individual spaces. Such a need is even more important for someone from a subculture who is working in the dominant culture. The person may feel a need to assert his or her cultural affiliation.

In collectivistic cultures, the need to mark individual territories would not be as great. Instead, the need would be to provide communal areas and ensure parity among different work areas.

Privacy and Intimacy

One of the uses of space, whether it be personal space or territory, is to preserve privacy. Privacy is not equivalent to isolation, and does not always mean being alone. Privacy is another concept that is determined by culture. In some cultures, physical isolation is possible, but in others, dense living conditions do not allow physical isolation. In these situations, the need for privacy might be signaled by a lack of talking, as occurs in Arab and English households, or by some other signal (Hall, 1982). In other cultures, people are concerned not with *individual* privacy, but with the privacy of the family. For example, in parts of rural Greece, which tends to be collectivistic and where the family and clan are the most important social units, no one has individual privacy. Instead, people work to maintain family privacy (Sciama, 1993).

Individual privacy did not appear in the West until about the 16th century. Before then, families lived in extended groups with their servants. Houses were centered around a general hall that served as living room, dining room, and work area. People did not have private bedrooms or areas that were their own. This began to change in the 16th century as rooms became specialized. Servants were separated from masters, children from parents, and individuals from each other (Rybezynski, 1986). This division of space went hand in hand with changes in philosophy and values. As a result, Anglo-Saxons began to equate individual privacy with individual freedom (Sciama, 1993).

One can look at how people divide space within their houses to see if the concept of individual privacy exists. In most Western cultures, the idea of the individual bedroom or territory does exist. These cultures value individual privacy. In many non-Western societies, where families live in one room or where rooms serve several functions, individual privacy does not exist. Privacy can be maintained without separate rooms or territories. In many Mediterranean cultures, people maintain privacy by avoiding physical and visual contact (McAndrew, 1993).

How one defines privacy also varies from culture to culture. Even if we take privacy to mean physical isolation, that does not mean that *all* the senses are denied input. In some societies, privacy requires only that one is out of *visual* range—behind a partition, or some distance away. In England and Japan, where walls often are paper thin, it is possible to have visual privacy and still hear others talking and going about their business. Germany, on the other hand, considers auditory privacy to be at least as important as visual privacy. As a result, buildings are well insulated, and office doors usually are kept shut (McAndrew, 1993). In individualistic cultures, the signs of privacy often are evident in the architecture and manipulation of the environment. In collectivistic cultures, where physical privacy often is not possible, privacy may be maintained through the close monitoring of self-disclosure. In other words, if a person has physical privacy, he or she may have no problem disclosing personal information, whereas someone who cannot acquire physical privacy may seek to maintain it by restricting self-disclosure (Gudykunst and Ting-Toomey, 1988).

EXERCISE 7.23 • Physical Privacy

At this point, you need to consider what people mean by "privacy."

In a small group, make a list of all the ways people can indicate that they want privacy. Spend a few days observing how people indicate privacy. Are there correlations between the signals they send and their situation, status, age, gender, race, or ethnicity?

Density and Crowding

Density refers to the number of people in a given area. The more people per square meter, the higher the density. Definitions of crowding, on the other hand, are culturally determined. Hong Kong is ten times denser than most European cities (Hall, 1971a). Cities are clearly more crowded than the countryside, but density is not the only factor. Environmental factors play an important role. If an area is closed off, stuffy, and hot, it will seem more crowded than an area of the same size that is open, cool, and has a fresh breeze blowing through. Whether or not one's presence in a situation is voluntary or involuntary will have a similar effect (Sommer, 1969). Consider the notion of "cabin fever." If one is stuck indoors and does not have the option of going outside, one is more likely to feel restless and confined than if one *chose* to stay indoors to finish reading a book or to work. In other words, crowding is more than a physical state connoting lack of space. It is an internal state that is situation specific and, in the United States, it often is given a negative connotation (Freedman, 1975). What we consider crowded depends on our culture's concept of interpersonal distance and on our individual personal space. In a society where social distance is small, a higher level of density can exist without people feeling crowded. If a person has a large personal space, then it will take only a small number of people to make him feel crowded in a small room.

EXERCISE 7.24 • Boundaries and Intrusions

The purpose of this exercise is to explore social space and how we signal that someone has entered ours. When such entry occurs, we need to recognize the other's presence and signal this recognition. Recognition signifies the possibility of social interaction and lets the other know that we are willing to interact with him or her.

At what point or distance do you feel the need to recognize someone else? What are the signals? Eye contact? A pause in the conversation? Stopping your actions? For each of the following situations, does the intruder need to be recognized? Does the occupant?

1. A person walks by an open office door.
2. A person walks by an open office door and looks in, seeing the occupant.
3. A person walks by an office door and looks in, catching the occupant's eye.
4. A person stops briefly at an open door but does not look in.
5. A person stops at an open door and looks in.
6. A person stops at an open door and looks in, catching the occupant's eye.
7. Two people are the only people in a large, open room.
8. Two acquaintances or colleagues are in a large, open room with other people.
9. Two acquaintances are in a large, open room with other people and catch each other's eye.
10. A person walks through the hallways past his or her friend.

Compare your answers with those of other people. How consistent are the answers? Discuss some of the reasons for any differences.

EXERCISE 7.25 • Crowding

We have already said that the concept of crowding is a social construct. At this point, you should determine your personal definition of crowding.

At what point is a space crowded? Find an elevator that you can ride repeatedly. Ride it alone, with one other person, with two other people, and with several people. How many people need to be in the elevator for you to feel crowded? How close do people stand to one another? Is there a difference based on size? Gender? Age? Race? Do people face each other? Do they face away from one another? Do they stand next to each other or apart?

When do you feel crowded in other situations? For example, how full does a bus or train have to be for you to consider it crowded? Which restaurants do you feel crowded in? Why? Does it have to do with the number of people per square foot, the space between tables, or the total size of the eating area?

EXERCISE 7.26 • Environmental Space

This exercise looks at how you evaluate environmental space.

What is your concept of an adequately sized home for an individual? For a couple? For a family of five? Drive through different neighborhoods and observe the different sizes of houses and house lots. In which neighborhoods could you find a house in which you would feel comfortable? How big do you expect a bedroom to be? How small can your office be if you are to feel productive? How many of your answers are a result of the amount of space you did or did not have when you were growing up? How many are the result of social values and expectations?

Groups and Boundary Crossing

The use of space can signal affiliation and togetherness. In many cultures, couples will stand within each other's personal space. How they orient themselves to each other also will depend on the culture. In the United States, couples tend to stand side by side, whereas in some Arabic and Asian cultures, the wife stands behind her husband and does not invade his personal space (Samovar & Porter, 1995).

How we orient ourselves to each other also is a function of the task. People occupied with the same task often will work side by side and create a work area. Conversational groups will stand facing each other and create a group area. People might lean toward each other or use their extremities or furniture to mark off the group's boundaries (Scheflen & Ashcroft, 1976).

There are unstated social rules about crossing boundaries and invading other territories. Crossing boundaries is often ritualized. For example, in most conversations, one simply stands at the edge of the group, waits for a pause, and then says "Excuse me" and proceeds. A person who wishes to enter an office or school to which he or she does not belong may need to go through a series of interviews or other procedures before being allowed into the institution. Crossing national boundaries requires one to go through passport control. Boundaries may also be maintained by making the intruder an honorary member of the group. For example, in the British House of Commons, women become fictive men (Ardener, 1993). Women are addressed and treated as men and wear the same attire.

EXERCISE 7.27 • Social Rules and Groups

This exercise focuses on how people cross social boundaries. The purpose is to observe the different techniques used and the success of each technique.

1. Observe how people form and mark off conversational groups. If possible, observe groups in both business and social settings. Note how people enter the groups. Does a person's status affect how he or she enters a group? Does gender, race, or ethnicity have an effect? Does it depend on the nature of the interruption?
2. Try joining conversational groups using some of the methods you have observed. Which were most successful? Why do you think that is?
3. Take note when other people try to join groups that you are in. How do you respond to the different types of intrusion?

Uses of Time and Space

Other people's use of time and space is a function not just of their nationality or culture, but of their gender, age, and physical abilities. How we *interpret* their use of time and space is a function of our own stereotypes about other races and ethnicities. It is important to realize that we interpret other people's actions based on our own unconscious rules and regulations. We might feel insulted by someone who kept us waiting for fifteen minutes, without realizing that the other person did not intend to insult us. We might not feel that a woman is standing too close, but a man at a similar distance might make us feel uncomfortable. Unfortunately, most of the comparative works on time and space deal with different nationalities. Although these findings can in some cases be extended to ethnic groups, these findings do not explain how other differences affect people's use of time and space. The rest of this chapter will explore the effects that membership in different groups can have on both our perceptions and on other people's intentions, with regard to time and space.

EXERCISE 7.28 • Recognizing Different Uses of Time and Space

The purpose of this exercise is to consider how individual needs and personalities affect the use and manipulation of time and space.

1. First consider time. Think of someone you know who is often late. What signs or clues suggest to you that the person has a different set of intervals for lateness than is generally accepted? Consider the person's history for being punctual and how the person acts when he or

she is late. Take into account the individual's character and the situation. One person may be "too nice a fellow" to insult someone purposely; another person may have "an ax to grind" and may use lateness as a way of irritating and insulting the other person.

Next, consider how people respond to deadlines. Some people are just bad at judging how much time a task requires. Others feel that deadlines do not apply to them. Still others—the ones with whom we are concerned—may have a different concept of time. They may mean to finish a project, but they get sidetracked by relational issues or other tasks. In other words, they have a polychronic sense of time. Take the time to sort out why someone you know is behind schedule on some task. If the person is late because he or she subscribes to polychronic time and you (or your organization) are monochronic, how can you help the person to be more monochronic at work? If the problem is that someone is polychronic, explaining how their missed deadlines affect other people and focusing on the relational effects may be more effective. Another strategy could be to clearly articulate priorities for different tasks.

2. Now, consider space. Conversational space, although not something that usually is consciously arranged, is something that people can work on. It also can produce great anxiety and unease. Notice the distance at which different people place themselves when undertaking different tasks. Consider the possibility that people may not participate in a conversation or meeting because they feel they are too far away. If people tend to advance or retreat when they are talking with you, adjust your distance so that they stop moving. How office space is used is, for most people, out of their control, but it still can produce ease or discomfort. Consider how far away chairs are placed. If they are far apart, they may seem intimidating or inhibitory. Some people will automatically move their chairs closer. How can you let people know that they can adjust their chairs to a comfortable distance?

Gender

It is commonly accepted that men and women view the world differently. For example, women often see the fine details, while men look more at the big picture. As we have pointed out repeatedly throughout this book, women and men are socialized differently, and their actions are perceived differently. How do such differences apply to concepts like time and space? In terms of time, it seems likely that women, who as a group tend to be more collectivistic and high-involvement than the dominant United States culture, are probably more polychronic. After all, most mothers cannot afford to look after their children and not also cook, wash dishes, vacuum, do laundry, or perform some other household task. If they approached their day in a purely monochronic manner, too many things would never get finished, much less started. Men, on the other hand, are in a better position to compartmentalize and to be purely monochronic. Until recently, they rarely were the ones who were called on when a child got sick or had an accident. Even now, men often will come home and expect to relax and read the paper, instead of getting dinner ready, seeing that the children do their homework, or doing the dishes from breakfast. The way men are socialized in our society, they are allowed to do one task at a time and to finish it before moving on to the next.

This gender difference also is seen in many traditional job categories. Support staff like secretaries and nurses, who tend to be women, have jobs that require multitasking. Although they must bow to the omnipresent schedule, they are not given the luxury of attending to only one task at a time. This does not mean that men do not have multitasked jobs. In many jobs, a man might be working on several projects at a time, all of which have different schedules and due dates.

EXERCISE 7.29 • Your Use of Time

The purpose of this exercise is to determine if you and a significant other tend to be monochronic or polychronic.

1. Make a list of all the tasks and activities that you perform in a day, noting the time that you attend to each one. Do you tend to work on many things at once, bounce from task to task, or do one thing at a time until it is finished? Does it matter if you are at work or at home?
2. Ask at least one person of the opposite gender to make a similar list of tasks. If you are married or involved with someone, it might be useful to have that person make a list. If you feel that you are not representative of your gender, you might ask someone of the same gender to make a list.
3. Compare your lists. Are they equally single-tasked or multitasked? Discuss your use of time and how you approach chores and jobs. You might be surprised at what or how much the other person is doing during the day.

Women and men also are socialized differently in terms of space. Consider the diagrams of your personal space that you constructed in Exercise 7.15. Did you allow men or women to stand close to you? In general, women have a smaller personal space. This is only partially because they are more comfortable with intimacy than men, who tend to be more aggressive and more stressed by personal space invasion. Women are seen as less threatening than men, and therefore more approachable (Freedman, 1975; Olmstead & Hare, 1978; McAndrew, 1993; Samovar & Porter, 1995). Women also are given less status in United States society. People of high status tend to be able to demand larger personal spaces. People of lower status often have their space determined by others. Therefore, women often have smaller personal spaces.

EXERCISE 7.30 • Others' Personal Spaces

The purpose of this exercise is to draw someone else's personal space.

Repeat Exercise 7.15, where you diagrammed your personal space, only this time make diagrams for other people, both men and women. Have the chosen subject stand in the middle of the space. Approach the subject. Record the points at which the subject says to stop. Approach from all directions, recording where you are told to stop.

What are the results? Do people of different gender have personal spaces that are significantly different? How does the gender of the approaching person affect the size of the other person's personal space?

EXERCISE 7.31 • Effects of Gender on Social Distances

The purpose of this exercise is to experiment with trying to alter personal or social space between individuals.

1. Review your findings from Exercise 7.18. Try narrowing the conversational space between you and men and women. Note how they react. Are there differences that can be attributed to gender?
2. Find a location with benches where people sit. Find a bench where one other person is sitting. Sit down. How far away from the person did you choose to sit? After at least five minutes, move closer. Keep moving closer until you note tension or discomfort in the other person. What distance are you at? Continue to move closer until you get a reaction. What kind of reaction did you get? Did the person move down the bench? Did he or she glare at you, say something, or even leave? Repeat the exercise in several different situations. Were certain reactions associated with specific genders? Have a friend of the opposite gender go through the experiment again while you stand someplace where you can observe. Does the gender of the intruder have an affect?

Class

No data exist concerning the different use of time and space by different social classes. One reason may be that other group affiliations are stronger, and have an overriding influence, at least in terms of time. Space, on the other hand, is clearly apportioned differently based on a person's class.

EXERCISE 7.32 • Territories and Class

The purpose of this exercise is to see whether the allocation of space relates to social class.

Go to some lower-, middle-, and upper-class neighborhoods near where you live. How large are the houses? Are they detached houses, townhouses, row houses, or apartments? How much land goes with each unit? How are the units separated and marked as separate? How does the allocation of space relate to the social class of the neighborhood?

EXERCISE 7.33 • Privacy and Class

In this exercise, we look at the relationship between privacy and social class.

Consider the neighborhoods and houses you looked at in Exercise 7.32. How is privacy maintained for each unit? Are fences, gates, and hedges used? Do people have play areas for their children in their lawns, or are public parks used? Are windows open, positioned at ground level, shuttered, or blocked?

Age

The main difference in the use of time and space in terms of age is between children and adults. The reason for this is that children have not yet internalized their culture's concepts and values concerning time and space. What does it matter to the average 5-year-old if the clock says nine o'clock or nine-fifteen? Children's concept of time is undeveloped. It is not until children are at least 3 or 4 years old that they can understand that *A* must happen *before B* can happen. Even by the time they enter high school, many are still developing a sense of time and chronology.

It also takes a while for children to internalize the rules and regulations concerning touching and contact that most of us take for granted. Young children have *not* learned not to touch or crowd people. They have no inhibitions about snuggling up to people. Contact between children of either sex is much higher than between adults, although the type of contact may be different. Fourteen-year-old boys and girls are more likely to slap or punch each other than they are to hug and hold hands, but although the touching is somewhat aggressive, it is affectionate in intent.

It is hard to tell if differences occur in the use of time and space between generations of adults. Fundamentally, cultures change little over an individual's lifetime, but some changes have occurred in the last 30 years that may affect our use of time and space. For one thing, communications are faster. E-mail takes a matter of minutes, whereas handwritten letters take days to reach their destination. In essence, we are no longer *able* to be out of touch with people—it is almost unheard of for someone today *not* to have an answering machine, and fax machines are becoming household items. In the United States, transactional time and communication time are continually becoming faster.

The concept of privacy is also changing. Although physical privacy is still possible, informational privacy is becoming harder to maintain. In office situations, what constitutes physical privacy is primarily visual. Cubicles allow an employee to be out of sight, but not out of hearing range. At the same time, monitors, in the form of hidden cameras or detectors, can even invade our visual privacy. In short, modern technology is changing many culturally accepted norms. These changes may result in generational differences in concepts of privacy.

Race and Ethnicity

Little work has been done that looks specifically at various ethnicities in terms of time and space, but a fair amount of data exists concerning different nationalities. It seems reasonable to suppose that, for example, in private settings Chinese Americans will view time according to Chinese concepts of time, but in public settings they will adopt the dominant United States culture's treatment of time. The same would be true for most ethnicities and, probably, most races. Of course, the degree to which a group adopts the dominant point of view is determined by the amount of time the group has spent in this country and the ease with which the group has been allowed to join the mainstream. People of southern European extraction, for example, who are readily accepted into the mainstream, dominant culture, might display the same use of time and space as white, Anglo-Saxon, Protestant males, whereas African Americans, who have not been allowed to merge with the mainstream, dominant culture, might be more African in their use of time and space out of self-preservation. In short, the situation can become quite complex, especially when gender and class are taken into consideration.

One clue that someone has a different concept of time and space might be how successful the person is in the workplace. A person who has not adopted the dominant culture's use of time and space will have trouble functioning successfully in the dominant culture. If someone who is smart, hardworking, and capable is not doing well, the reason may relate to their use of time and space.

Time: Cultural Variations

In the United States, punctuality is associated with success and likableness. Similar values seem to hold for the Japanese and German-speaking cultures. The same is not true for other countries and might not be true for some of the subcultures found in the United States. In Brazil, lateness, not punctuality, is associated with success. A person who shows up late is seen to be relaxed, happy, and likable (Keyes, 1991). Africans have a polychronic sense of time, which is reflected in African American vernacular terms like *hang-loose time* (Samovar & Porter, 1995). Native Americans are completely aschedule. They start events when the time is ripe (Hall, 1966b, 1971b; 1982; Samovar & Porter, 1995). In short, most people who come from polychronic cultures will have larger intervals for lateness and will be less likely to stress punctuality. Other cultures that would not value punctuality are Arabic, Mediterranean, and Latin American cultures.

Another aspect of different concepts of time that people need to be aware of is pace. In general, polychronic cultures will have a slower pace than monochronic cultures. Time orientation also will have an affect. Future-oriented societies always will be faster paced than past- or present-oriented societies, because people are rushing to get on to the next activity. This orientation will also affect future planning and time scales. People from past-oriented societies see the past and present in greater depth than other people. Future-oriented cultures, the ones to which most North Americans belong, have a short concept of past and future. They want things done now!

Personal Space: Cultural Variations

Personal space can be invaded in several ways. One can walk into it, talk into it, stare into it, invade it through the use of strong perfumes, with smell, or invade it through assaulting some other sense. What people consider an invasion is culturally determined, and it is quite common for people from different cultures to invade each other's personal space without intending to do so. Therefore, it is important to remember that some cultures, like North American and Arabic cultures, expect people to look directly at each other, while most Asian cultures consider direct eye contact to be insulting (Triandis, 1996). Arabs also expect to be able to smell each other's breath (Hall, 1982), while North Americans object to bad breath and body odor. Remember, too, that conversational distances, which are related to personal space, are determined by language. Two people who are speaking Spanish will stand closer together than two people who are speaking English. Even when they are speaking English, Hispanics generally will stand closer together than Anglo-Americans (McAndrew, 1993).

EXERCISE 7.34 • Ways of Being Invaded

The purpose of this exercise is to try to become aware of different ways of deliminating conversational space.

1. Make a list of all the senses that are used to determine distance between people. (You might want to review some of the exercises from

earlier in the chapter.) For each sense, such as sight, how do we make contact with someone? With sight, contact is made through vision, eye-to-eye.

2. Go to a public place that is frequented by an ethnic group that is different from your own, such as a shopping area or a playground. Observe people in conversation. Consider each of the senses and the different ways of contact. What types of senses appear to be used for determining conversational distance? At what distance do people display evidence of invasion? (Evidence of invasion may be expressed by jitteriness, moving away, a louder voice, or any other clue that you may notice.)

Remember that the size of a person's personal space can be influenced by situations. It also is linked to whether a culture is collectivistic or individualistic. Most North American subcultures tend to be more collectivistic than the dominant culture. This is definitely true for Latino, African American, and Native American cultures. As a result, people from such cultures tend to stand closer together (Samovar & Porter, 1995). Their personal space will be smaller when they are interacting with each other, although it will be likely to expand when they are interacting with members of different cultures. The status of the individuals involved also will affect the size of personal space. People with greater status are given larger space out of respect.

Privacy: Cultural Variations

It is important to remember that privacy can relate to physical space or to information. In cultures or situations where physical privacy is not possible, people often use silence to establish a sense of privacy. Both Arabs and Britons will stop talking when they wish to have privacy (Hall, 1982). In the United States, not talking usually is interpreted differently. Sometimes it indicates anger, embarrassment, or deference. North Americans are often considered insincere and shallow by people of other cultures because they frequently impart personal information. Therefore, it is important to remember that how much one talks, and in what situations one talks, can have different meanings, depending on one's culture. People who come from high-density settings, who do not have the ability to isolate themselves physically, will use silence to acquire privacy.

Conclusion

The use of time and space is so basic to our culture that we rarely are aware of how we use it. Instead, we tend to react emotionally to invasions and misuses of what we consider (unconsciously) normative behavior. Therefore, whenever you feel tense or irritated because of someone's use of time and space, take a moment to consider whether or not that person shares your values and norms. If not, ask what he or she intended. This way you can avoid misunderstandings.

The best way to avoid problems in the way people use time and space is to recognize how discomfort is signaled. Arousal or anger can signal discomfort, especially with regard to time. Movement, either toward or away from you, signals discomfort with regard to space. Look for such reactions in both yourself and the other person, and adjust your behavior accordingly. Obviously, it is harder to stand still while someone advances toward you than it is to remain calm when someone enters a meeting 30 minutes late, but looking for the reasons behind the actions may help you to avoid a destructive reaction. Telling the other person how you interpreted his or her actions may lead the person to change how he or she acts or at least to apologize for the actions.

APPENDIX A

Commonly Agreed-upon Ethnic Identities of U.S. Subcultures

African Americans

- interdependence
- emotional vitality
- collective survival
- oral tradition
- rhythm
- improvisation
- spirituality

Latinos

- interdependence
- conformity
- avoidance of interpersonal conflict
- strong attachment, loyalty
- clearly defined gender roles
- obedience to authority
- flexible attitudes toward time
- support to extended family
- collective identity

Asian/Americans

- precedence of group interests over individual interests
- harmonious relationships
- importance of fulfilling obligations
- respect for elders
- control of undesirable emotions
- outward calmness
- open expression and confrontation avoidance
- high value on education

Native Americans

- privateness
- present orientation
- harmony with nature
- generosity
- cooperation
- interrelatedness of all life
- belief in mind/body/spirit relationship with Supreme Creator
- power of the spoken word
- support of families
- shared child-rearing to establish bases of collective responsibility
- more visual than auditory
- importance of silence

Anglo Americans

- independence
- autonomy
- direct communication

Adapted from:

Attneave, C. (1982). American Indians and Alaska Native families: Emigrants in their own homeland. In M. McGoldrick, J. Pearce, & J. Giordano (Eds.), *Ethnicity and family therapy* (pp. 55–83). New York: Guilford.

Marin, G., & Marin, B. (1991). *Research with Hispanic populations.* Thousand Oaks, CA: Sage.

Uba, L. (1994). Asian Americans: *Personality patterns, identity, and mental health.* New York: Guilford.

White, L., & Parham, T. (1990). *Psychology of blacks: An African American perspective*. Englewood Cliffs, NJ: Prentice-Hall.

APPENDIX B

Ecomap

The major premises of the ecological perspective are: (1) An individual is a system in him- or herself, composed of interacting components or subsystems such as the cognitive, affective, and physiological arenas; (2) an individual is a component of past and current family systems, which in turn are components within larger social systems such as the school, workplace, and community; (3) these larger social systems are shaped by sociocultural elements.

The ecomap displays the multiple contexts that shape an individual's self-identity. Adapt it to your own situation in order to complete Exercise 2.1. In the core microsystem (at the center of the ecomap), you can see how you are embedded in your primary family, school, and work systems. The mesosystem represents the interface of the microsystem with the larger exosystem, which is embedded in an even larger macrosystem comprising cultural attitudes and ideologies, race, class, ethnicity, geographical region, and so forth. The two-way arrows indicate the reciprocal influences of all these systems, or their mutual interaction.

ECOMAP

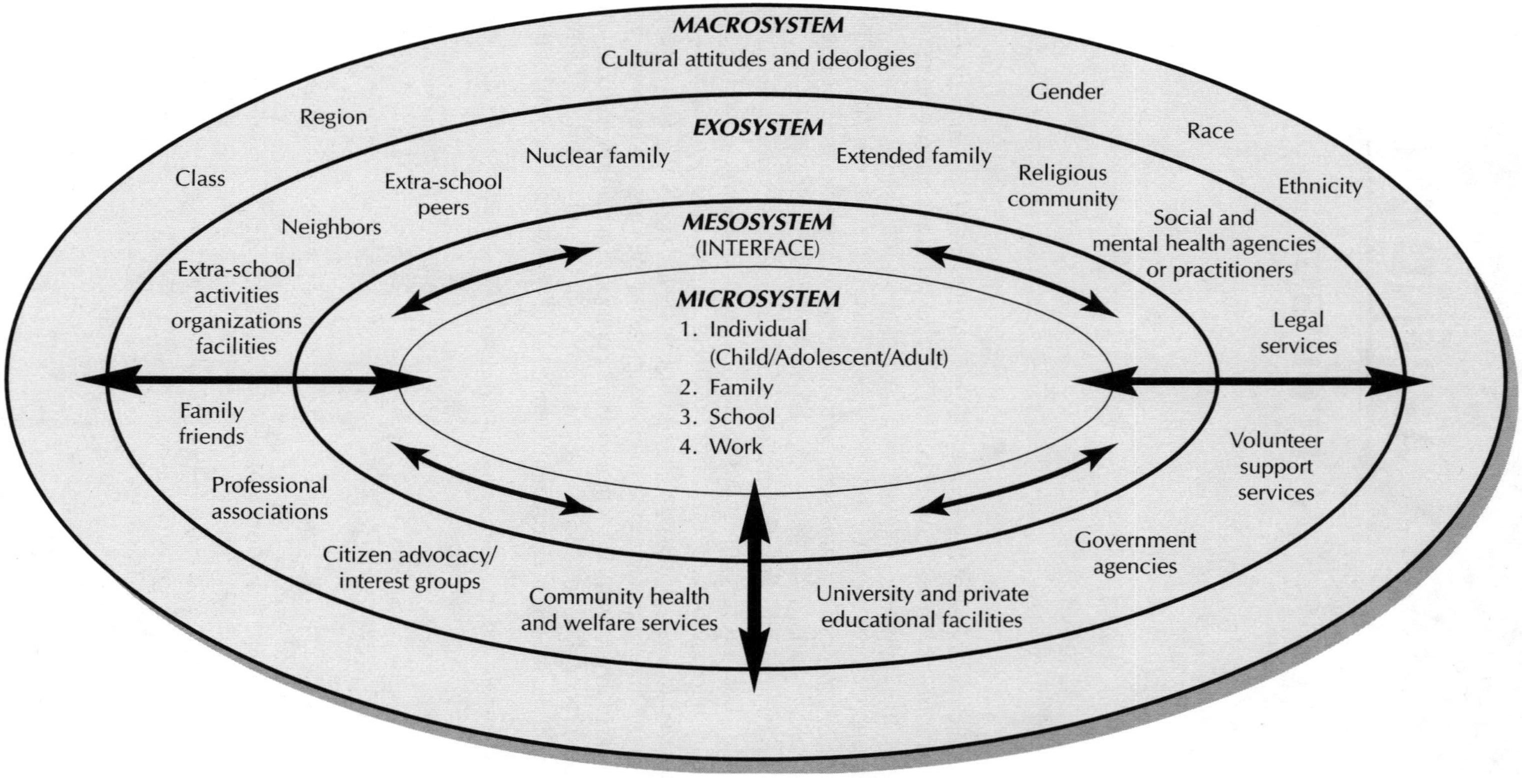

MACROSYSTEM
Cultural attitudes and ideologies
Class
Region
Gender
Race
Ethnicity
EXOSYSTEM
Nuclear family
Extended family
Extra-school peers
Neighbors
Religious community
Social and mental health agencies or practitioners
Extra-school activities organizations facilities
Legal services
Family friends
Volunteer support services
Professional associations
Government agencies
Citizen advocacy/ interest groups
Community health and welfare services
University and private educational facilities
MESOSYSTEM
(INTERFACE)
MICROSYSTEM
1. Individual (Child/Adolescent/Adult)
2. Family
3. School
4. Work

Source: Based on Knoff (1986).

References

Abu-Lughod, L., & Lutz, C. A. (1990). Introduction: Emotion, discourse, and the politics of everyday life. In C. A. Lutz & L. Abu-Lughod (Eds.), *Language and the politics of emotion* (pp. 1–23). New York: Cambridge University Press.
Agar, M. (1994). *Language shock: Understanding the culture of conversation.* New York: Morrow.
Ainsworth, M., Bell, S. M., & Stayton, D. (1974). Infant-mother attachment and social development. In M. P. Richards (Ed.), *The introduction of the child into a social world* (pp. 95–135). London: Cambridge University Press.
Alexander, A., Cronen, V., Kang, K., Tsou, B., & Banks, B. J. (1986). Patterns of topic sequencing and information gain: A comparative study of relationship development in Chinese and American cultures. *Communications Quarterly, 34*(1), 66–78.
Ardener, S. (Ed.). (1993). *Women and space. Ground rules and social maps.* Oxford: Berg.
Argyle, M. (1988). *Bodily communication.* London: Methuen.
Armstrong, K. (1993). *A history of God.* New York: Knopf.
Atkinson, D. R., Morten, G., & Sue, D. W. (Eds.). (1993). *Counseling American minorities* (4th ed.). Madison, WI: Brown and Benchmark.
Babad, E. Y., & Wallbutt, H. G. (1986). The effects of social factors on emotional reactions. In K. R. Scherer, H. G. Wallbutt, & A. B. Summer (Eds.), *Experiencing emotion: A cross-cultural study* (pp. 154–172). New York: Cambridge University Press.
Barnulund, D. C. (1975). *Public and private self in Japan and the United States.* Tokyo: Simul Press.
Barton, S. (1994). Chaos, self-organization and psychology. *American Psychologist, 49,* 5–14.
Bataille, G., & Sands, K. (Eds.). (1984). *American Indian women telling their stories.* Lincoln, NE: University of Nebraska Press.
Berne, E. (1963). *The structure and dynamics of organization and groups.* Philadelphia: J. Lippincott.
Boyd-Franklin, N. (1989). *Black families in therapy: A multisystems approach.* New York: Guilford.

Brettell, C. (1993). *When they read what we write: The politics of ethnography*. Connecticut: Bergin & Garvey.

Brody, L. R., & Hall, J. A. (1993). Gender and emotion. In M. Lewis & J. M. Haviland (Eds.), *Handbook of emotions* (pp. 447–460). New York: Guilford.

Broude, G. J. (1994). Marriage, family and relationships: A cross-cultural encyclopedia. In D. Levinson (Ed.), *Encyclopedia of the human experience*. Santa Barbara, CA: ABC-CLIO.

Brown, D. E., Werner, C. M., & Altman, I., (1994). Close relationships in environmental context. In A. L. Weber and J. H. Harvey (Eds.), *Perspectives on close relationships* (pp. 340–358). Boston: Allyn & Bacon.

Brown, P., & Levinson, S. (1987). *Politeness: Some universals in language usage*. Cambridge: Cambridge University Press.

Cantor, M. H., Brennan, M., & Sainz, A. (1994). The importance of ethnicity in the social support systems of older New Yorkers: A longitudinal perspective (1970 to 1990). *Journal of Gerontological Social Work*, *22*(3–4), 95–128.

Caple, R. (1985). Counseling and the self-organizational paradigm. *Journal of Counseling and Development, 64,* 173–178.

Carlson, J. G., & Hatfield, E. (1992). *Psychology of emotions*. New York: Harcourt, Brace & Jovanovich.

Carter, R. (1990). The relationship between racism and racial identity among white Americans. *Journal of Counseling and Development, 69,* 46–50.

Carter, R. T. (1995). *The influence of race and racial identity in psychotherapy: Toward a racially inclusive model.* New York: Wiley.

Castex, G. M. (1994). Providing services to Hispanic/Latino populations: Profiles in diversity. *Social Work*, *39,* 288–296.

Cathcart, R. S., & Samovar, L. A. (1992). *Small group communication: A reader*. Dubuque, IA: W. C. Brown.

Comas-Diaz, L., & Greene, B. (Eds.). (1994). *Women of color: Integrating ethnic and gender identities in psychotherapy.* New York: Guilford Press.

Cooley, C. H. (1956). *Human nature and the social order.* New York: Free Press.

Cose, E. (1992). *A nation of strangers: Prejudice, politics, and the populating of America.* New York: Morrow.

Crohn, J. (1995). *Mixed matches: How to create successful interracial, interethnic, and interfaith relationships.* New York: Fawcett Columbia.

Cupach, W. R., & Metts, S. (1994). *Facework*. Thousand Oaks, CA: Sage.

De Jongh, E. M. (1991). Foreign language interpreters in the courtroom: The case for linguistic and cultural proficiency. *Modern Language Proficiency, 75*(3), 285–295.

Del Castillo, A. (1993). Covert cultural norms and sex/gender meaning: A Mexico City case. *Urban Anthropology and Studies of Cultural Systems and World Economic Development, 22,* 237–258.

Desouza, E. R. (1997). Presentation on cross-cultural research, Northeastern University, November 1.

DuBois, W. E. (1961/1903). *The souls of Black folk*. Greenwich, CT: Fawcett.

Ehrenreich, B. (1986, September 7). Is the middle class doomed? *The New York Times Magazine*, pp. 44, 50, 54, 62, 64.

Ekman, P. (1972). Universal and cultural differences in facial expressions of emotion. In J. R. Cole (Ed.), *Nebraska Symposium on Motivation*, 1971 (pp. 209–283). Lincoln: University of Nebraska Press.

Ekman, P. (1993). Facial expression and emotion. *American Psychologist*, *48*(4), 384–392.

Ekman, P. (1994). Strong evidence for universals in facial expressions: A reply to Russell's mistaken critique. *Psychological Bulletin, 115*(2), 268–287.

Ekman, P., & Friesen, W. V. (1975). *Unmasking the face: A guide to recognizing emotions from facial clues*. Englewood Cliffs, NJ: Prentice Hall.

Erber, R., & Gilmour, R. (1994). *Theoretical frameworks for personal relationships.* Hillside, NJ: Lawrence Ehrlbaum.

Erchak, G. (1992). *The anthropology of self and mind.* New Brunswick, NJ: Rutgers University Press.

Erikson, E. (1968). *Identity: Youth and crisis.* New York: Norton.

Espin, O. (1995). Women immigrants. Panel at "The Cultural Context of Psychology" symposium, New York, NY, August 8–10.

Fairchild, H. H., Yee, A. H., Wyatt, G. E., & Weizman, F. (1995). Readdressing psychology's problems with race. *American Psychologist, 50,* 46–47.

Fanon, F. (1967). *Black skin, white masks*. New York: Grove.

Fast, J. (1970). *Body language*. New York: Evans.

Frankenberg, R. (1993). *White women, race matters: The social construction of whiteness*. Minneapolis: University of Minnesota Press.

Freedman, J. (1975). *Crowding and behavior. The psychology of high density cities.* New York: Viking.

Fried, J. (1995). *Shifting paradigms in student affairs*. Lanham, MD: University Press of America.

Frye, B. A., & D'Avanzo, C. D. (1994). Cultural themes in family stress and violence among Cambodian refugee women in the inner city. *Advances in Nursing Science, 16*(3), 64–77.

Gailey, C. (1993). Lecture in Workshop on Multicultural Perspectives in Curriculum Development and Teaching Strategies. Boston, MA: Northeastern University.

Geertz, C. (1983). *Local knowledge.* New York: Basic Books.

Geertz, C. (1986). On the nature of anthropological understanding. In R. Shweder & R. LeVine (Eds.), *Culture theory*. New York: Cambridge University Press.

Gerstner, L. V., Semerad, R. D., & Doyle, D. P. (1995). *Reinventing education: Entrepreneurship in America's public schools.* New York: Plumsock Mesoamerican Studies.

Gibson, B., Harris, P., & Werner, C. (1993). Intimacy and personal space: A classroom demonstration. *Teaching of Psychology, 20*(3), 180–181.

Giele, J., & Smock, A. (1977). *Women: Roles and status in eight countries* (pp. 3-31). New York: John Wiley.

Gilligan, C. (1982). *In a different voice*. Cambridge, MA: Harvard University Press.

Ginzburg, E. S. (1967). *Journey into the whirlwind.* New York: Harcourt Brace.

Goffman, E. (1967). *Interaction ritual: Essays on face-to-face behavior.* New York: Pantheon.

Goodenough, W. H. (1981). *Culture, language and society.* Reading, MA: Benjamin Cummings.

Gottfried, A. E., & Gottfried, A. W. (Eds.). (1994). *Redefining families: Implications for children's development.* New York: Plenum Press.

Gray, J. (1993). *Men are from Mars, women are from Venus.* New York: HarperCollins.

Gudykunst, W. B., & Kim, Y. Y. (1992). *Communicating with strangers.* New York: McGraw-Hill.

Gudykunst, W. B., & Ting-Toomey, S. (with E. Chun). (1988). *Culture and communication*. Newbury Park, CA: Sage.

Haley, J. (1963). *Strategies of psychotherapy.* New York: Grune & Stratton.
Hall, E. T. (1959). *The silent language*. New York: Doubleday.
Hall, E. T. (1966a). *The hidden dimension*. New York: Doubleday.
Hall, E. T. (1966b). *The silent language* (7th ed.). Greenwich, CT: Fawcett.
Hall, E. T. (1971a). Environmental communication. In A. H. Esser (Ed.), *Behavior and environment* (pp. 247–256). New York: Plenum.
Hall, E. T. (1971b). *Beyond culture*. New York: Anchor/Doubleday.
Hall, E. T. (1981). *Beyond culture.* New York: Doubleday.
Hall, E. T. (1982). *The hidden dimension*. New York: Anchor/Doubleday.
Hall, N. (1980). *The moon and the virgin.* New York: Harper.
Hansen, L. S. (1997). *Integrative life planning.* San Francisco: Jossey-Bass.
Harding, M. E. (1971). *Women's mysteries ancient and modern.* New York: Harper.
Helms, J. (Ed.). (1990). *Black and white racial identity attitudes: Theory, research and practice.* Westport, CT: Greenwood Press.
Helms, J. (1994). The conceptualization of racial identity. In E. Trickett, R. Watts, & D. Birman (Eds.), *Human diversity: perspectives on people in context.* San Francisco: Jossey-Bass.
Ho, D. (1995). Internalized culture, cultocentrism and transcendence. *The Counseling Psychologist, 23*(1), 4–24.
Hoare, C. (1991). Psychosocial identity development and cultural others. *Journal of Counseling and Development, 70,* 45–53.
Hochschild, A. R. (1997). *The time bind: When work becomes home and home becomes work*. New York: Metropolitan Books.
Hofstede, G. H. (1984). *Culture's consequences, international differences in work-related values*. Thousand Oaks, CA: Sage.
Hofstede, G. H. (1996). Gender stereotypes and partners preferences of Asian women in masculine and feminine cultures. *Journal of Cross-Cultural Psychology, 27,* 533–546.
Iannacone, L. R. (1995). Risk, rationality, and religious portfolios. *Economic Inquiry, 33,* 285–295.
Ibrahim, F. A. (1985). Effective cross-cultural counseling and psychotherapy: A framework. *The Counseling Psychologist,* 13, 625–638.
Izard, C. E. (1977). *Human emotions.* New York: Plenum Press.
Izard, C. E. (1994). Innate and universal facial expressions: Evidence from developmental and cross-cultural research. *Psychological Bulletin, 115*(2), 288–299.
Johnson, D. W., & Johnson, F. P. (1997). *Joining together: Group theory and group skills* (6th ed.). Needham Heights, MA: Allyn & Bacon.
Johnson, F. (1985). The western concept of self. In A. Marsella, G. DeVos, & F. Hsu (Eds.), *Culture and self: Asian and western perspectives* (pp. 91–138). New York: Tavistock.
Johnstone, B., Ferrara, K., & Bean, J. M., (1992). Gender, politeness and discourse management in same-sex and cross-sex opinion poll interviews. *Journal of Pragmatics, 18*(5), 405–430.
Kagan, J. (1984). The idea of emotion in human development. In C. E. Izard, J. Kagan, & R. J. Zajonc (Eds.), *Emotions, cognition, and behavior* (pp. 38–72). New York: Cambridge University Press.
Kantor, D., & Lehr, W. (1975). *Inside the family*. San Francisco: Jossey-Bass.
Katz, J. (1995). *Messengers in the wind*. New York: Ballantine.
Keyes, R. (1991). *Timelock: How life got so hectic and what you can do about it.* New York: HarperCollins.

Knoff, H. (Ed.). (1986). *The assessment of child and adolescent personality.* New York: Guilford.

Knowles, M., & Knowles, H. (1965). *Introduction to group dynamics.* New York: Association Press.

Kochman, T. (1981). *Black and white: Styles in conflict.* Chicago: University of Chicago Press.

Kraut, R. E., & Johnston, R. E. (1979). Social and emotional messages of smiling: An ethnological approach. *Journal of Personality and Social Psychology 37*(9), 1539–1553.

Kuschel, R. (1992). "Women are women and men are men." How Bellonese women get even. In K. Bjorkvisl and P. Niemela (Eds.), *Of mice and women: Aspects of female aggression*. San Diego, CA: Academic Press.

LaFrance, M., & Mahzuin, B. (1992). Toward a reconsideration of the gender-emotion relationship. In M. S. Clark, *Emotion and social behavior: Review of personality and social psychology* (Vol. 14). Newbury Park, CA: Sage.

Langston, D. (1995). Tired of playing monopoly? In M. Anderson & P. Collins (Eds.), *Race, class and gender* (2nd ed.) (pp. 100-110). Belmont, CA: Wadsworth.

Lederer, W. J., & Burdick, E. (1958). *The ugly American.* New York: Norton.

Lee, Y. T., Jussim, L. J., & McCauley, C. R. (1995). *Stereotype accuracy: Toward appreciating group differences.* Washington, DC: American Psychological Association.

Lemon, D. S., Newfield, N. A., & Dobbins, J. E. (1993). Culturally sensitive family therapy in Appalachia. *Journal of Systemic Therapies, 12*(4), 8–26.

Lerner, H. (1985). *The dance of anger*. New York: Harper.

Lewis, M., & Saarni, C. (1985). Culture and emotions. In M. Lewis & C. Saarni (Eds.), *The socialization of emotions* (pp. 1–17). New York: Plenum Press.

Lutz, C. A. (1990). Engendered emotion: Gender, power, and the rhetoric of emotional control in American discourse. In C. A. Lutz & L. Abu-Lughod (Eds.), *Language and the politics of emotion* (pp. 69–91). New York: Cambridge University Press.

Lynch, O. M. (1990). Introduction: Emotions in theoretical contexts. In O. M. Lynch (Ed.), *Divine passions: The social construction of emotions in India* (pp. 3–34). Los Angeles: University of California Press.

Malatesta, C. Z., & Haviland, J. M. (1985). Signals, symbols, and socialization: The modification of emotional expression in human development. In M. Lewis & C. Saarni (Eds.), *The socialization of emotions* (pp. 89–116). New York: Plenum Press.

Mantsios, G. (1995). Class in America: Myths and realities. In P. Rothernberg (Ed.), *Race, class and gender in the United States*. New York: St. Martin's Press.

Margolis, M. (1979). *Viable democracy*. New York: St. Martin's Press.

Markus, H. R., & Kitayama, S. (1991). Culture and the self: Implications for cognition, emotion, and motivation. *Psychological Review 98*(2), 224–253.

Matsumoto, D. (1994). *People: Psychology from a cultural perspective*. Pacific Grove, CA: Brooks/Cole.

Matsumoto, D. (1996a). *Culture and psychology*. Pacific Grove, CA: Brooks/Cole.

Matsumoto, D. (1996b). *Unmasking Japan: Myths and realities about the emotions of the Japanese*. Stanford, CA: Stanford University Press.

Mauss, M. (1985). A category of the human mind: The notion of person; the notion of self. In M. Carruthers, S. Collins, & S. Lukes (Eds.), *The category of the person*. New York: Cambridge University Press.

McAndrew, F. T. (1993). *Environmental psychology*. Pacific Grove, CA: Brooks/Cole.

McCloud, J. (1995). You defend what's sacred to you. In J. Katz (Ed.), *Messengers of the wind* (pp. 272–283). New York: Ballantine Books.

McGill, D. (1997). Personal communication, Cambridge Hospital, June 5.

McGoldrick, M. (1982). Ethnicity and family therapy: An overview. In M. McGoldrick, J. K. Pearce, & J. Giordano (Eds.), *Ethnicity and family therapy*. New York: Guilford.

McGoldrick, M., Giordano, J., & Pearce, J. K. (Eds.). (1996). *Ethnicity and family therapy* (2nd ed.). New York: Guilford.

McIntosh, P. (1989). *White privilege: Unpacking the invisible knapsack*. Working paper, Wellesley College Center for Research on Women, Wellesley, MA.

McMiller, W., & Weisz, J. R., (1996). Help-seeking preceding mental health clinic intake among African-American, Latino, and Caucasian youths. *Journal of the American Academy of Child and Adolescent Psychiatry 35,* 1086–1094.

McNeill, D. (1992). *Hand and mind: What gestures reveal about thought.* Chicago: University of Chicago Press.

Mead, G. H. (1964). *On social psychology: Selected papers.* Chicago: University of Chicago Press.

Merelman, R. (1984). *Making something of ourselves.* Berkeley, CA: University of California Press.

Ming-Dao, D. (1992). *365 Tao daily meditations.* San Francisco: HarperCollins.

Moore, M., Britt, T., & Leary, M. (1997). Integrating social and counseling psychology perspectives on the self. *The Counseling Psychologist 25,* 220–239.

Morris, D. (1994). *Body talk*. New York: Crown.

Naipaul, V. (1977). *India: A wounded civilization.* New York: Knopf.

Neihard, J. (1972). *Black Elk speaks*. New York: Simon and Schuster.

Ogbu, J. (1990). Cultural model, identity and literacy. In J. Stigler, R. Shweder, & G. Herdt (Eds.), *Cultural psychology* (pp. 520-541). New York: Cambridge University Press.

Okun, B. F. (1996). *Understanding diverse families: What practitioners need to know.* New York: Guilford.

Okun, B. F. (1997). *Effective helping: Interviewing and counseling techniques* (5th ed.). Pacific Grove, CA: Brooks/Cole.

Okun, B. F., & Rappaport, L. (1980). *Working with families: An introduction to family therapy.* Monterey, CA: Brooks/Cole.

Okun, M. L. (1990). *The early Roman frontier in the Upper Rhine area: Assimilation and acculturation on a Roman frontier.* Oxford, England: B.A.R. International Series 547.

Olmstead, M. S., & Hare, A. P. (1978). *The small group.* New York: Random House.

Oyserman, D., Gant, L., & Ager, J. (1995). A socially contexualized model of African American identity: Possible selves and school persistence. *Journal of Personality and Social Psychology 69,* 1216–1232.

Perls, F. (1969). *Gestalt therapy verbatim.* Lafayette, CA: Real People Press.

Peterson, I. (1988). Namaste. [Greeting card]. Eugene, OR.

Phinney, J. S. (1996). When we talk about American ethnic groups, what do we mean? *American Psychologist, 51*(9), 918–928.

Plais, A. J., & Sanders, E. (1994). Transplanting God: Asian immigrants are building Buddhist and Hindu temples across the United States. *Far eastern economic review 157,* 34–35.

Plomin, R. (1994). *Genetics and experience: The interplay between nature and nurture*. Thousand Oaks, CA: Sage.

Poortinga, Y. H., Shoots, N. H., & Van de Koppel, J. M. (1993). The understanding of Chinese and Kurdish emblematic gestures by Dutch subjects. *International Journal of Psychology, 28*(1), 31–44.

Poyatos, F. (1983). *New perspectives in nonverbal communication*. New York: Pergamon.

Poyatos, F. (1992). *Advances in nonverbal communication*. Philadelphia/Amsterdam: John Benjamin.

Pryor, J. B., Desouza, E. R., Fitness, J., Hutz, C., Kumpf, M., Lubbert, K., Pesonen, O., & Erber, M. W., (1997). Gender differences in the interpretation of social-sexual behavior: A cross-cultural perspective of sexual harassment. *Journal of Cross-Cultural Psychology, 28*(5), 509–534.

Quintero, G. A. (1995). Gender, discord and illness: Navajo philosophy and healing in the Native American church. *Journal of Anthropological Research, 51,* 69–89.

Roland, A. (1988). *In search of self in India and Japan*. Princeton, NJ: Princeton University Press.

Root, M. P. P. (Ed.). (1997). *Filipino Americans: Transformation and identity*. Thousand Oaks, CA: Sage.

Russell, J. A. (1994). Is there universal recognition of emotion from facial expression? A review of cross-cultural studies. *Psychological Bulletin, 115,* 102–141.

Rutter, M., & Rutter, M. (1993). *Developing human minds: Challenge and continuity across the lifespan*. New York: Basic Books.

Rybezynski, W. (1986). *Home: A short history of an idea*. New York: Viking Penguin.

Sabine, G. (1961). *A history of political theory* (3rd ed.). New York: Holt, Rinehart & Winston.

Samovar, L. A., & Porter, R. E. (1995). *Communication between cultures*. Belmont, CA: Wadsworth.

Sapir, E. (1958). *Culture, language and personality*. Berkeley, CA: University of California Press.

Sarris, G. (1994). *Mabel McKay*. Berkeley, CA: University of California Press.

Scheflen, A. E., & Ashcroft, N. (1976). *Human territories: How we behave in space-time*. Englewood Cliffs, NJ: Prentice-Hall.

Schiele, J. H. (1996). Afrocentricity: An emerging paradigm in social work practice. *Social Work, 41*(3), 284–294.

Schwartz, R. (1987, March–April). Our multiple selves: Applying systems thinking to the inner family. *The Family Therapy Networker 11,* 25–31, 80–83.

Sciama, L. (1993). The problem of privacy in Mediterranean anthropology. In S. Ardener (Ed.), *Women and space: Ground rules and social maps* (pp. 87–111). Oxford: Berg.

Scollon, R., & Scollon, S. (1995). *Intercultural communication*. Cambridge, MA: Blackwell.

Sexton, T. (1994). Systemic thinking in a linear world: Issues in the application of interactional counseling. *Journal of Counseling and Development, 72,* 249–258.

Shimanoff, J. (1994). Cited in S. Ting-Toomey, *The challenge of facework*. Albany, NY: State University of New York Press.

Shweder, R. (1991). *Thinking through cultures*. Cambridge, MA: Harvard University Press.

Smith, H. (1994). *The illustrated world's religions*. San Francisco: HarperCollins.

Smith-Hefner, N. J., (1994). Ethnicity and the force of faith: Christian conversion among Khmer refugees. *Anthropological Quarterly, 67,* 24–37.

Sommer, R. (1969). *Personal space: The behavioral basis of design.* Englewood Cliffs, NJ: Prentice-Hall.

Steele, C. M. (1997). A threat in the air: How stereotypes shape intellectual identity and performance. *American Psychologist 52*(6), 613–630.

Sue, D. W., & Sue, D. (1990). *Counseling the culturally different: Theory and practice.* New York: Wiley.

Tannen, D. (1990). *You just don't understand: Women and men in conversation.* New York: Morrow.

Tarpley, M. L. (1993). On Culture. Position paper presented by the Multi-Cultural Advisory Committee's First Annual Symposium of Mental Health Professionals of Color. Belmont, MA: Department of Mental Health.

Thich Nhat Hanh (1992). *Touching peace.* Berkeley, CA: Parallax Press.

Ting-Toomey, S. (1994). *The challenge of facework.* Albany, NY: State University of New York Press.

Triandis, H. C. (1994). *Culture and social behavior.* New York: McGraw-Hill.

Tseng, W. S., & Hsu , J. (1991). *Culture and family: Problems and therapy.* New York: Haworth Press.

Ucko, L. G. (1994). Culture and violence: The interaction of Africa and America. *Sexroles, 31*(3–4), 185–204.

Valentine, P. (1995). *Women's working worlds: A case study of a female organization.* Albany, NY: State University of New York Press.

Wallbott, H. G., Ricci-Bitti, P. E., & Banninger-Huber, E. (1986). Nonverbal reactions of emotional experiences. In *Experiencing emotion: A cross-cultural study* (pp. 98–116). European Monographs in Social Psychology. New York: Cambridge University Press.

Wheatley, M. (1994). *Leadership and the new science.* San Francisco: Berrett-Koehler.

Whipple, V. (1987). Counseling battered women from fundamentalist churches. *Journal of Marital and Family Therapy 13*(3), 251–258.

White, M. T., & Levine, R. A. (1986). What is an "ik ko" (good child)? In H. W. Stevenson, H. Azuma, and K. Hakuta (Eds.), *Child development and education in Japan* (pp. 55-62). New York: W. H. Freeman.

Whorf, B. L. (1956). *Language, thought and reality.* Cambridge, MA: MIT Press.

Wilber, K. (1996). *A brief history of everything.* Boston: Shambala.

Wilbur, M., Kulikowitch, J., Roberts-Wilbur, J., & Torres-Rivera, E. (1995). Chaos theory and counselor training. *Counseling and Values, 39,* 129–144.

Wiseman, R., & Koester, J. (1973). *Intercultural communication competence.* London: Sage Public.

Wolcott, H. E. (1991). Propriospect and the acquisition of culture. *Anthropology and Educational Quarterly, 22,* 251–278.

Yontef, G. (1982). Gestalt therapy: Its inheritance from Gestalt psychology. *Gestalt Theory, 4,* 23–39.

Author Index

Subject Index

Personal Notes

Personal Notes

Personal Notes

Personal Notes

Personal Notes

Personal Notes

Personal Notes

Personal Notes

Personal Notes

Personal Notes

Personal Notes

Personal Notes

Personal Notes

Personal Notes

Personal Notes

Personal Notes

Personal Notes

Personal Notes

Personal Notes

Personal Notes

Personal Notes

Personal Notes

Personal Notes

Personal Notes

Personal Notes

Personal Notes

Personal Notes

Personal Notes

Personal Notes

Personal Notes

TO THE OWNER OF THIS BOOK:

We hope that you have found *Understanding Diversity: A Learning as Practice Primer* useful. So that this book can be improved in a future edition, would you take the time to complete this sheet and return it? Thank you.

School and address: ______________________________

Department: ______________________________

Instructor's name: ______________________________

1. What I like most about this book is: ______________________________

____

____

2. What I like least about this book is: ______________________________

____

____

3. My general reaction to this book is: ______________________________

____

4. The name of the course in which I used this book is: ______________________________

____

5. Were all of the chapters of the book assigned for you to read? ______________

If not, which ones weren't? ______________________________

6. In the space below, or on a separate sheet of paper, please write specific suggestions for improving this book and anything else you'd care to share about your experience in using the book.

____

____

____

____

____

Optional:

Your name: ________________________ Date: ________________________

May Brooks/Cole quote you, either in promotion for *Understanding Diversity: A Learning as Practice Primer* or in future publishing ventures?

Yes: __________ No: _________

Sincerely,

Barbara F. Okun
Jane Fried
Marcia L. Okun

FOLD HERE

NO POSTAGE
NECESSARY
IF MAILED
IN THE
UNITED STATES

BUSINESS REPLY MAIL

FIRST CLASS PERMIT NO. 358 PACIFIC GROVE, CA

POSTAGE WILL BE PAID BY ADDRESSEE

ATT: *Barbara F. Okun, Jane Fried, & Marcia L. Okun*

Brooks/Cole Publishing Company
511 Forest Lodge Road
Pacific Grove, California 93950-5098

FOLD HERE